I0793020

IMAGES
*of America*

# THE WELSH HILLS

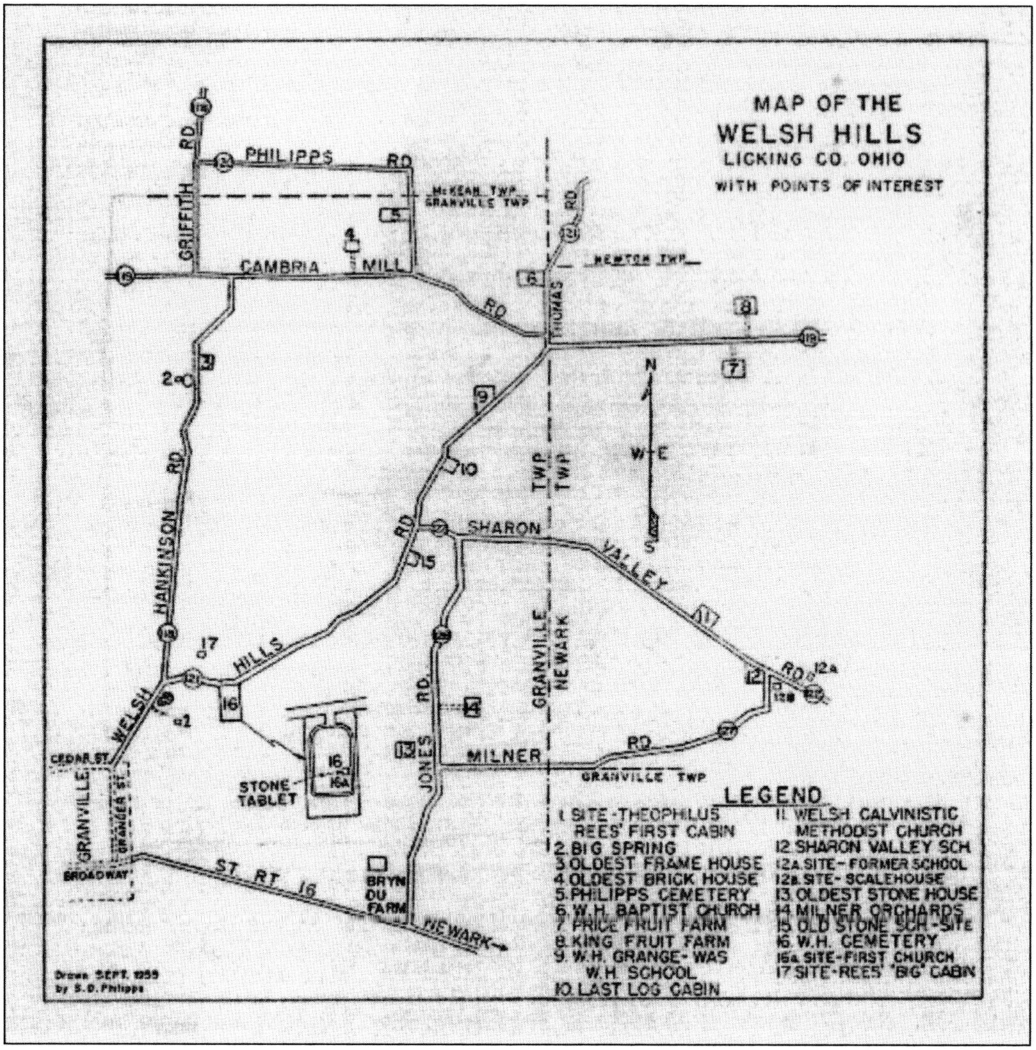


Samuel David Philipps prepared this map of the Welsh Hills in 1955 for the sesquicentennial celebration (150 years) for Granville and the Welsh Hills. A surveyor, Philipps prepared the map to help people find their way through the area. His home at the time, located on Welsh Hills Road, had originally been Jacob Frederick's house. Prior to the creation of this map, every road in the Welsh Hills was called Welsh Hills Road. Most of the routes indicated were named for a family farm found on the roadway. Cambria Mill Road bears the name of the mill once located on the road. The legend identifies many landmark sites located throughout the Welsh Hills. (Courtesy of the Granville Historical Society.)

**On the Cover:** Gertrude Harlan Price was a breeder of White Holland turkeys at the Price farm, also known as Evergreen Farm, in the Welsh Hills. She was known nationally for her prize-winning turkeys, including competitions at Madison Square Garden. She was married to Homer Price, who ran the family orchard. In this photograph, Gertrude is weighing one of the birds. (Courtesy of T. David Price, grandson of Gertrude and Homer.)

IMAGES
*of America*

# THE WELSH HILLS

Janet Philipps Procida

ARCADIA
PUBLISHING

ISBN 978-0-7385-7817-0

Published by Arcadia Publishing
Charleston SC, Chicago IL, Portsmouth NH, San Francisco CA

Printed in the United States of America

Library of Congress Control Number: 2009943566

For all general information contact Arcadia Publishing at:
Telephone 843-853-2070
Fax 843-853-0044
E-mail sales@arcadiapublishing.com
For customer service and orders:
Toll-Free 1-888-313-2665

Visit us on the Internet at www.arcadiapublishing.com

*To my father, Thomas Evans Philipps, who provided the encouragement to write about the Welsh settlement and stories and memories of growing up in the Welsh Hills, and to Ruth Valentine Sipe for allowing me to finish the work that she began.*

# Contents


| | | |
|---|---|---|
| Acknowledgments | | 6 |
| Introduction | | 7 |
| 1. | The Land | 9 |
| 2. | The People | 17 |
| 3. | Children | 39 |
| 4. | Welsh Churches | 53 |
| 5. | Welsh Schools | 61 |
| 6. | Homes and Farms | 71 |
| 7. | Welsh Cemeteries | 89 |
| 8. | Industry | 97 |
| 9. | Livestock and Pets | 107 |
| 10. | Celebrations and Entertainment | 115 |
| Bibliography | | 127 |

# ACKNOWLEDGMENTS

The opportunity arose to document and share images of the early days in the Welsh Hills thanks to the generosity of so many people who hold these cherished photographs. This book would never have occurred without the hard work of my sister, Carol Philipps, and my father, Thomas E. Philipps, who carefully scanned each photograph and identified the content. I must also thank Lloyd Philipps, Ruth Valentine Sipe, Philip "Bucky" Philipps, Lynda Villars Abbott, Mary Philipps Villars, Jennifer Philipps Welsh, Karen Harden, Patty Wheeler Andrews, T. David Price, Mary Ellen Everett, and the volunteers at the Granville Historical Society for sharing their photographs. I must acknowledge my grandfather, Thomas W. Philipps, an avid amateur photographer responsible for photographing many of the scenes contained in this book. Historical facts and stories were contributed by Thomas E. Philipps (age 91), Philip "Bucky" Philipps (age 80), Clarence "Pete" Hankinson (age 103), Donald Griffith (age 84), T. David Price (age 74), and Ruth Valentine Sipe (age 94). The enthusiasm and support of Maggie Brooks, Theresa Overholser, and Florence Hoffman from the Granville Historical Society has been and will continue to be greatly appreciated throughout the effort to rediscover and celebrate the early Welsh settlers.

# INTRODUCTION

*The portion of Licking County in which the first Welsh settlers located, has ever since been known and designated as the Welsh Hills settlement.*

—from *The History of Licking County 1881*, A.A. Graham, Publisher, N.N. Hill Jr., Compiler

Prior to 1787, Wales was experiencing civil unrest and religious dissension. The Church of England under King George III was attempting to suppress religious freedom throughout Great Britain. John H., Thomas, and Erasmus Philipps, sons of Thomas Philipps, were attending school in Wales around this time. It is reported that John H. wrote letters criticizing the British government and was therefore considered treasonous. In 1787, the three brothers left for America. After considerable appeals from his sons to join them, Thomas Philipps agreed to leave Wales and convinced his friend Deacon Theophilus Rees to accompany him. Rees was then serving as the deacon at Salem Chapel, a nonconformist Baptist church. As they were both Baptists, it is thought that Thomas Philipps and Rees met through the church.

Through the generosity of Philipps and Rees, many of their Welsh neighbors accompanied them to America. On April 1, 1796, they boarded the ship *Amphion*, under the command of Captain Williams. After arriving in New York 44 days later on May 14, they traveled to Chester County, Pennsylvania, where a large Welsh community was already established. In the fall of 1797, the immigrants led by Philipps and Rees relocated to Beulah, in Cambria County, Pennsylvania, where they purchased land and established businesses. Since the soil in Cambria County was extremely rocky and not conducive to farming, many of the Welsh families began looking for better homesteads by 1800, when word reached the community about land that had recently opened in Ohio.

In August 1801, Theophilus Rees sent Simon James, David Jones, and his own son, John Rees, to examine this tract. When they returned with a favorable report, John H. Philipps traveled to Ohio to negotiate for the purchase of this property on behalf of several Welsh families residing in Beulah. On September 4, an agreement was reached in Ebensburgh, Pennsylvania, with landowner Sampson Davis, a Welshman from Philadelphia who dealt extensively in western tracts. Theophilus Rees purchased 988 acres; Thomas Philipps, 799 acres; Elizabeth Conroy, 200 acres; Henry Jenkins, 100 acres; David Roberts, 400 acres; William Roberts, 100 acres; and Walter Griffith, 100 acres. At the time, Elizabeth Conroy and Henry Jenkins were residents of Philadelphia, and Walter Griffith and David Roberts resided in New York. With the exception of Elizabeth Conroy, all purchasers were of Welsh extraction.

In 1802, the first who migrated to the territory were Theophilus Rees and his family; his two sons-in-law, "Big" Davy Thomas and David Lewis, and their families; and Simon James. Along the way, they stopped in Wheeling, where they met frontiersman and Indian fighter Jimmy Johnson. Thinking Johnson would be useful in their new wilderness home, Rees invited him to join the group and offered Johnson 100 acres of land, which he accepted. In 1803, James Evans, James James, and a man named Shadwick settled in the Welsh Hills. Thomas Cramer and his brother Peter Cramer from western Virginia arrived in 1804. In 1805 and 1806, John Price, Benjamin Jones, John H. Philipps (Thomas Philipps's son), and Thomas Powell were added to the list of Welshmen in the settlement. Thomas Philipps did not move to the Welsh Hills until after closing his business affairs in Beulah in 1806. Samuel Joseph Philipps (Thomas Philipps's son), Thomas Owens, Jacob Reily, and a Mr. McLane moved to the Welsh Hills in 1807 and 1808. In 1809 and 1810, "Little" Davy Thomas (Theophilus Rees's son-in-law), and Samuel White (Thomas Philipps's son-in-law) joined the community. White had been living in his native Massachusetts. In 1812, Daniel Griffith arrived from Wales, followed by Walter and Nicodemus Griffith (1815), David Pittsford (1816), Hugh Jones (1819), Edward Price and Edward Glynn (1821), and Rev. Thomas Hughes (1822). Most of these early settlers were born in Wales, spoke Welsh, and had little or no experience with the English language, which helped establish a strong bond in the community. Later arrivals of Welsh families kept the language alive in the Welsh Hills until the 1880s. Isaac Smucker discussed these early settlers in *History of the Welsh Settlements in Licking County, Ohio* in 1869:

> From the foregoing it will be seen that the purchase of Messrs Rees and Phillips formed the nucleus of the Welsh settlement in Licking county. Theophilus Rees settled upon his half of the purchase, and surrounded himself by his sons Theophilus and John and his sons-in-law the two David Thomas' and David Lewis, and his hunter "Jimmy Johnson," giving to each of them a hundred acres or thereabouts, of his land.
>
> Mr. Thomas Phillips, settled upon his portion of the purchase, and likewise surrounded himself by his sons and sons-in-law, giving to each of his sons John H. and Samuel J., about one hundred acres and to his sons-in-law, Thomas Owens, Samuel White, William Morrison and John Evans, an equal quantity, the two latter however never occupied it.

When the first immigrants arrived on "the Hills" in 1802, they immediately set about clearing land and building the first cabins to house the families that would follow soon after. Early cabins also served as a school and church until 1809, when a log structure was built for that purpose on a site now occupied by the Welsh Hills Cemetery. The Welsh settlers were devoutly religious. Welsh Hills Baptist Church was formed on September 4, 1808, and Theophilus Rees was elected its first deacon. Rees's great-great-great-great-grandson, Lloyd Philipps, serves as deacon of the Welsh Hills Baptist Church today. In 1833, Welsh families living in Sharon Valley organized the Welsh Calvinistic Methodist Church and constructed a wooden structure to house their congregation in 1837.

Education was important to the people in the Welsh Hills. Completed in 1825, the first permanent school, called the Old Stone Schoolhouse, was built by local craftsmen from locally quarried stone. This structure became the cultural center of the Welsh Hills, and the formation of the Welsh Hills Agriculture and Historical Society occurred within its walls. Many of its teachers came from the families in the Welsh Hills.

Compared to the nearby towns of Granville and Newark, the Welsh Hills area has changed very little in the past 200 years. Most of the early large farms have been divided into smaller parcels, with housing developments constructed in some. To a large extent, the fields and woods still predominate. Descendants of the early settlers reside in the Welsh Hills or nearby towns and claim a kindred spirit to "the Hills."

# *One*

# The Land

In 1869, Isaac Smucker wrote about the Welsh Pioneers in Licking County:

> The country known as the Welsh Hills as its title implies, belongs to the class designated as hilly, but it may be regarded as rather fertile, particularly in the production of the cereals. It was originally all heavily timbered, but is now mostly cleared land. Farms generally are not large, and some timber, sufficient for present and prospective purposes, is found on each of them with rare exceptions. A considerable quantity of level and slightly undulating land is found on most of the farms, which produces corn and different varieties of grasses well. Soft water springs abound, and it may be considered one of the best watered sections of Licking county, although the streams are small.

The area of Ohio called the Welsh Hills is noted for landscape similar to that seen in south central Wales, where Theophilus Rees and Thomas Philipps emigrated from Carmarthenshire. Both terrains contain fertile soil conducive to growing wheat, rye, and other grains. Early documents note that after acreage was purchased in Licking County, Theophilus Rees sent his son John to erect a cabin and clear some plots for sowing wheat. The wheat would be necessary for the making of bread by the Welsh pioneers. The region does not contain any large bodies of water or rivers, but the natural springs that abound in the Welsh Hills feed many streams. In 1900, David D. Jones wrote that there were still 103 natural springs on the Hills, four of which were hard water springs. Forests present at the time of settlement were cleared to create farmland and the wood used to build homes, barns, and wagons. The area has remained predominantly rural, but most land is no longer farmed, and forested country has returned to the Welsh Hills.

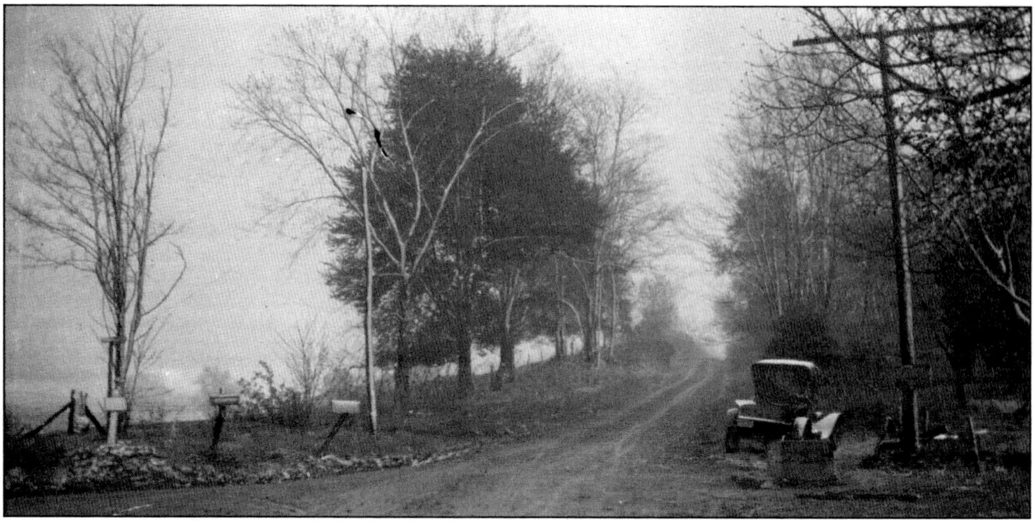

The above photograph shows a view of Welsh Hills Road near the intersection with Hankinson Road. Welsh Hills Road remained a dirt road until the late 1930s. This photograph was taken in front of Jake Frederick's home at the site of the first cabin built by Theophilus Rees on his arrival in the Welsh Hills. The water trough behind the car served passing buggies and local boys' nighttime skinny-dipping escapades. Tom Philipps recalls bootleggers making their midnight deals at this intersection. The photograph below was taken in front of the Welsh Hills Cemetery, looking west on Welsh Hills Road. The road branching to the left is the entrance to the cemetery. The wood fence on the adjacent farm was known as "snake and cross," which did not require setting posts in the ground. (Courtesy of Lloyd Philipps.)

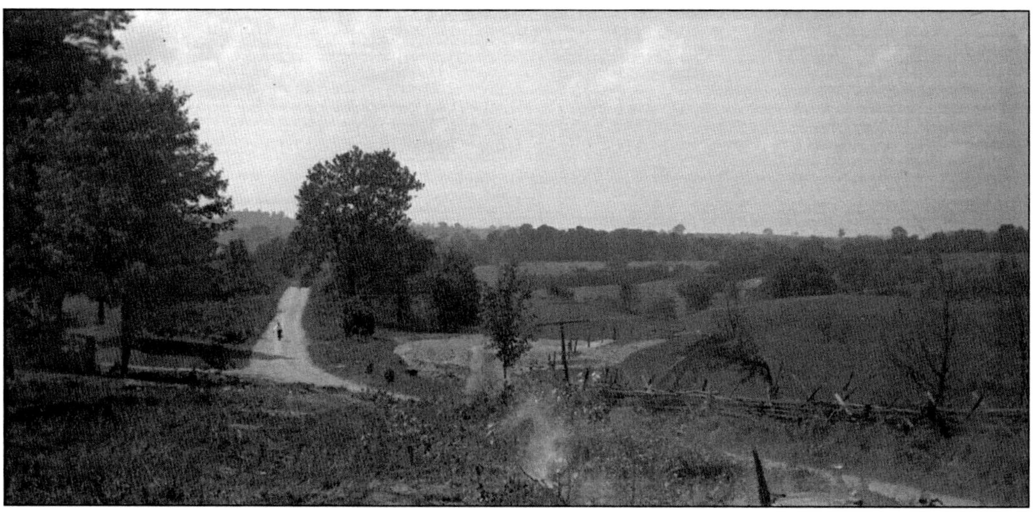

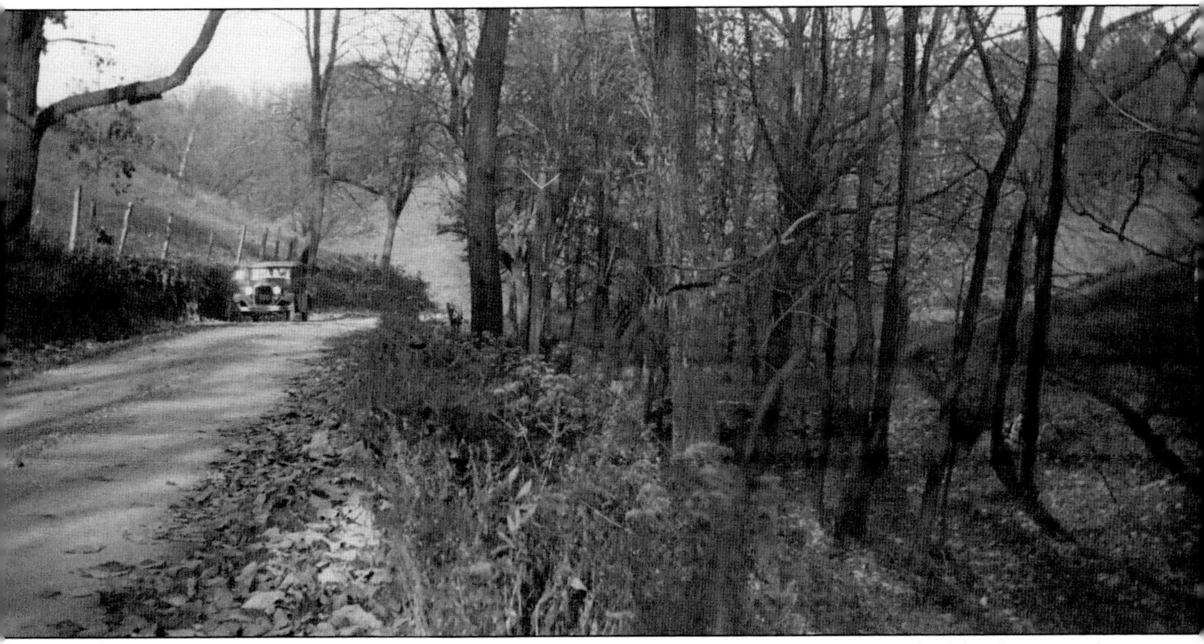

Thomas Warren Philipps, who worked as a surveyor for Licking County, took this photograph of Welsh Hills Road in the early 1930s, prior to the rebuilding of the road toward the end of the decade. This section crosses land once owned by Theophilus Rees. This north-facing view clearly shows the definition of the hills and valleys found throughout the Welsh Hills. Because many of the trees found on the hills in 1801 were cleared for farming, livestock, construction, heating, and cooking, those in this photograph would be second or third growth. By 1930, much of the land had naturally reforested, as farming moved to other areas of the county. (Courtesy of Lloyd Philipps.)

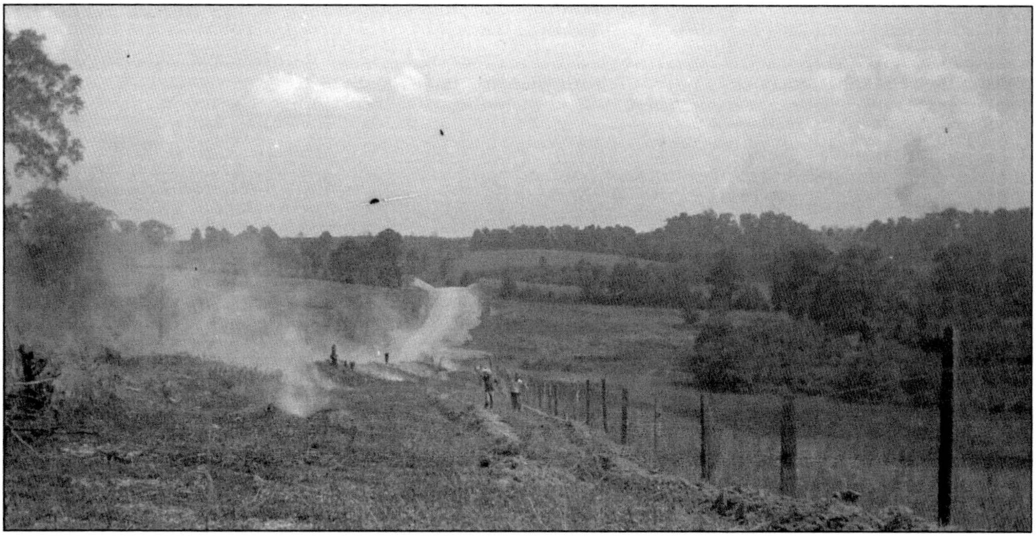

The photograph above is a view of Welsh Hills Road taken between the Welsh Hills Cemetery and Sharon Valley Road. During the mid-1930s, WPA (Works Progress Administration) projects throughout the United States put citizens to work. Welsh Hills Road from the town of Granville to Cambria Mill Road was widened and paved as part of the WPA projects. Local farmers who owned draft horses were hired by the federal government to assist with earthmoving operations. The photograph below shows a section of Welsh Hills Road that has already been widened. This view faces west, and Welsh Hills Cemetery is located beyond the line of trees on the left. (Courtesy of Lloyd Philipps.)

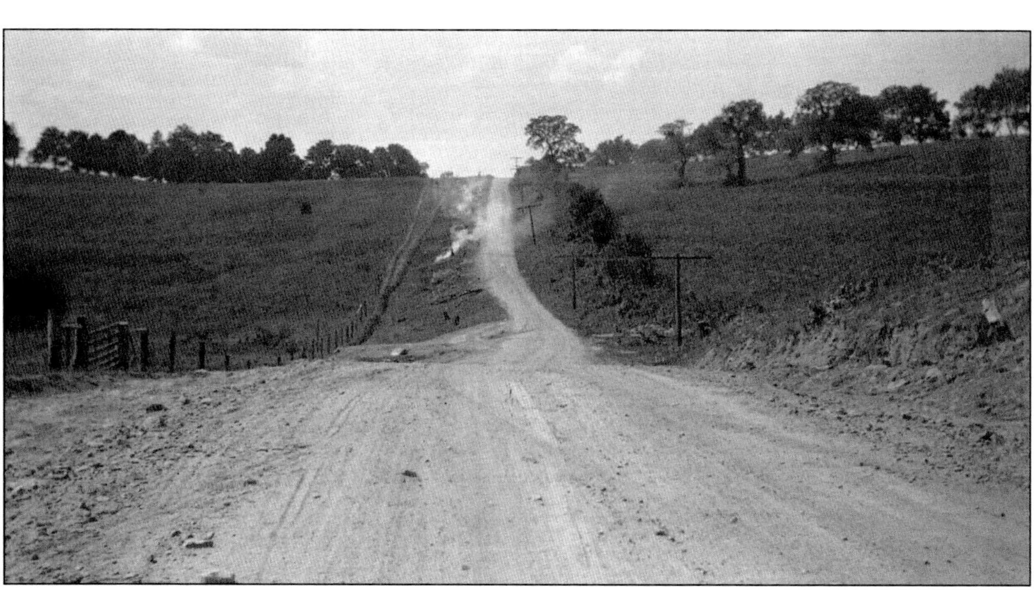

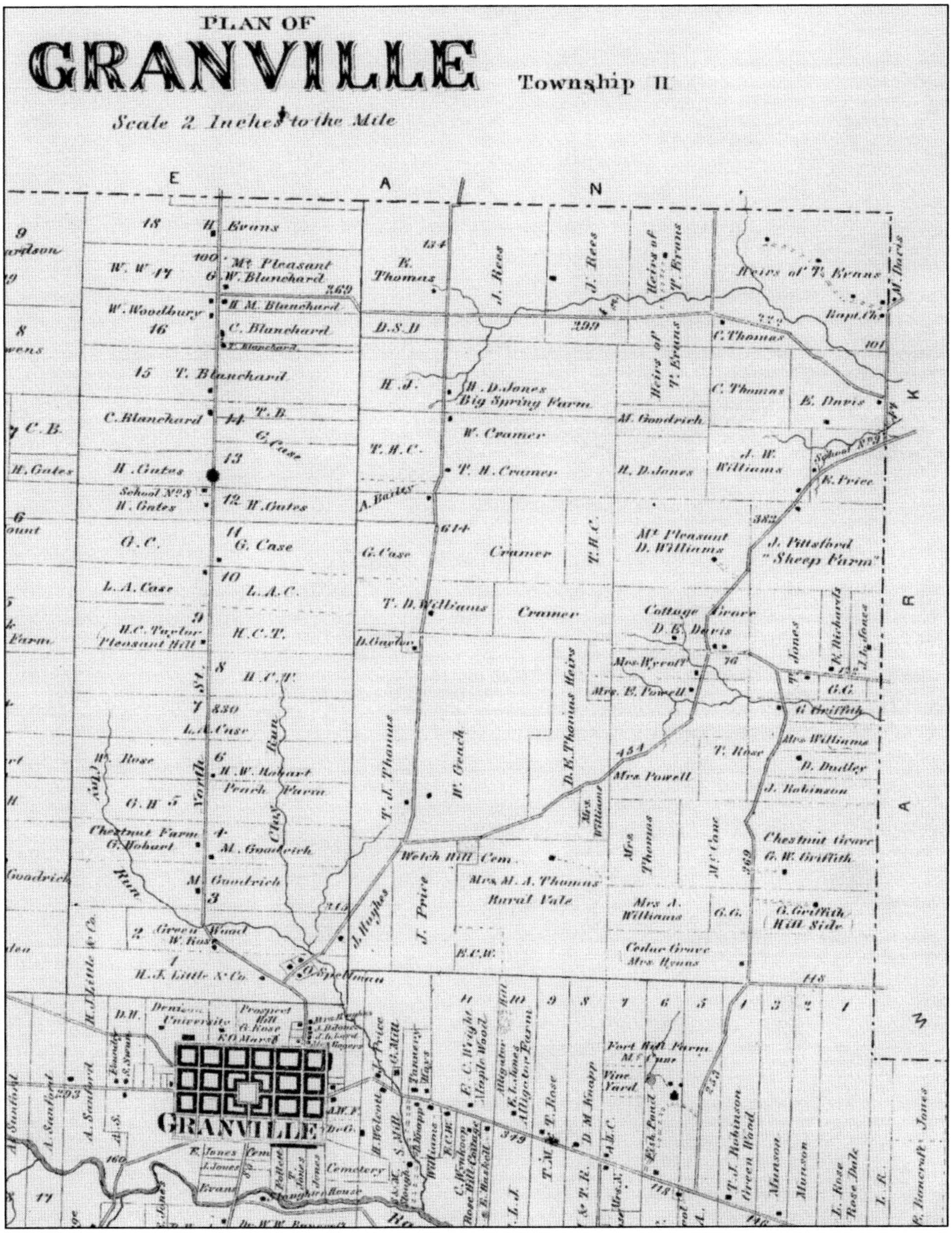


This map segment appears in an 1866 atlas of Licking County and shows the northeastern quadrant of Granville Township that is a portion of the Welsh Hills. This area was the land originally purchased by Theophilus Rees and Thomas Philipps. Among the 1866 property owners identified is T. J. Thomas, Rees's grandson. Most of the Philipps' property passed on to other families, many from Wales, who arrived in the mid-1800s. Farms at the time included Hill Side, Cedar Grove, Rural Vale, Mt. Pleasant, and Big Spring Farm. Noted historian Ben Jones writes about the "line-fence war" that carried on for many years and created animosity between Tommy J. Thomas and his neighbor William Geach. The grid at the lower left is the town of Granville. Welsh Hills extends east into Newark Township, north into McKean Township, and northeast into Newton Township. (Courtesy of T. David Price.)

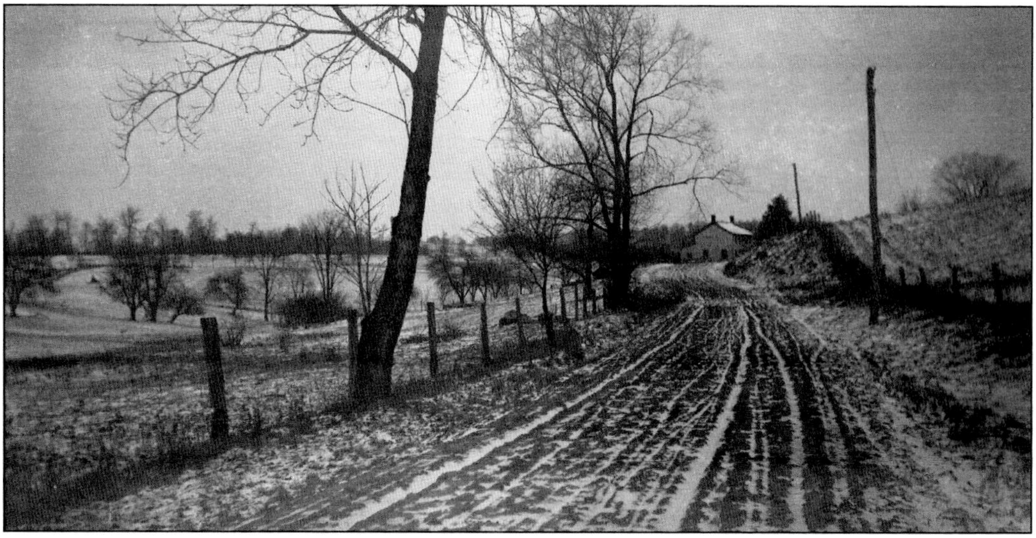

Very little changed along this section of Hankinson Road from the early 1900s (above) to the present day (below). Thomas Cramer and his father, William Cramer, purchased land in this area from the descendants of Theophilus Rees. Thomas established several of the farmsteads located along the road, including one where his sister Adaline Rebecca Cramer and her husband, William Hankinson, lived. Their son Hayes owned the farm in the older image, and several other of their seven children inhabited farms along Hankinson Road. Marshall Hankinson, Hayes's son, owns the place in the newer photograph. (Courtesy of Thomas E. Philipps.)

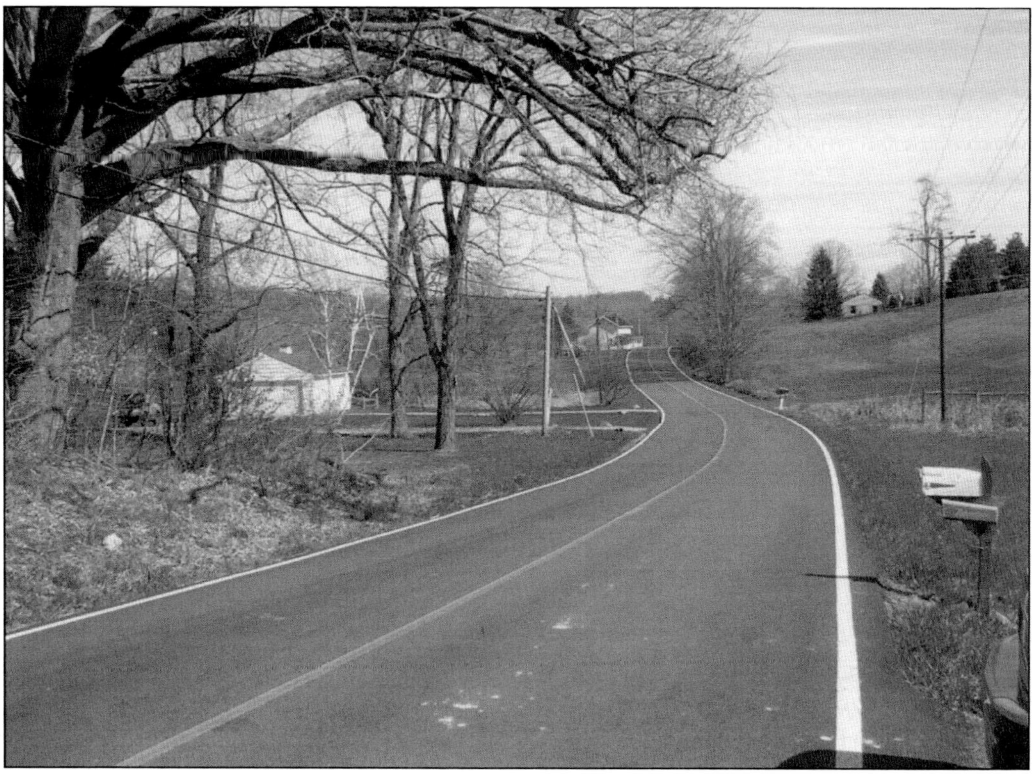

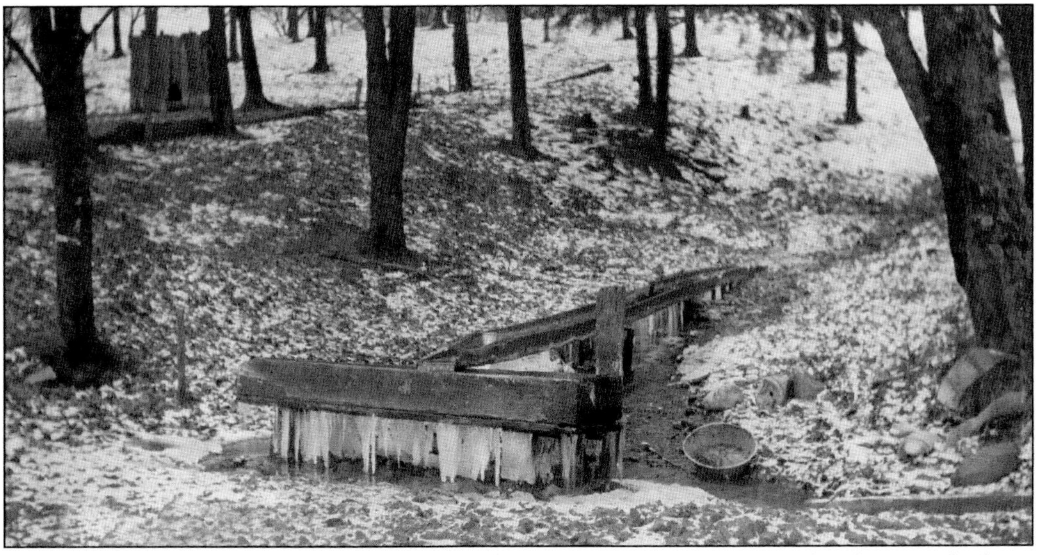

The Big Spring is located on Hankinson Road opposite Big Spring Farm. The photograph above was taken in the early 1900s, and the image below shows the Big Spring as it looks today. Isaac Smucker wrote the following:

> Among the large springs are several north of Centerville street, in Granville township; and another, or rather two that form one, on the Welsh hills, being the head or source of the Goose Pond run. The two rise within two feet of each other, and flowing together, make one spring. The one is what is called hard water, and the other soft water, thus presenting the anomalous feature of being hard water on one side and soft water on the other. It is on the farm of William Cramer in Granville township. It had a copious flow of water in early times, and was reckoned among the largest springs of the county.

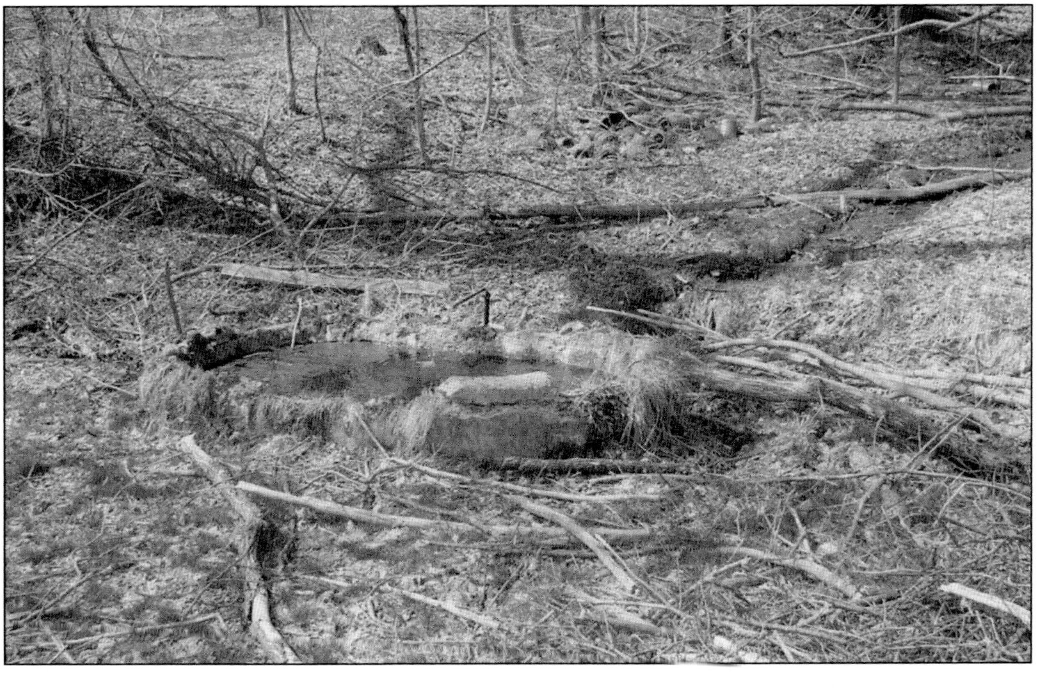

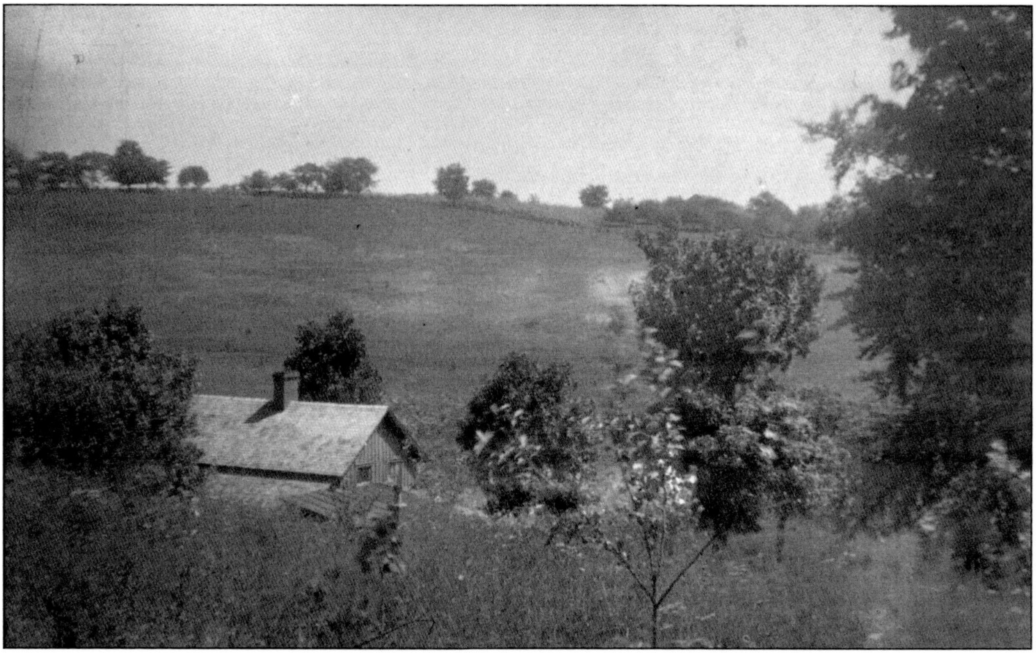

The image above, taken around 1900, is a view of the Welsh Hills taken from the hill overlooking the Samuel Jones Philipps farm and looking east toward present-day Philipps Road. Samuel was the great-grandson of Thomas Philipps, who originally purchased this land in 1801 and divided it among his children. This property is now owned by Kenneth Philipps, grandson of Samuel Jones Philipps. Below is the view from the porch of the house presently on the site. The Philipps cemetery, originally set up by Samuel Joseph Philipps, is found at the top of the hill and to the right. (Below photograph courtesy of Carol Philipps.)

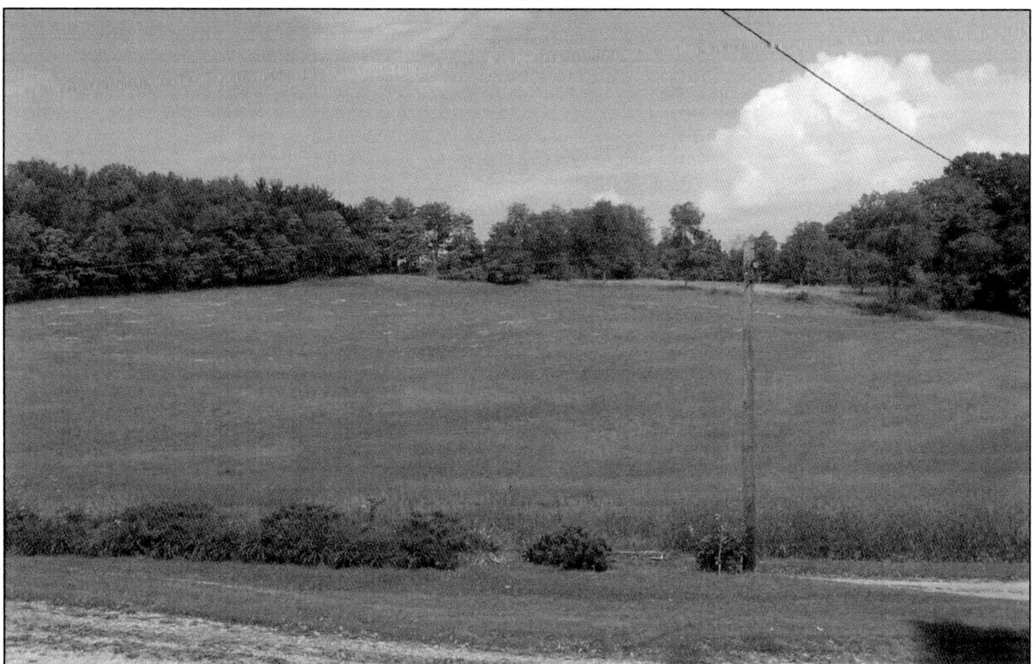

# *Two*

# The People

The early settlers of the Welsh Hills were predominantly immigrants from Wales. Most of the immigrants, with a few exceptions, spoke only their native Welsh, which tended to create both a kinship bond with locals and isolation from surrounding communities. Later generations quickly learned English in order to communicate outside their locale. Settlers were very religious, adhering generally to the Baptist, Methodist, or Congregational churches and being mostly Calvinist in their views. The Welsh settlers were well-educated and firm believers in promoting mental and moral improvement. Nearly every adult settler in the Welsh Hills had learned a trade before coming to America. Farming skills had to be developed out of necessity but were adapted quickly and efficiently.

The first settlers had to endure great hardships in both reaching their new home and managing the first few years. They cut roads in order to reach their destination, felled trees to construct the first cabins, and cleared land to plant the first crops. Wild animals such as wolves, bears, and panthers plagued settlers, who recorded stories about such events. Native Americans often visited the first settlers but were not hostile.

Generally the first Welsh settlers, as characterized by William Harvey Jones, were "honest, upright and trustworthy in business; kind, humane and considerate in their relations with others."

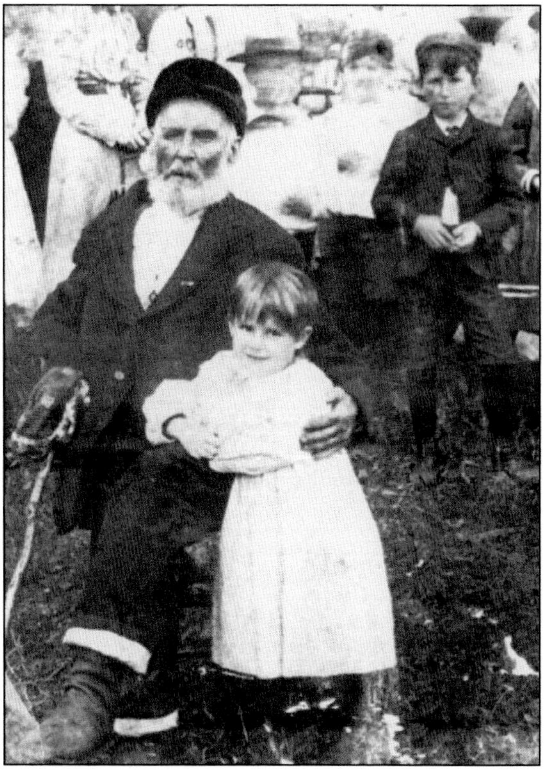

Samuel Griffith Philipps, grandson of Thomas Philipps, was born in Beulah, Pennsylvania. During the migration to the Welsh Hills, Samuel traveled in one saddlebag and his sister Mary in the other. Their mother, Lydia Griffith Phillips, holding baby Erasmus, rode the horse, while their father, Samuel Joseph Philipps, walked alongside. Samuel G. was a farmer and helped organize one of the first farmers' cooperatives in the area. He also worked on the construction of the Ohio Canal. The photograph at left shows Samuel with his granddaughter Edith and his grandson Tom in the background. The photograph below shows Samuel with his wife, Susannah Reily. Susannah's mother, Sallie Tilton, was said to be the first white child born in Ohio. Samuel died in 1899 at age 93, while Susannah died in 1892 at age 86. (Courtesy of Sylvia McClain.)

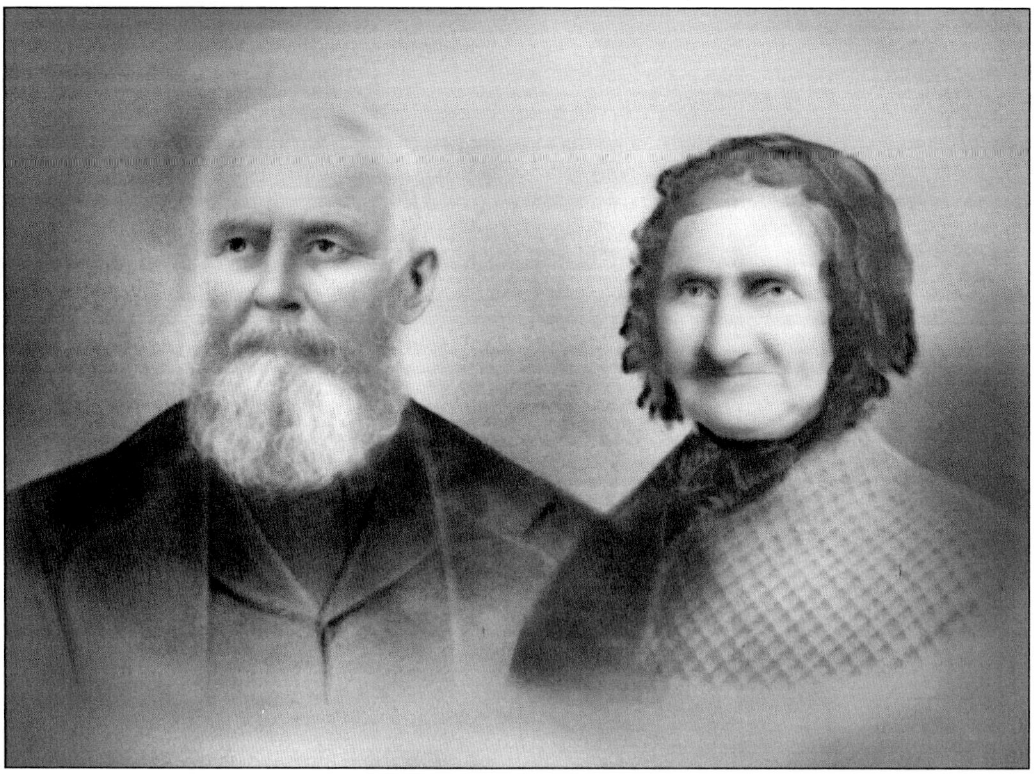

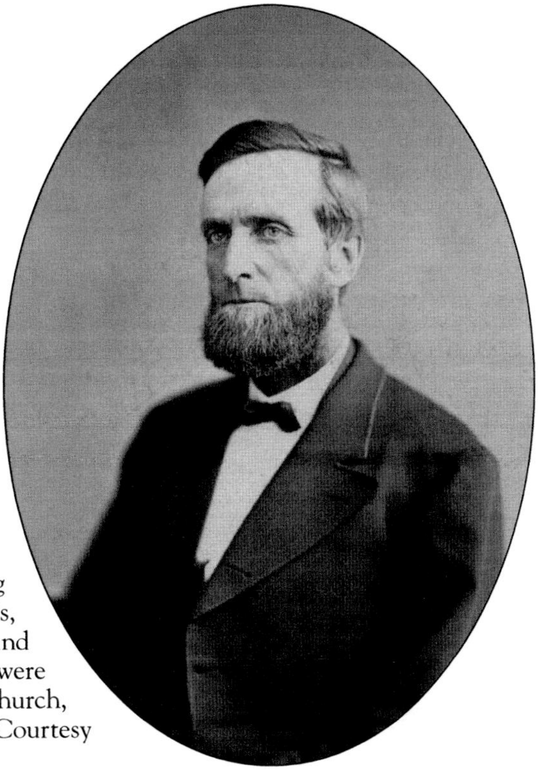

Thomas Davis Price was born in the Welsh Hills in 1826 at the Price farm. His grandfather Thomas Price I was born in Wales in 1754 and married Sarah Ann Powell in 1780. Their six children were born in Wales, including Edward, father of Thomas Davis Price. The senior Thomas Price arrived in the Welsh Hills in 1823 and purchased 87 acres from S. Turner on Cambria Mill Road in Newark Township. In 1832, Thomas deeded his son Edward 80 acres. Thomas Davis Price (at right) married Sarah Jane Jones (below) in 1855. During his life, he taught in the Welsh Hills schools, worked the family farm, raised Merino sheep, and became a fruit specialist. Thomas and Sarah were active members of the Welsh Hills Baptist Church, where Thomas served as clerk for 44 years. (Courtesy of T. David Price.)

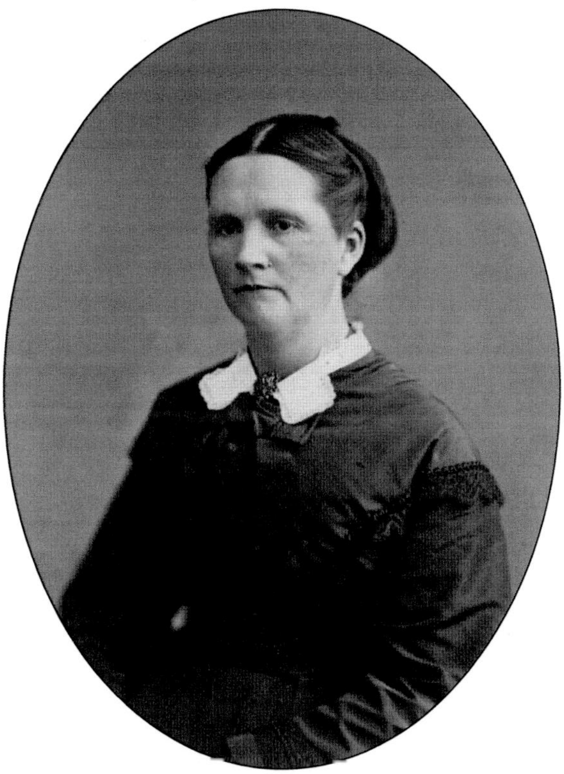

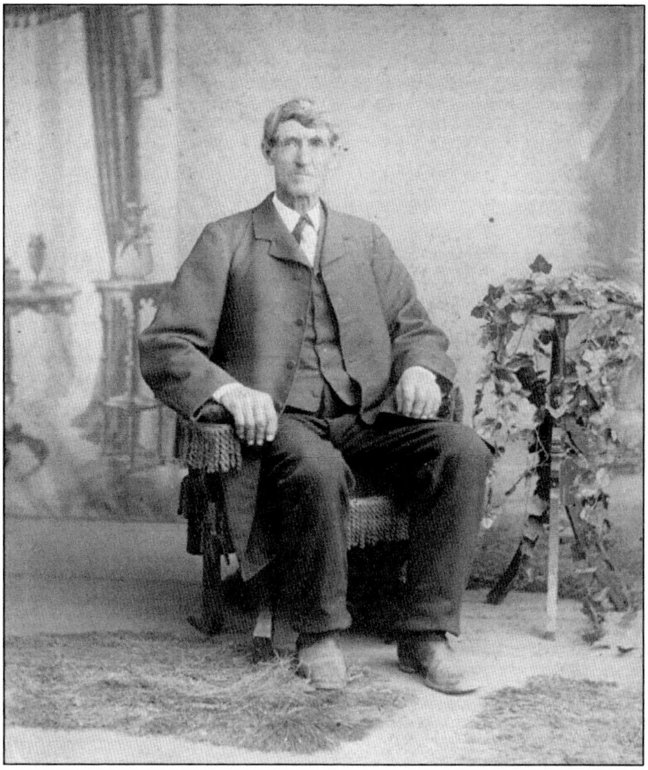

Simeon and Susannah Hankinson came to the Welsh Hills in 1875, when they purchased 53 acres on Dry Creek Road in Newton Township from their son Samuel for $2,400. Simeon Hankinson and Susannah Collingham were born and met in New Jersey. Susannah moved to Ohio in 1837 with relatives, followed in 1838 by Simeon. They married later the same year and lived in Perry County, then Franklin County, before moving to the Welsh Hills. They had 11 children, most of whom lived long lives and resided in the area. Simeon was a farmer his entire life and raised most of his sons to be farmers as well. (Courtesy of Ruth Valentine Sipe.)

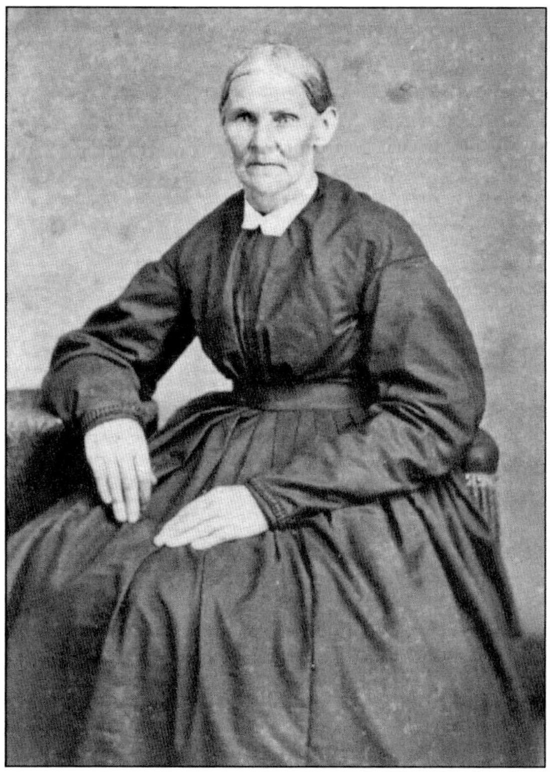

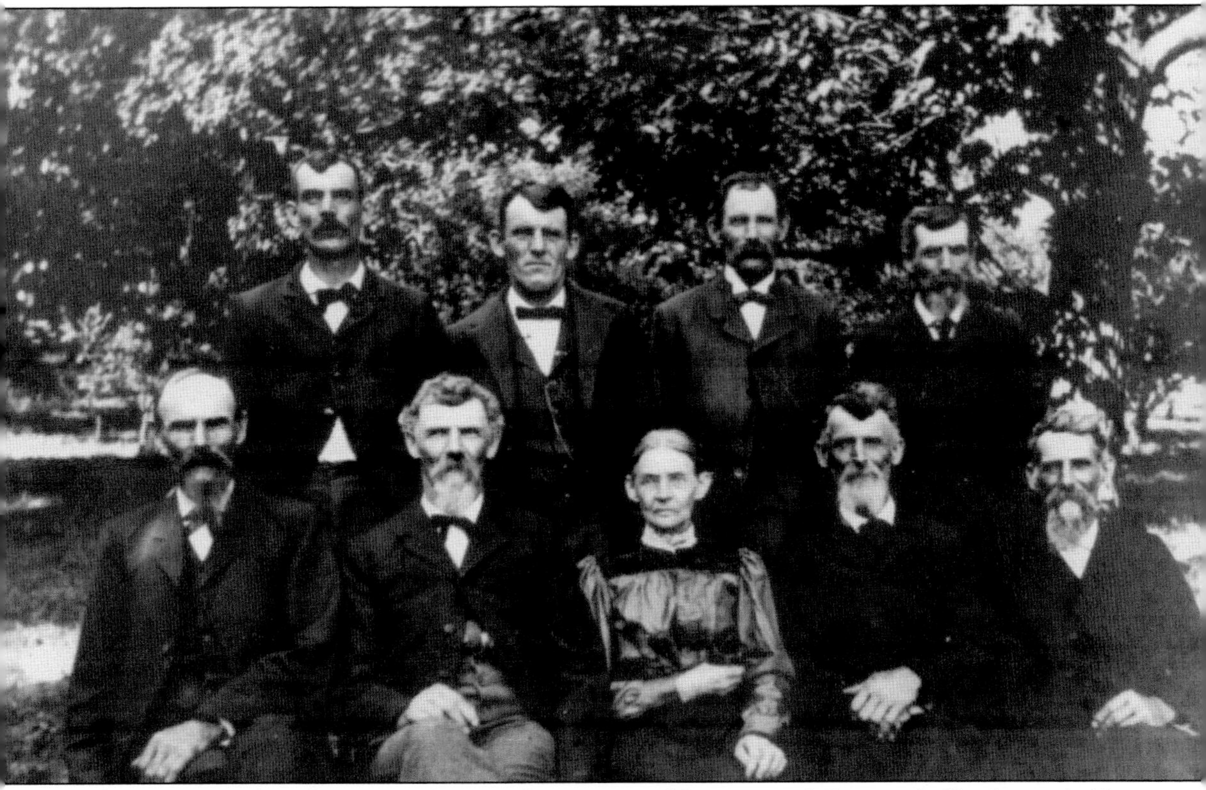

This photograph, taken around 1900, shows nine of Simeon and Susannah Hankinson's 11 children. They are, from left to right, (first row) Joseph, Samuel, Margaret (known as "Aunt Mag"), William, and George; (second row) Titus, Joshua, Simeon Jr., and David. Missing from this photograph are John and Mary Ellen. Mary Ellen passed away in 1884, at age 34, at the Columbus State Hospital. All of the brothers married and raised families. Aunt Mag, who lived to be 81, never married. She lived at her brothers' homes, moving from one house to the next. William and Rebecca Hankinson set aside a room in their home for Mag. Titus was Simeon and Susannah's youngest son. Still living in the Welsh Hills, 103-year-old Clarence (known as "Pete") is Titus's youngest child. (Courtesy of Ruth Valentine Sipe.)

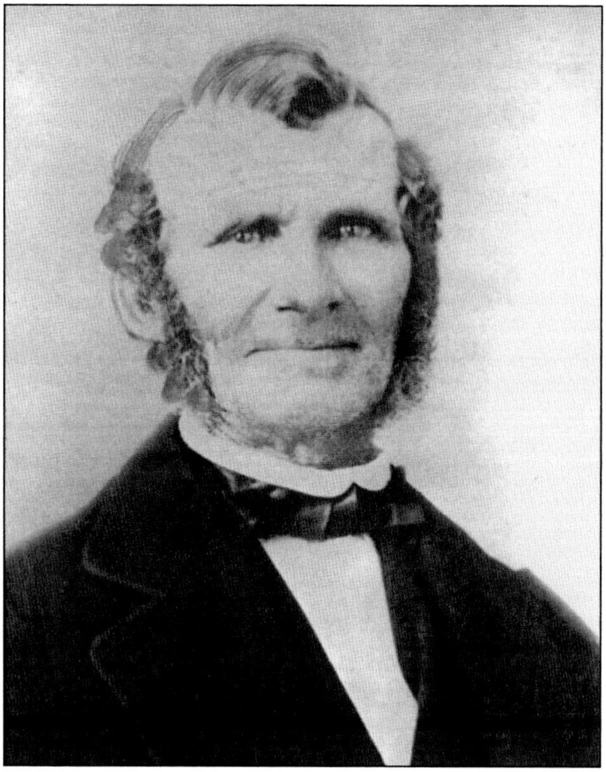

William (Billy) Cramer and Adaline Knight Cramer were married December 11, 1827. William was the grandson of Jimmy Johnson, who accompanied Theophilus Rees to Ohio. Adaline's ancestors have been traced back to the 1670s in her native Maine. William Cramer constructed the frame house known as Big Spring Farm, and he and Adaline raised five children. Their daughter Rebecca married William Hankinson and received one of the farms her father started on Hankinson Road. William was remembered as fabricating some of the best yarns in the Welsh Hills, tales always supported by his wife.

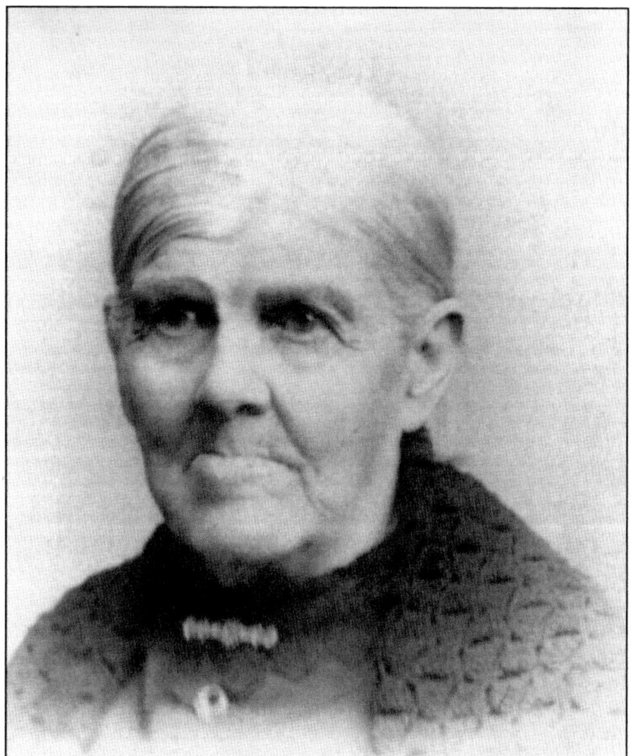

Born in Cardigan, South Wales, in 1787, David R. Jones came to America in 1800. Before moving to the Welsh Hills in 1839, he was a resident of Remsen, New York. Jones was one of the later Welsh residents to settle in the area, bringing his wife, Susan Thomas Jones, and 11 children. All of his sons had the middle name David. Jones served as a deacon for Welsh Hills Baptist Church. (Courtesy of Ruth Valentine Sipe.)

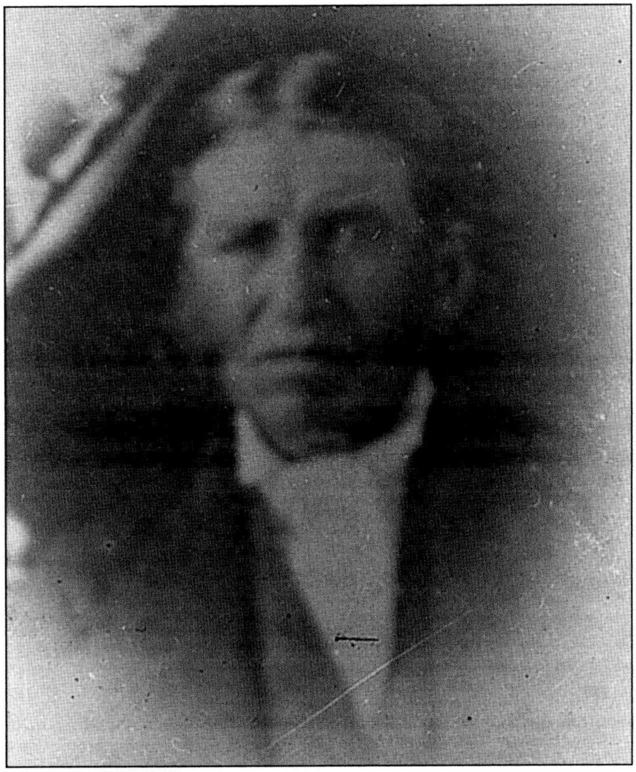

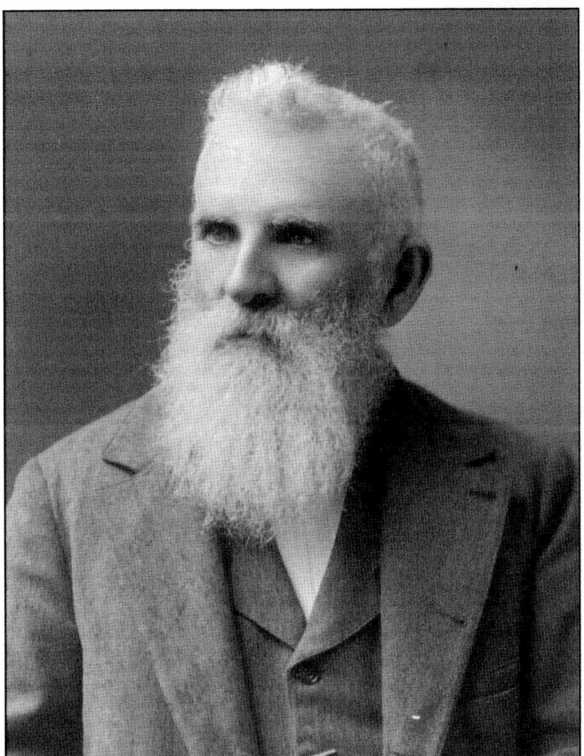

David D. Jones, one of the sons of David R. and Susan Thomas Jones, was a child when his parents moved the family from Remsen, New York. The Jones family moved into Big Spring Farm in 1839. It was during the time on the farm that David D. met Sarah Amanda Philipps, daughter of Samuel Griffith Philipps. (Courtesy of Ruth Valentine Sipe.)

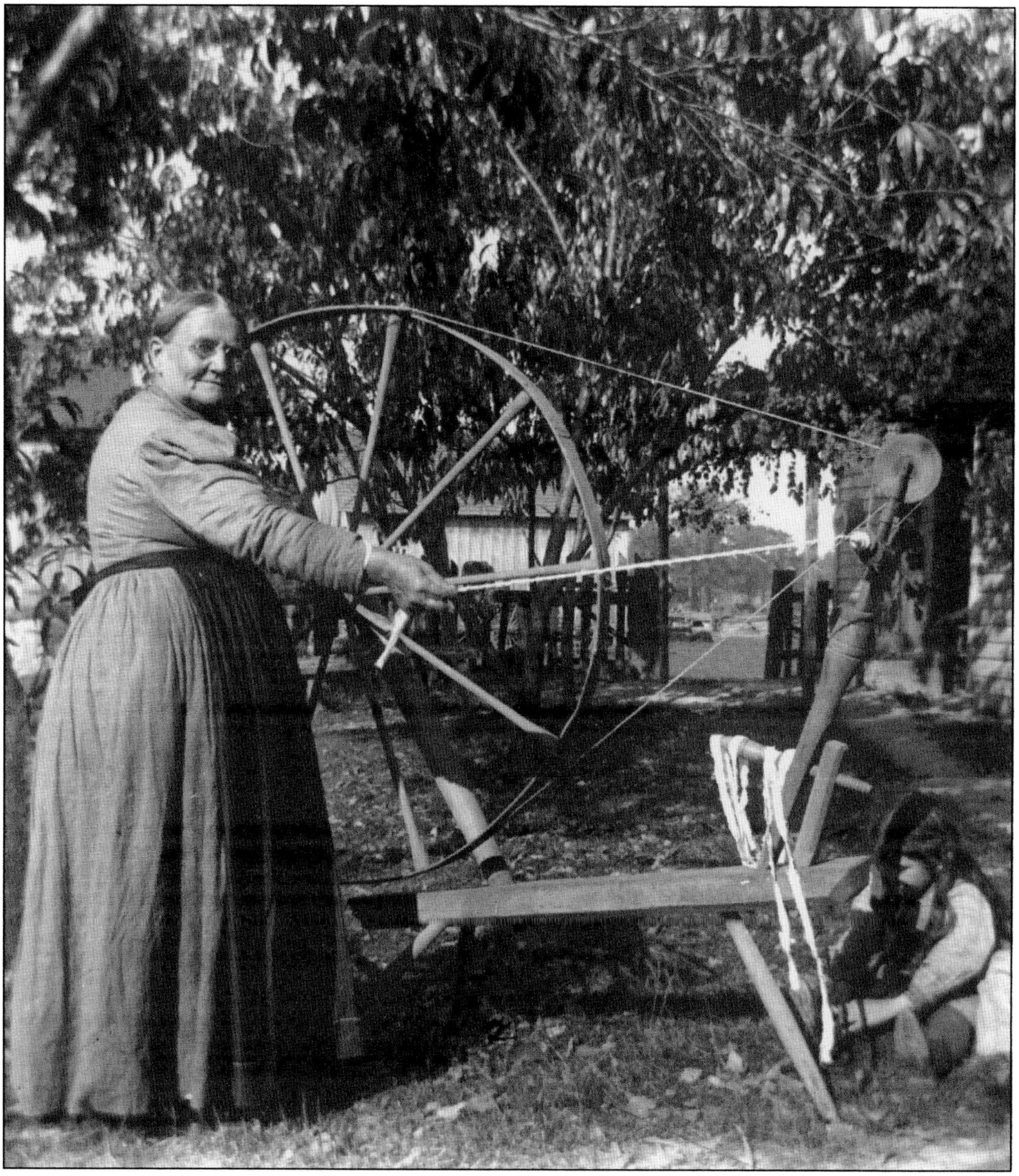

Sarah Amanda Philipps was the great-granddaughter of Thomas Philipps. She married David D. Jones on September 5, 1852. They remained in the Welsh Hills for a short time and had four daughters before moving to Fulton in Morrow County, Ohio, where they raised sheep and turkeys. Sarah is shown at the spinning wheel with one of their granddaughters. David and Sarah's daughter Lilah, who took up photography as a hobby, made this image around 1890. Numerous glass negatives are still in the family's possession. (Courtesy of Ruth Valentine Sipe.)

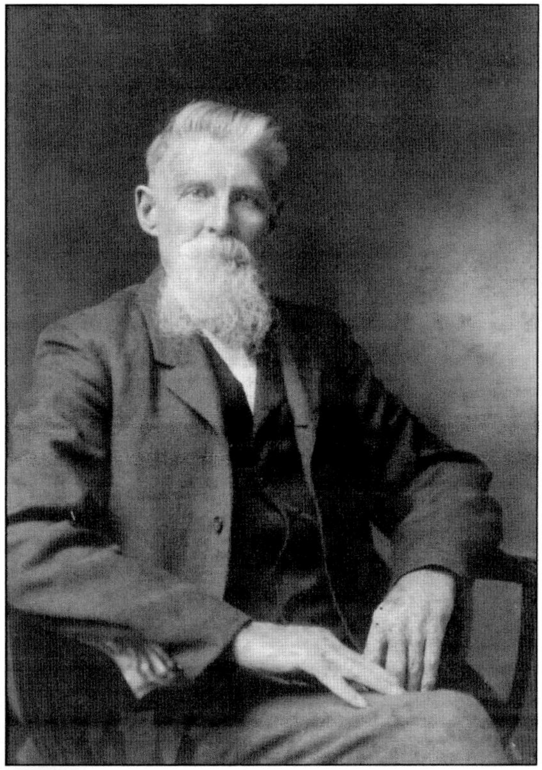

David Lewis Evans and Ariadne Davis Evans were lifelong residents of the Welsh Hills. David was the oldest son of Thomas and Elizabeth Evans and a grandson of Joseph and Ann Evans, who migrated from Carmarthenshire, Wales, on January 12, 1801. His maternal grandparents were "Little" Davy Thomas and Elizabeth Rees, and his maternal great-grandfather was Theophilus Rees. Ariadne Davis was the daughter of David and Isabella Davis, natives of South Wales. David Evans owned 73 acres in the Welsh Hills, 25 of those in McKean Township. He devoted his entire life to farming the land on which he and Ariadne lived. They were members of Welsh Hills Baptist Church, where David served as a trustee.

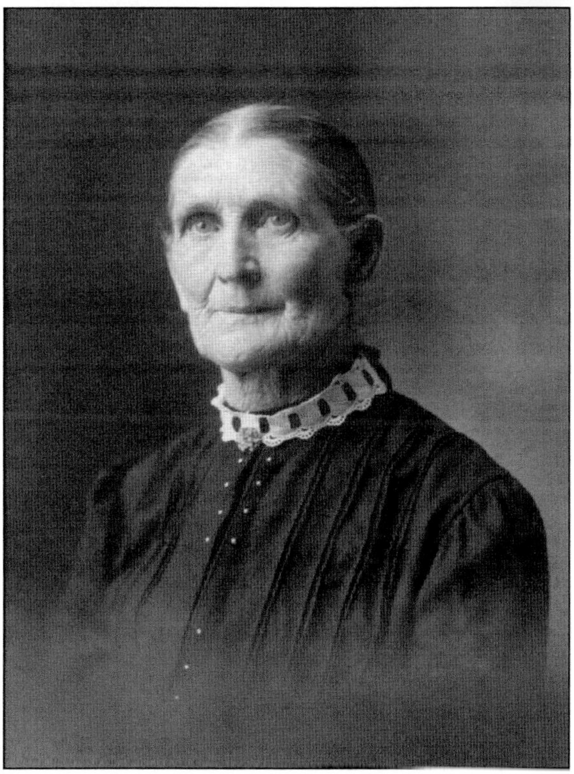

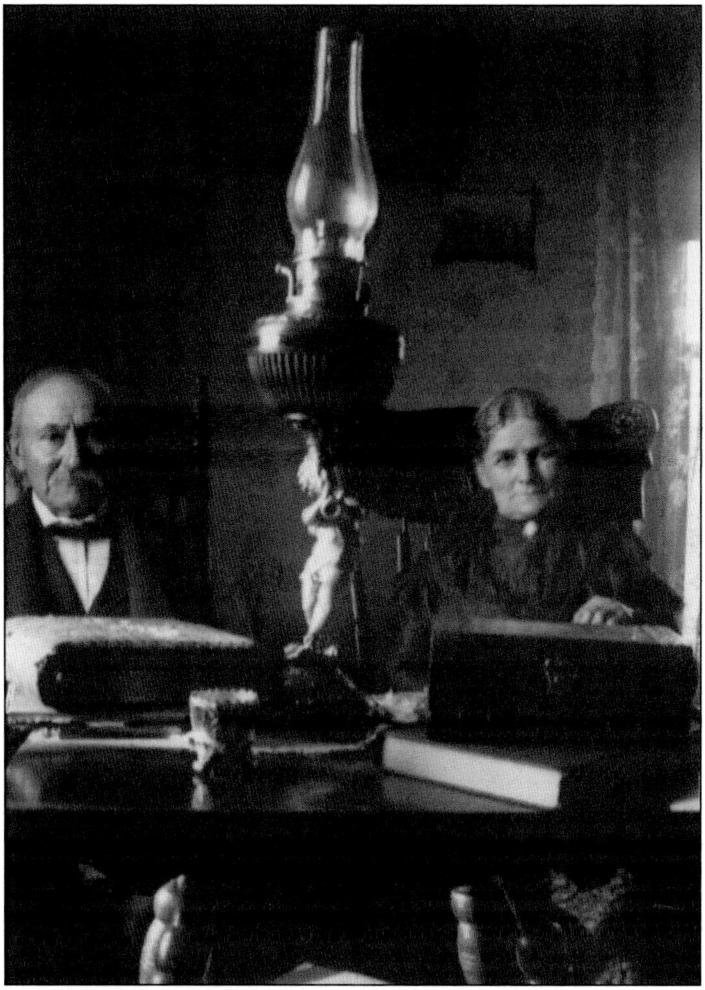

Jacob ("Jake") and Nellie Frederick built their home on Welsh Hills Road, where both of these photographs were taken—the image at left taken around 1890 and the one below around 1910. Nellie was a great-granddaughter of Thomas Philipps. Jacob George Frederick was born in Newton Township in 1836. His family moved between Illinois and Ohio several times before Jake returned to the Welsh Hills. On November 25, 1863, Jake was wounded and lost his left arm in the Battle of Missionary Ridge. In 1865, Jake married Nellie. As a young couple they lived in Illinois until 1877, when they returned to the Welsh Hills, where they remained. Even with one arm, Jake managed to make a living as a house painter. He and Nellie had four children. One daughter died at age three. (Courtesy of Ruth Valentine Sipe.)

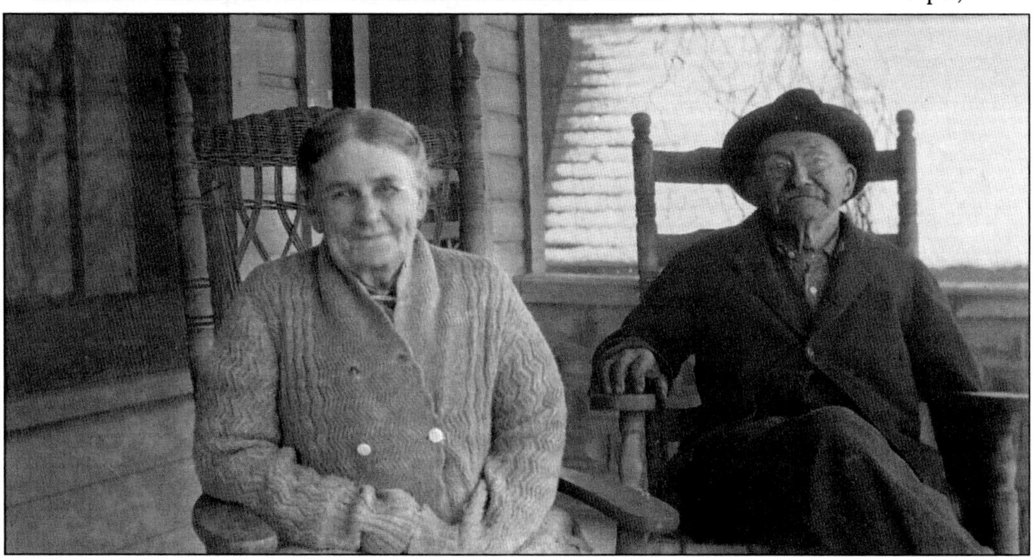

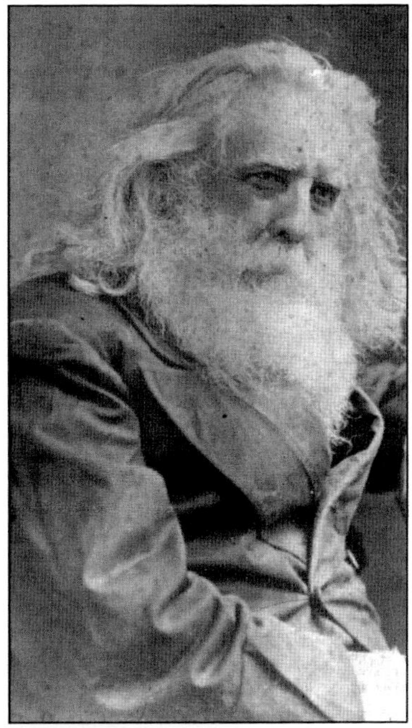

Thomas "Tom" D. Jones (right), son of David R. and Susan Thomas Jones, was a renowned sculptor. Born in Remsen, New York, he spent the early part of his life in the Welsh Hills. The photograph below shows an early sculpture representing his mentor and first employer, Erasmus Philipps, a stonemason who taught Tom his trade. During his life, Tom created two works of art that are proudly displayed at the state capitol in Columbus. The first is a white Carrara marble bust of Abraham Lincoln, based on a plaster likeness created at Lincoln's home, where Lincoln would ask Jones to comment on his speeches. The second sculpture is a high relief scene of the surrender at Vicksburg. Jones is buried in the Welsh Hills Cemetery. (Courtesy of Ruth Valentine Sipe.)

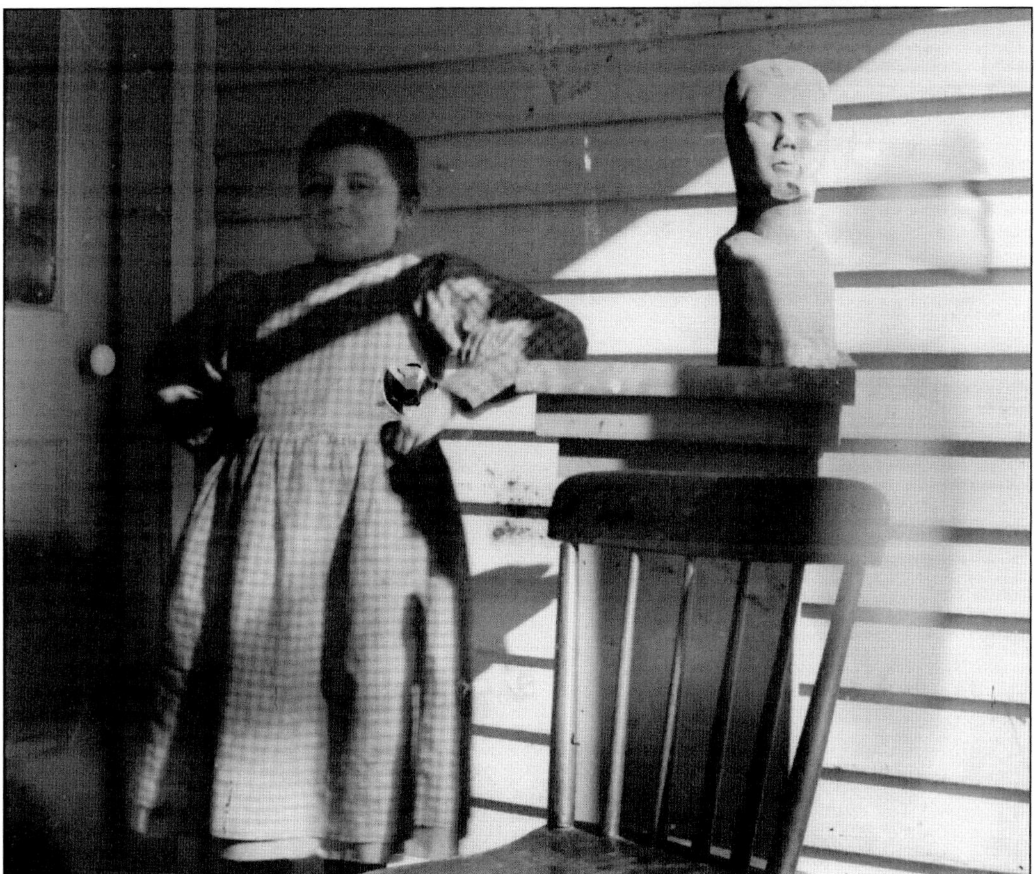

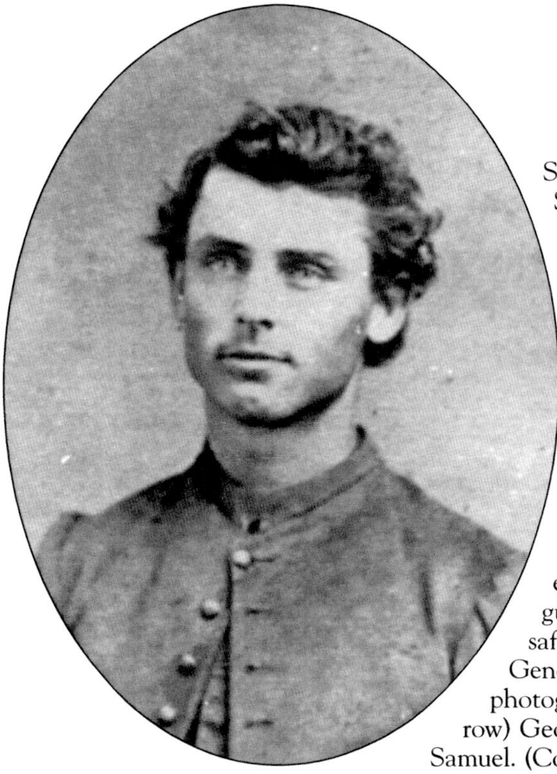

Simeon and Susannah Hankinson's sons, Samuel G., William Austin (pictured at left), Joseph F., and George C., served with the Union army during the Civil War. Samuel enlisted in 1861 in Company D, 18th Regiment U.S. Infantry and received a medical discharge after contracting measles. William enlisted in 1864 and served in Company F, 1st Regiment of the U.S. Veteran Volunteer Engineers. Joseph and George enlisted in 1864 in Company C, 10th O.V. Cavalry. Joseph lied about his age; he was only 16. He was captured by the Confederate army but managed to escape by hiding in a field of high grass as the guards searched for him. He returned to Ohio safely, as did his brothers. George accompanied General Sherman on his "March to the Sea." The photograph below shows, from left to right, (first row) George and William, (second row) Joseph and Samuel. (Courtesy of Ruth Valentine Sipe.)

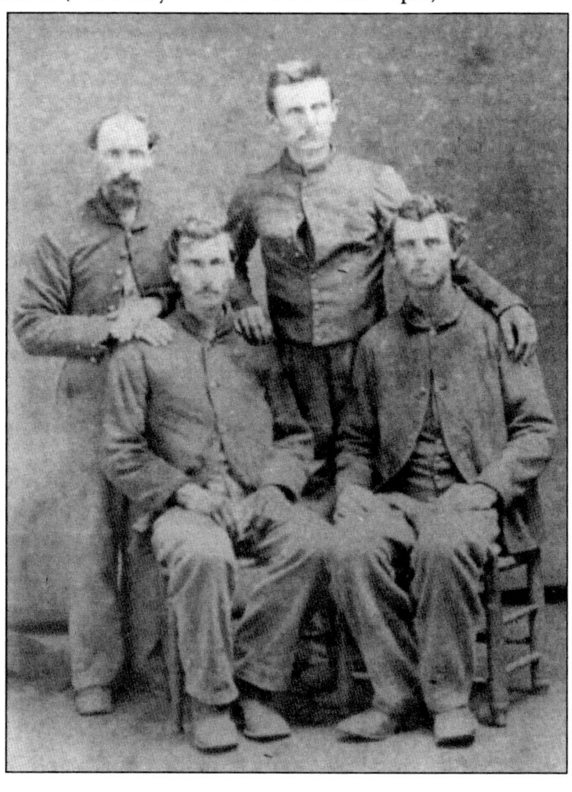

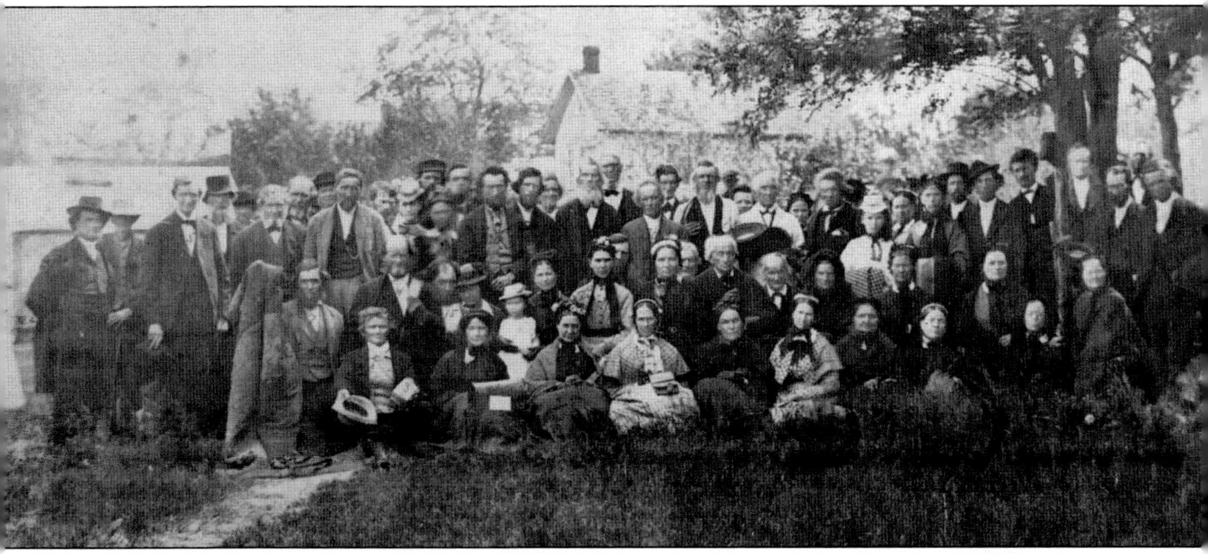

Most of the people in this early 1890s photograph trace their ancestry to the first Welsh settlers. Theophilus Rees's descendants include grandsons David Rees Thomas (second row, first on left) and his brother Thomas J. Thomas (second row, third from left); granddaughter Elizabeth Rees (first row, third from left), and her husband, James Black (third row, second from left); and great-grandson George Washington Evans (back row, sixth from left). Price Glynn (third row, sixth from left) is Thomas Price I's great-grandson. Samuel Jones Philipps, great-grandson of Thomas Philipps, is thought to be the man standing at the left of the tree. There is a ghostly image in front of the tree that appears to have been placed after the photograph was taken. (Courtesy of the Granville Historical Society.)

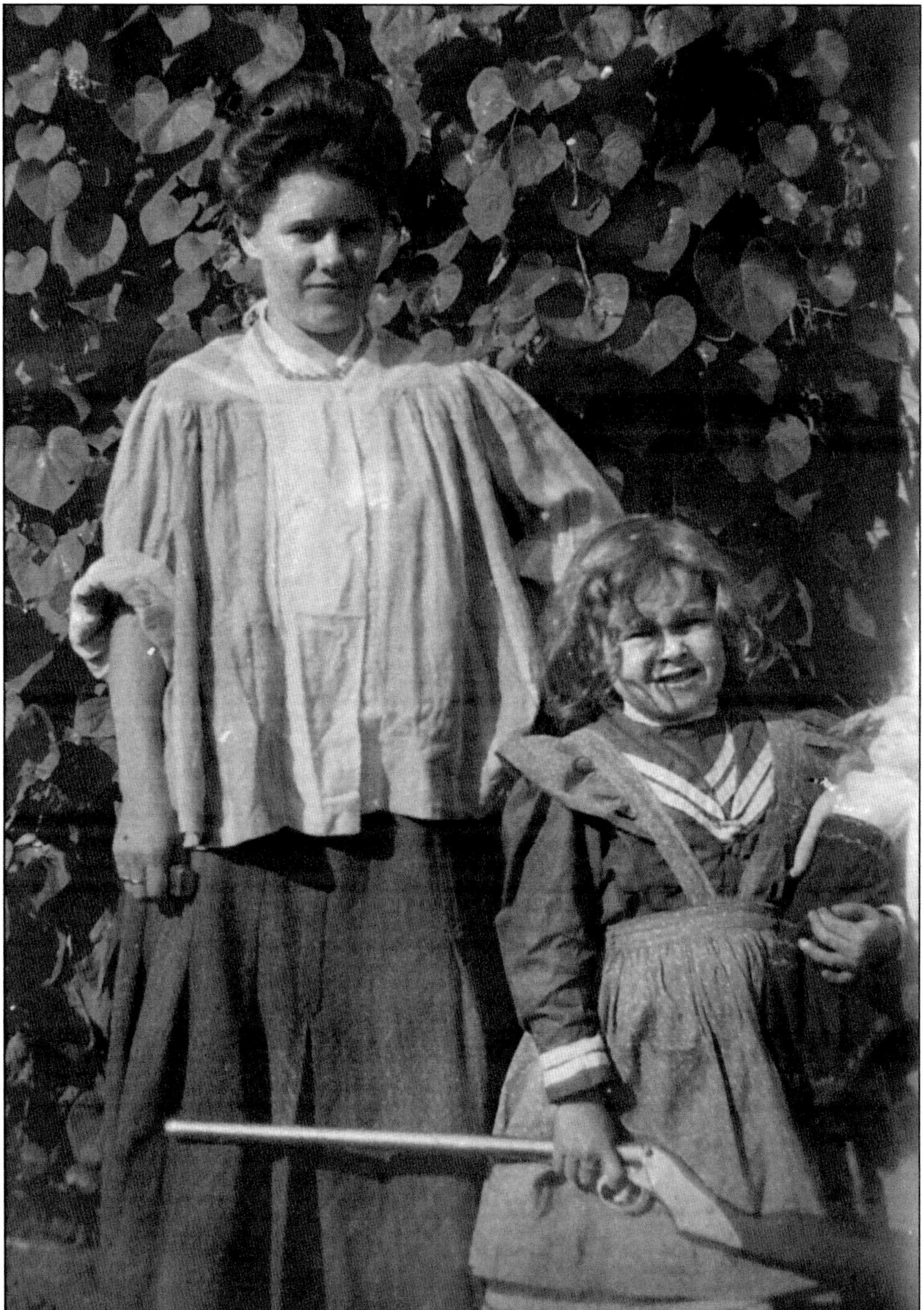

Shown with her daughter Madeline Inez in this photograph from around 1906, Victoria Belle Philipps was the second surviving of 10 children born to Samuel and Wilhelmina Williams Philipps. Victoria married George Franklin Stoner. Madeline Inez married Carl William Nutter, and their daughter Victoria Louise married Richard Spaulding and relocated the family to California. Victoria and Richard Spaulding's daughter Mary is the mother of Cpl. Patrick Tillman. This picture was taken at the Samuel Jones Philipps home on Philipps Road.

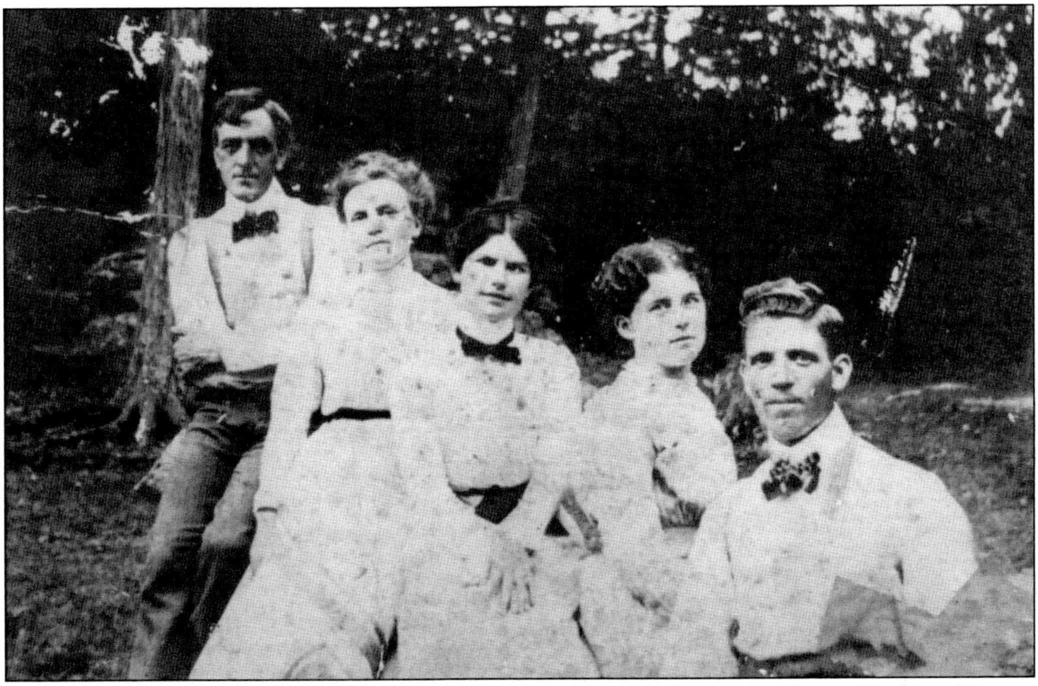

In this group of friends from the early 1900s are, from left to right, Homer Price, Florence Hoover Osburn, Mamie (Mary Oolaita) Philipps, Dora Hankinson, and Oscar Osburn. Homer was married to Gertrude Harlan Price (shown on the cover of this book). Florence married Oscar Osburn. Samuel Jones Philipps's second child, Mamie, married Samuel Crane Wheeler. Dora—William and Mary Hankinson's third eldest—married Samuel Sipe. (Courtesy of T. David Price.)

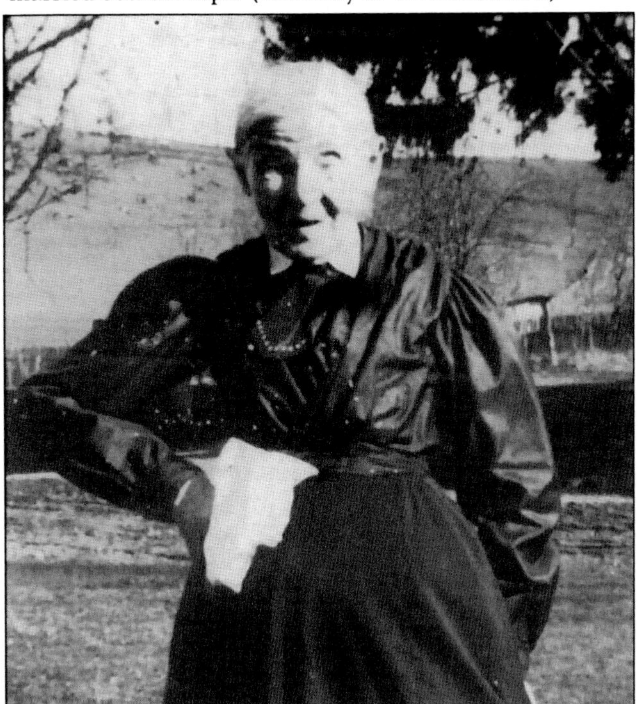

Esther Jones Williams was born in Cardiganshire, Wales, on November 24, 1823. She came to Ohio with her parents, David and Gwen Jones, in 1824, and married John W. Williams in 1840. Esther and John had 11 children and lived at the family home in the Welsh Hills. Esther was baptized at age 13 in the Welsh Hills Baptist Church, where she remained a faithful member until her death at age 93.

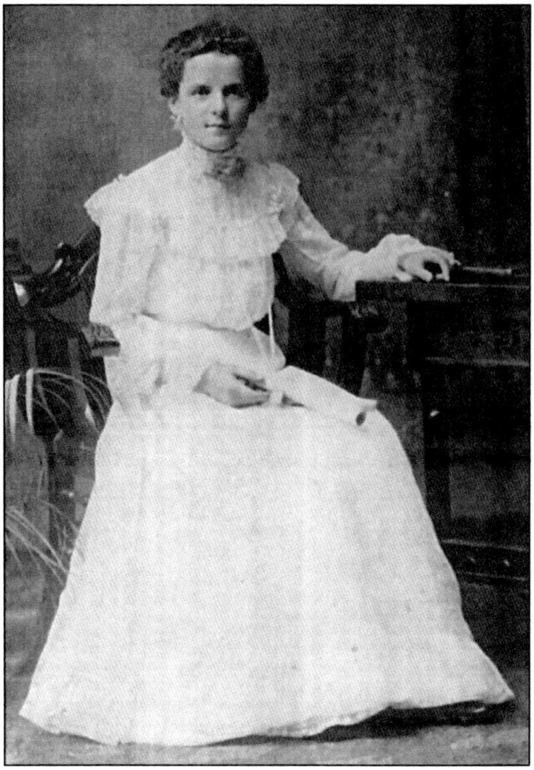

First cousins Elsie Lodena Hankinson (left) and Ada Blanche Hankinson (below) were both born in 1896. The fifth child of William and Rebecca Hankinson, Elsie died at 27 from consumption (tuberculosis). She was married to Philip Philipps. Titus and Ellen Hankinson's eldest child, Ada, married Edgar Taylor in 1911. Her youngest brother, Clarence, known to his family as "Pete," is the last survivor of this generation and still resides at the family farm at age 103. (Courtesy of Ruth Valentine Sipe.)

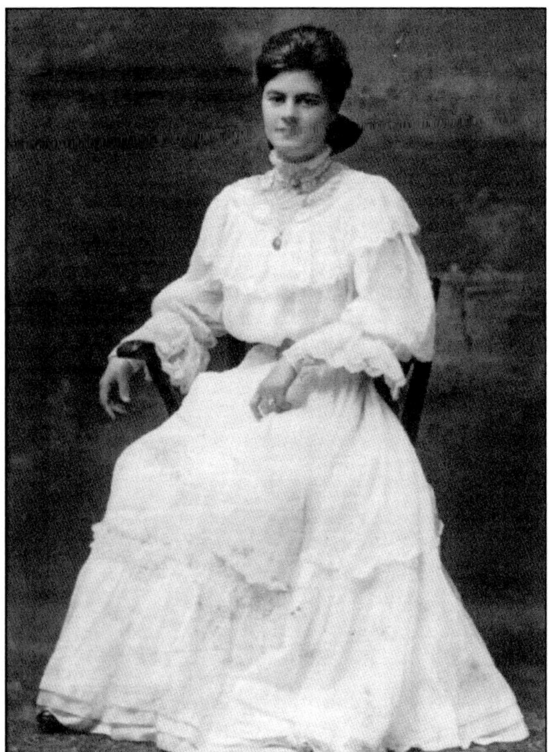

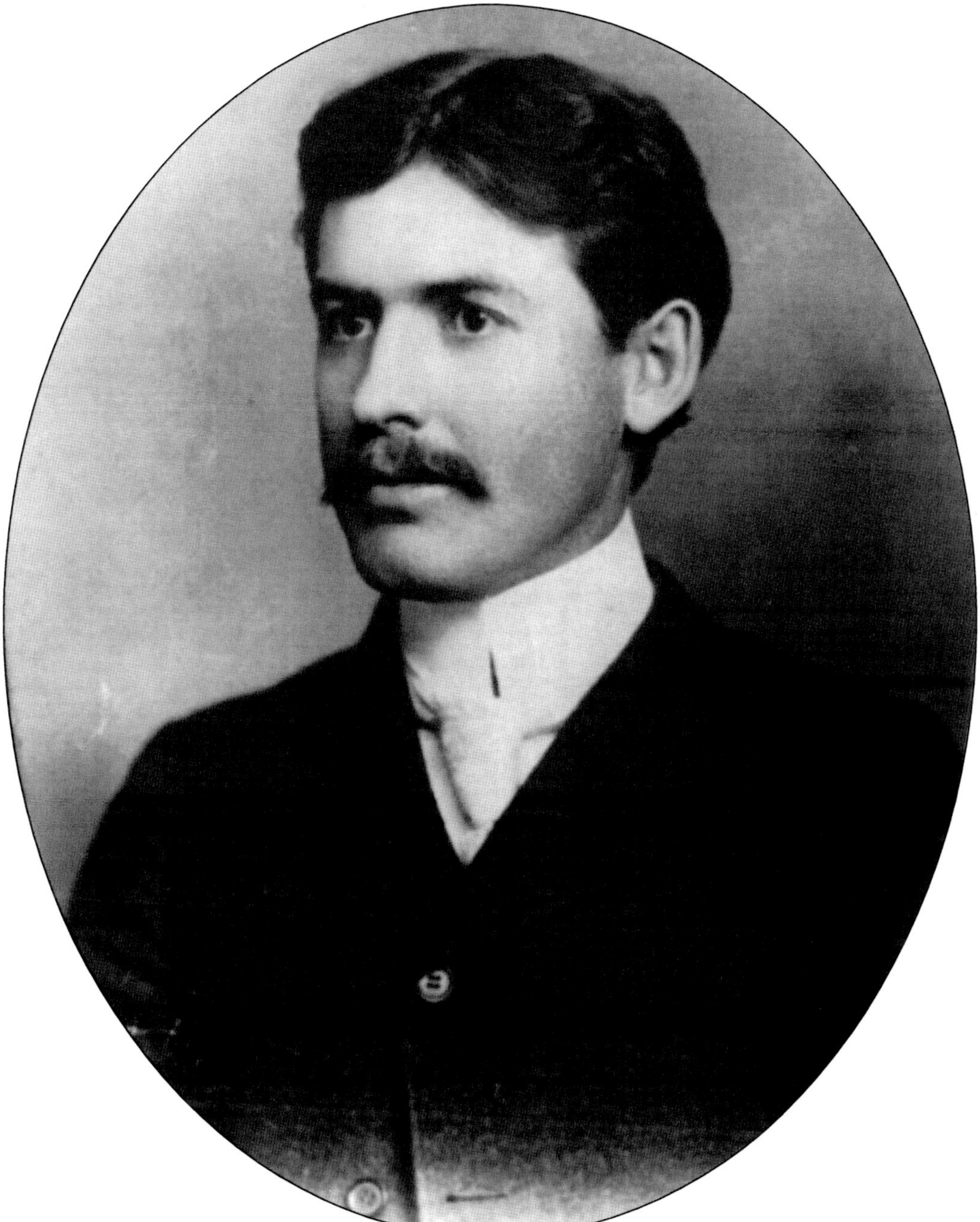

A grandson of David R. Jones (one of the early settlers), Columbus attorney William Harvey Jones was a noted local historian. He was raised in the Welsh Hills and attended Denison University in Granville. William penned an article titled "The Welsh Hills, The Story of a Pioneer Community," that he presented at a Jones family reunion in 1935 and wrote a three-part feature about other Welsh communities in Ohio that appeared in a newspaper called the *Cambrian* from July to September 1907. He encouraged his uncle David D. Jones to chronicle his memories of the Welsh Hills in 1905. This narrative was published in the *Granville Times* in 1931. William's brother Ben Jones was a noted historian and writer as well.

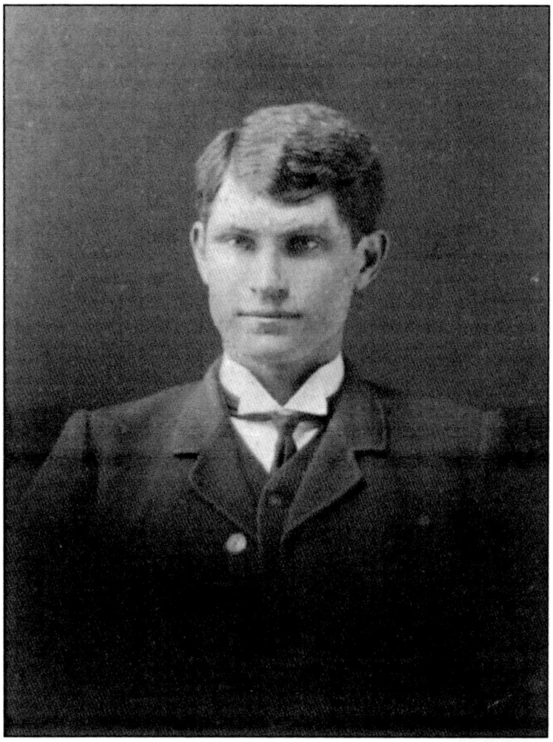

Born in 1862, Thomas David Evans was the son of David Lewis and Ariadne Davis Evans and a descendant of Theophilus Rees. Tom had one brother and two sisters. He married Mary A. Hankinson in 1892. They had two children, Grace and Gene, and resided on Hankinson Road in a house built by her grandfather Cramer. Mary was the daughter of William and Rebecca Hankinson and granddaughter of Simeon and Susannah Hankinson. Tom Evans was a carpenter and constructed many homes in the town of Granville and also worked on the Granville Inn. For many years, he served on the Licking County Fair board. He is remembered by his grandson Thomas Philipps for having a great sense of humor.

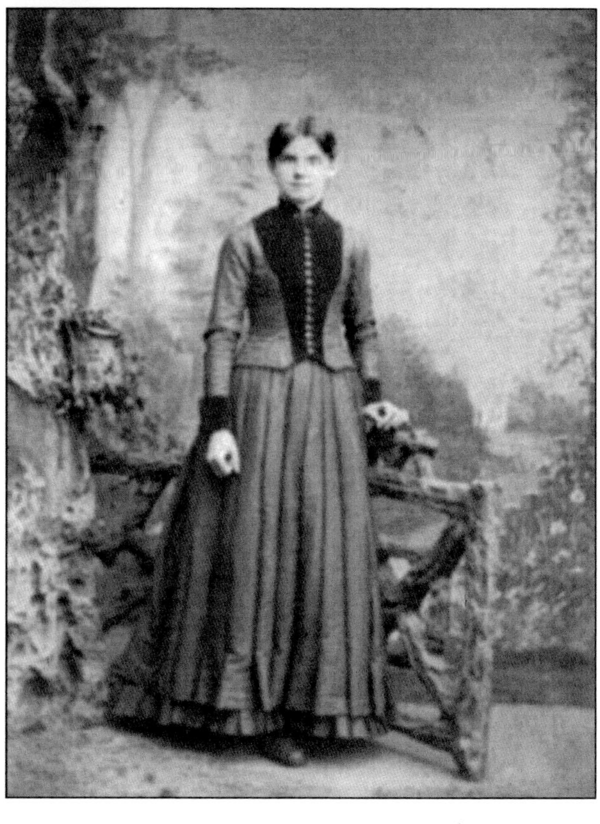

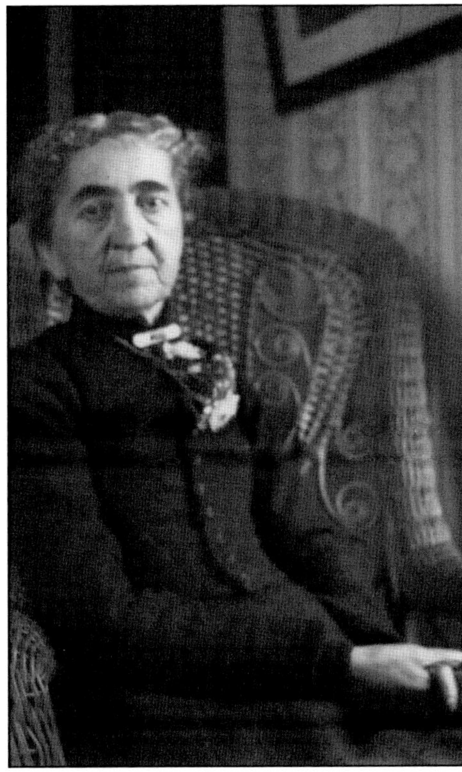

Sisters Susan Pittsford (right) and Mary Eunice Pittsford (below) were granddaughters of David Pittsford, a native of Wales. Their father, James, was born in Beulah, Pennsylvania, and came to the Welsh Hills with his family in 1816. In addition to Susan and Mary, the other children were David, Phoebe Ann, Enoch J., William H., and Frank J. The Pittsford farm, where the family raised sheep, was located on Welsh Hills Road, not far from the Welsh Hills School. Mary married Henry H. Hillbrandt, a farmer from Union Station, Ohio. Never married, Susan taught at the Welsh Hills Old Stone Schoolhouse and served for many years as matron of the Ohio Orphan Asylum. With the exception of Frank, the Pittsford children all became teachers.

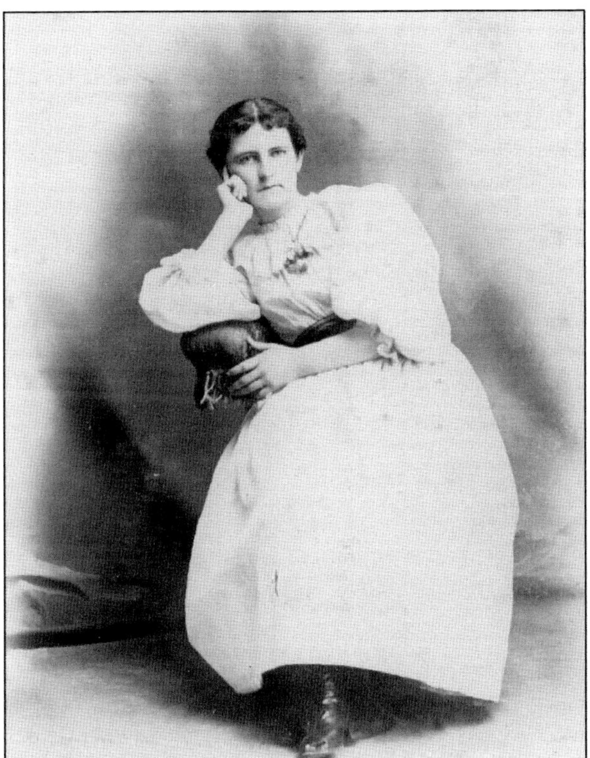

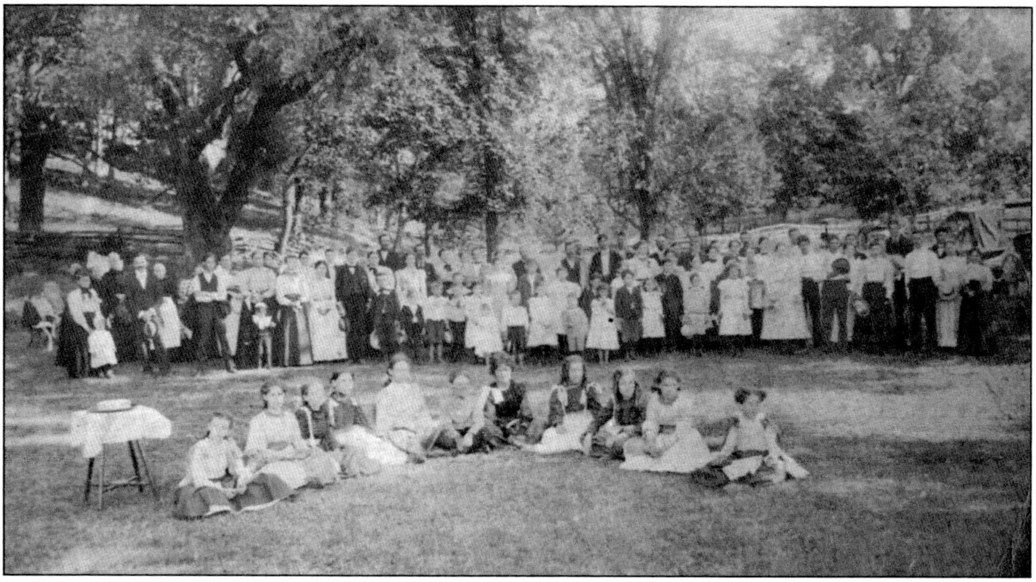

Nellie Philipps Frederick (far left, in a bonnet) enjoys a Sunday school picnic with other members of the Welsh Hills Baptist Church. Other people in this photograph are from the Hankinson, Griffith, Price, Williams, Evans, and Philipps families.

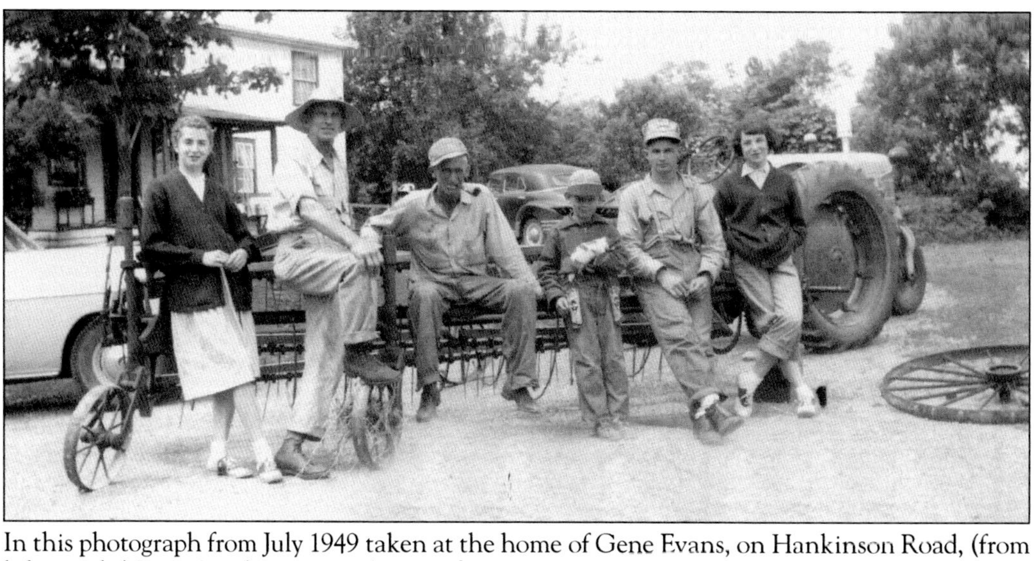

In this photograph from July 1949 taken at the home of Gene Evans, on Hankinson Road, (from left to right) Janet Hankinson, Archie Hankinson, Gene Evans, David Evans, Eddie Hankinson, and Rebecca Hankinson rest on a hay rig. Janet, Eddie, and Rebecca are the children from Archie's second marriage, to Florella Wacker. He and Mildred Jones, his first wife who died at age 35, had four children—William, Marian, Elizabeth, and Archie.

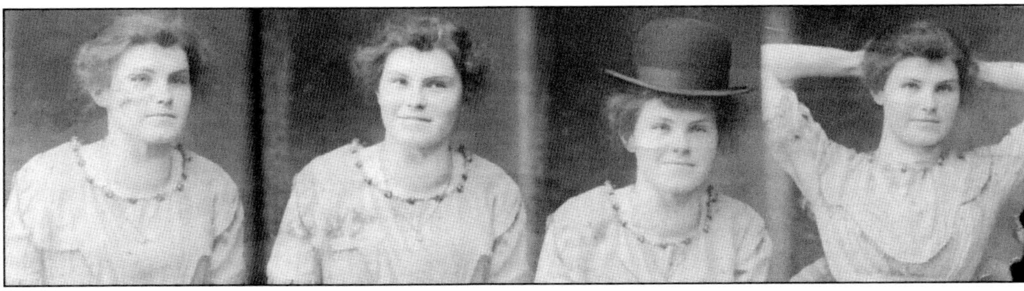

Grace Evans Philipps, a fifth-generation descendant of Welsh settler Theophilus Rees, married Thomas Warren Philipps in 1914 and raised five children. This was one of the marriages between direct descendants of the founding fathers of the Welsh Hills. The four photographs of Grace above were taken during her youth and shows her playful character. One of the rare females in the area who obtained a college education, she graduated from Denison University. The photograph below shows Grace with some of her cousins at the Frederick home on Welsh Hills Road. They are, from left to right, Lorna and Dorothy Jones (daughters of Gertrude Evans and Ben Jones), Grace Evans (daughter of Tom and Mary Evans), and Hazel and Cecil Hankinson (daughters of Jane Evans and Simeon Hankinson). Grace was a member of the DAR (Daughters of the American Revolution).

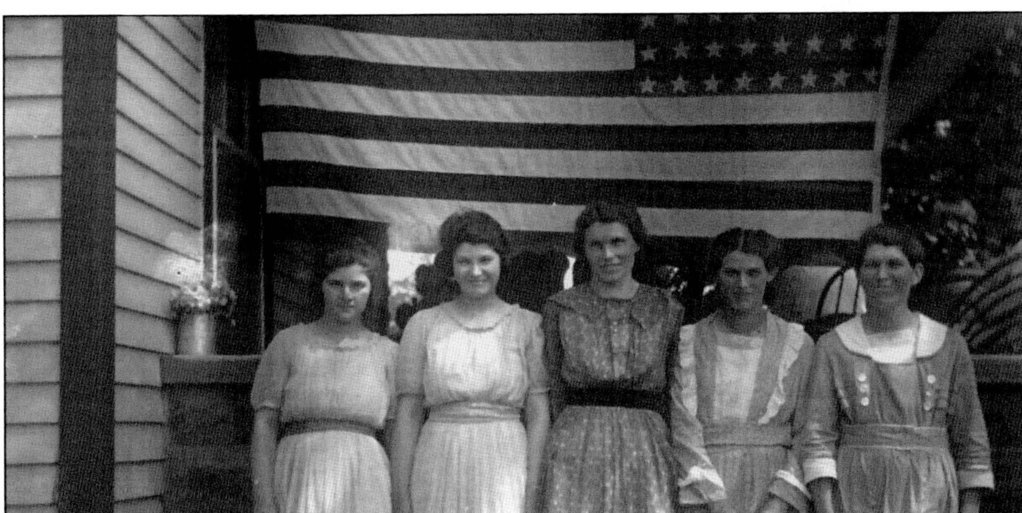

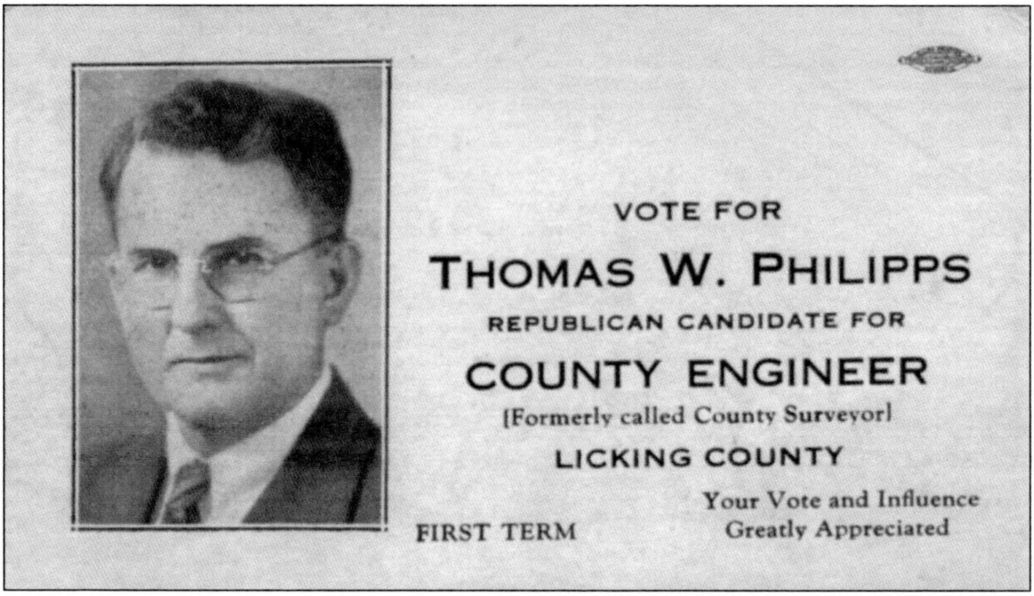


Thomas Warren Philipps, fourth-generation descendant of Welsh settler Thomas Philipps, was the winning candidate on the Republican ticket for Licking County engineer in 1940. During construction on a new bridge on North Street, he was hit in the head by a steel beam and died in June 1941 at age 52. A graduate of Denison University, Philipps became a schoolteacher, high school principal, surveyor, and politician. He was also a member of the Masonic lodge, patron of the Order of Eastern Star, and a member of the Welsh Hills Grange. (Courtesy of Janet Philipps Procida.)

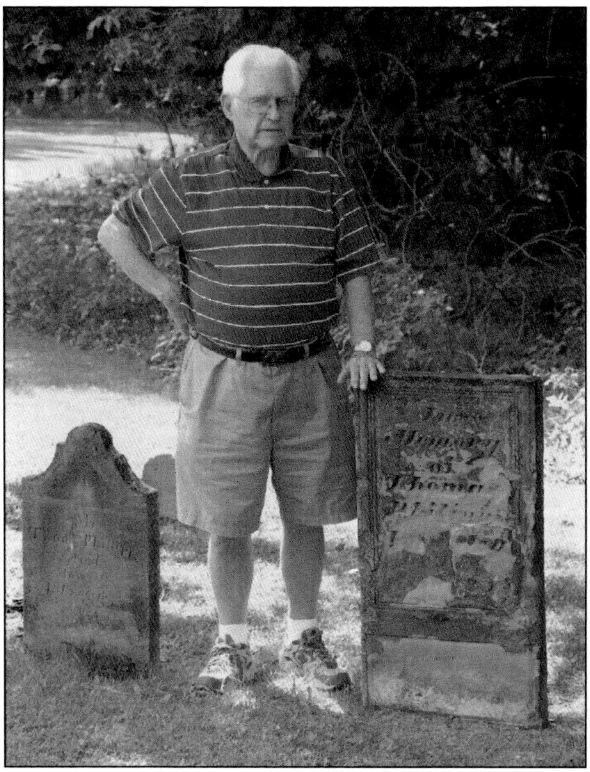

Thomas Evans (Tom) Philipps is standing next to the grave of his great-great-great-grandfather Thomas Philipps, located in the Philipps cemetery. His parents were Thomas Warren Philipps and Grace Evans Philipps, a descendant of Theophilus Rees. Tom, now 91, still resides near the Welsh Hills. (Photograph by Janet Philipps Procida.)

# *Three*

# CHILDREN

Adventurous and mischievous youth in the pioneer days were not so different from children in the Hills today. Most early settlers had large families, with many children surviving into adulthood. Though they helped with the farm chores, youngsters still found time to play. Parents disciplined but still doted on their offspring. Some parents spent time and money to have professional photographs taken that are still treasured today. These images offer a glimpse back to the early days and show that, despite hardships, children were often happy.

Families taught their children strong moral values, and formal education was very important to the early settlers of the Welsh Hills. Even though most of the children of the early settlers worked on the family farms, time was devoted to schooling. Many young people from the community went on to attend colleges and become prominent citizens in the community. The Welsh Hills produced doctors, lawyers, politicians, writers, teachers, and artists.

Dr. Samuel Wheeler, a descendant of Thomas Philipps, wrote about his boyhood at the home of his uncle Phil Philipps in the Welsh Hills during the early 1920s. His stories detail the various chores required of children on farms as well as the playful adventures they experienced.

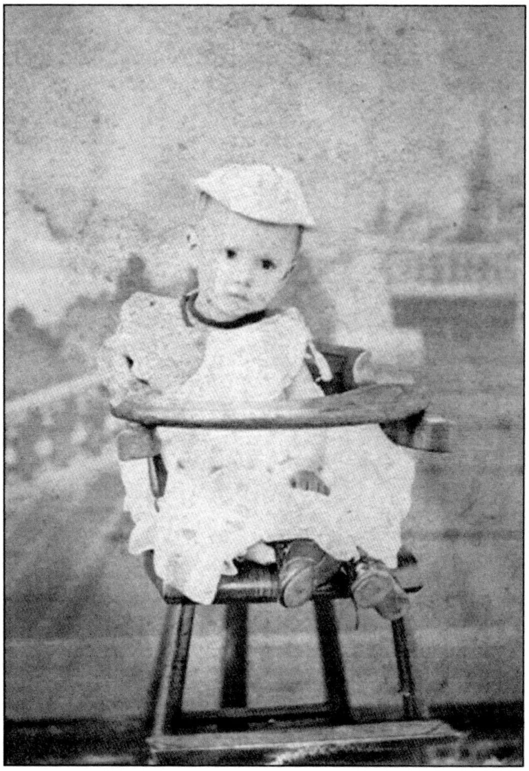

Seen here as infants in the 1870s, Arthur Frederick (left) and his sister, Nellie (below), were children of Jacob George and Ellen (Nellie Philipps) Frederick. Born when the family lived in Illinois, Arthur and Nellie grew up in the house their father built on Welsh Hills Road. Arthur married Hattie McFarland and raised two children, Laura and Robert. Nellie raised one son, John Leonard Briggs, from an 1895 marriage to Edward Franklin Briggs. She celebrated her 100th birthday in 1975 and died in 1976, having survived three husbands.

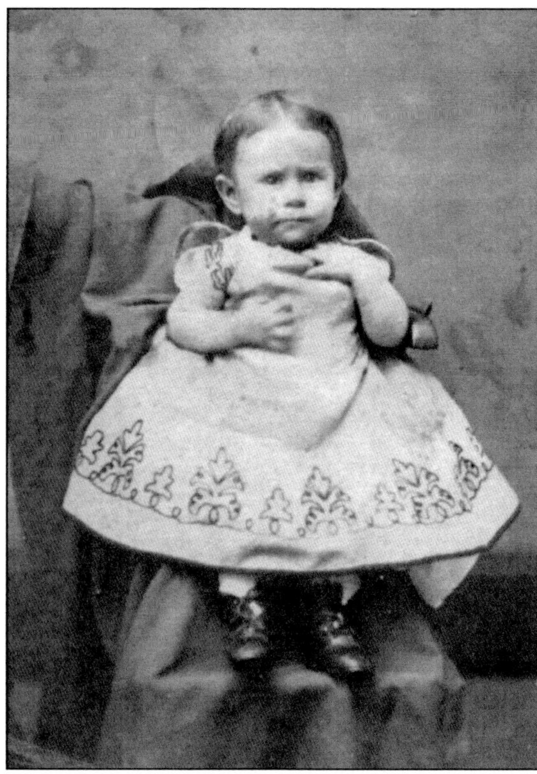

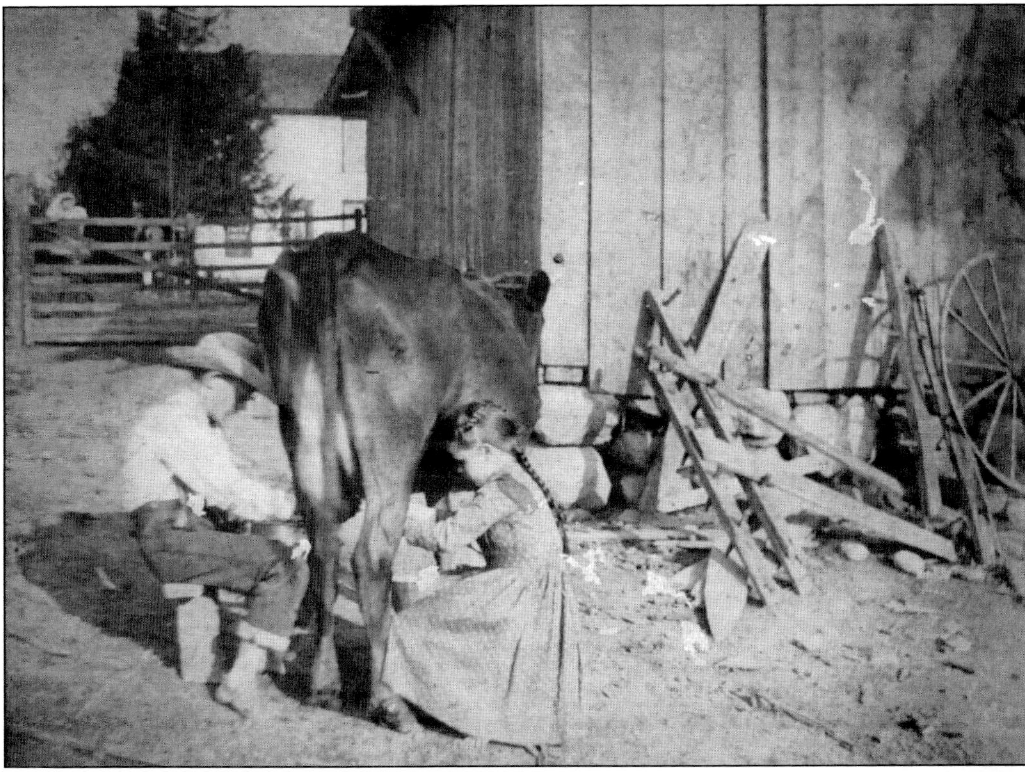

Archie Hankinson and Grace Evans share the chore of milking one of the family cows. Grace's mother was Mary Hankinson Evans. Only four years older than Grace, Archie was one of Mary's younger brothers and Grace's uncle. The house in the background in the image above is the Hankinson home on Hankinson Road, where Grace and her brother, Gene, were raised.

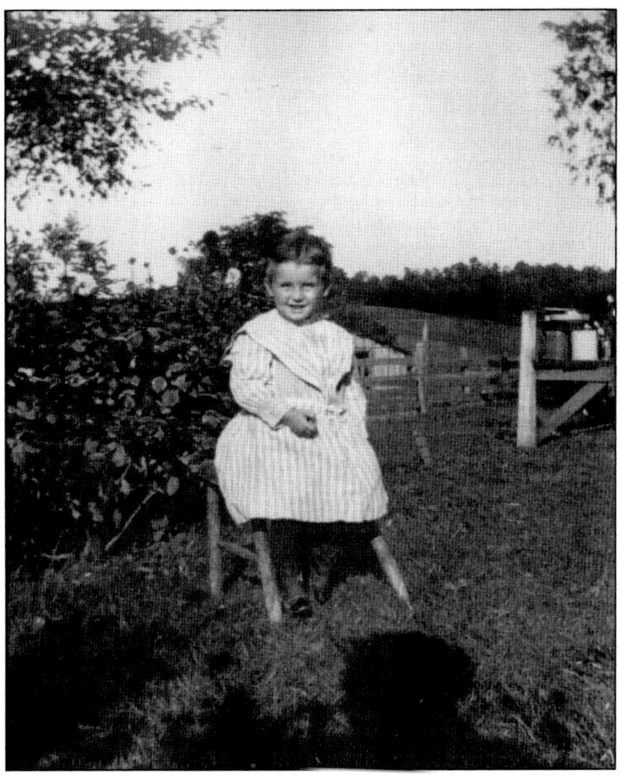

Born William Robert Eugene Evans in 1901, Gene was the younger brother of Grace Evans. It was common into the early 1900s to outfit young boys in dresses. It is also possible that he inherited this outfit from his sister. In his adult life, Gene married Burdelle Hobbs and raised a son, David, who still resides near the Welsh Hills. (Courtesy of Mary Ellen Everett.)

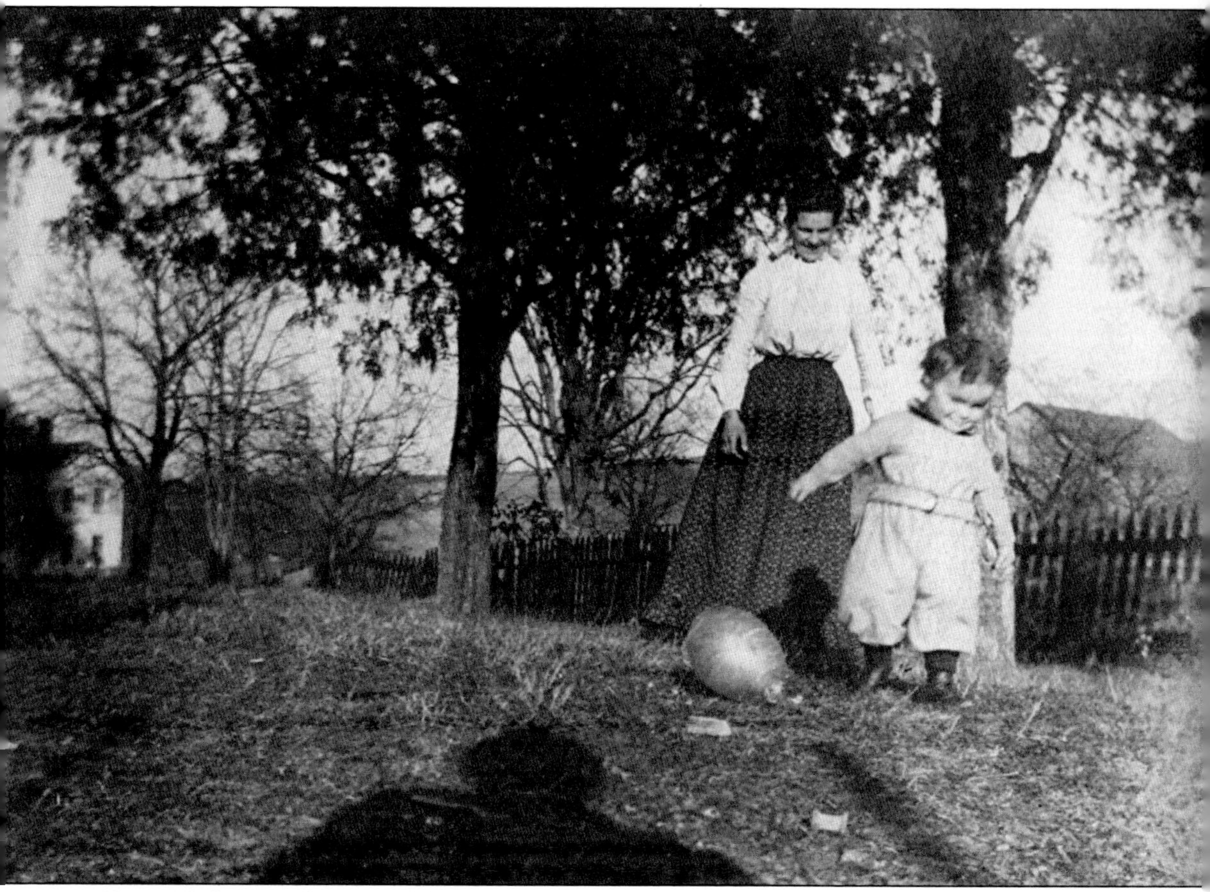

Young Wilbur Hankinson is followed closely by his mother, Mami Eigher Hankinson. Wilbur and his sister, Lucy, grew up on one of the Hankinson farms on Hankinson Road. Their father was Rutherford Hayes Hankinson, son of William Hankinson. After their mother died in 1907, Wilbur and Lucy's father married Bertha Fleming in 1909. The couple had a son named Marshall. In 1922, Wilbur married Marie Tschanen; their son, Lamarre, died in Belgium in 1945 during World War II. The photographer's shadow can be seen in the foreground. (Courtesy of Mary Ellen Everett.)

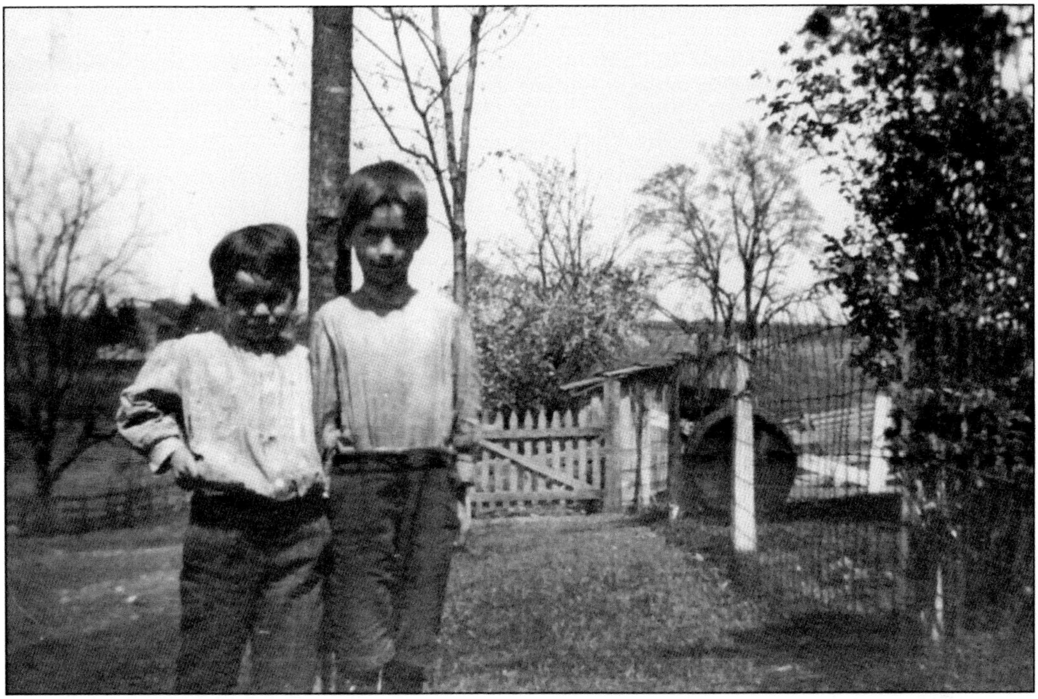

Gene Evans (right) and Wilbur Hankinson were first cousins. This photograph was taken near the barn at the house on Hankinson Road where Gene was raised. Norman Kennedy now owns this home. (Courtesy of Mary Ellen Everett.)

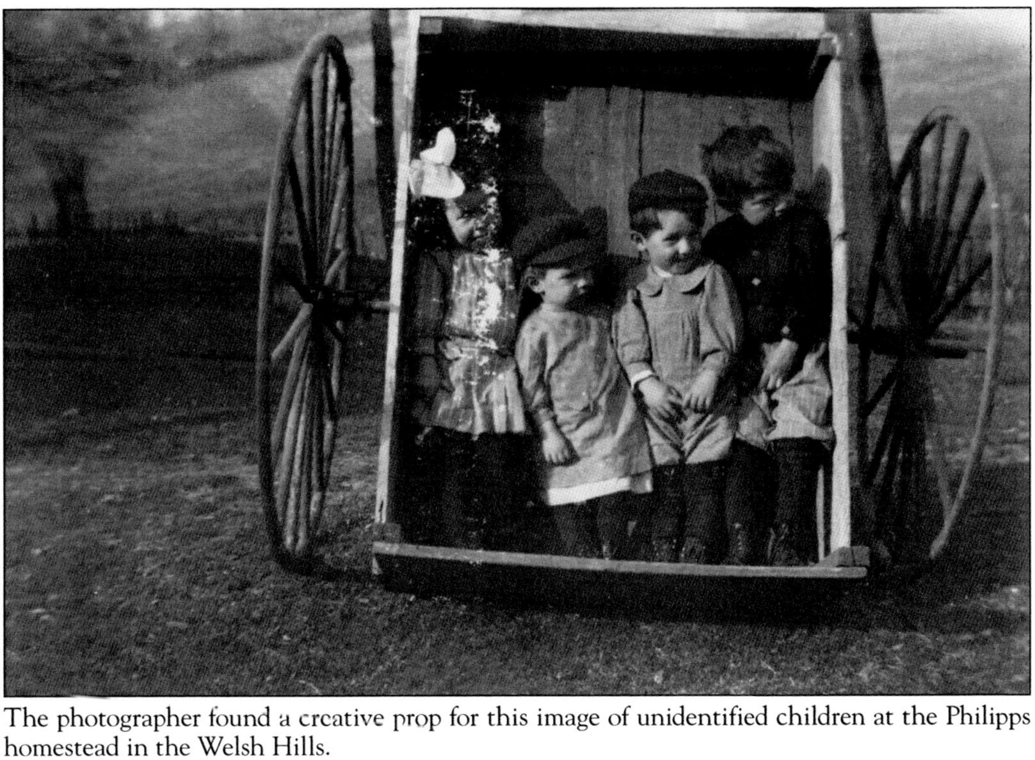

The photographer found a creative prop for this image of unidentified children at the Philipps homestead in the Welsh Hills.

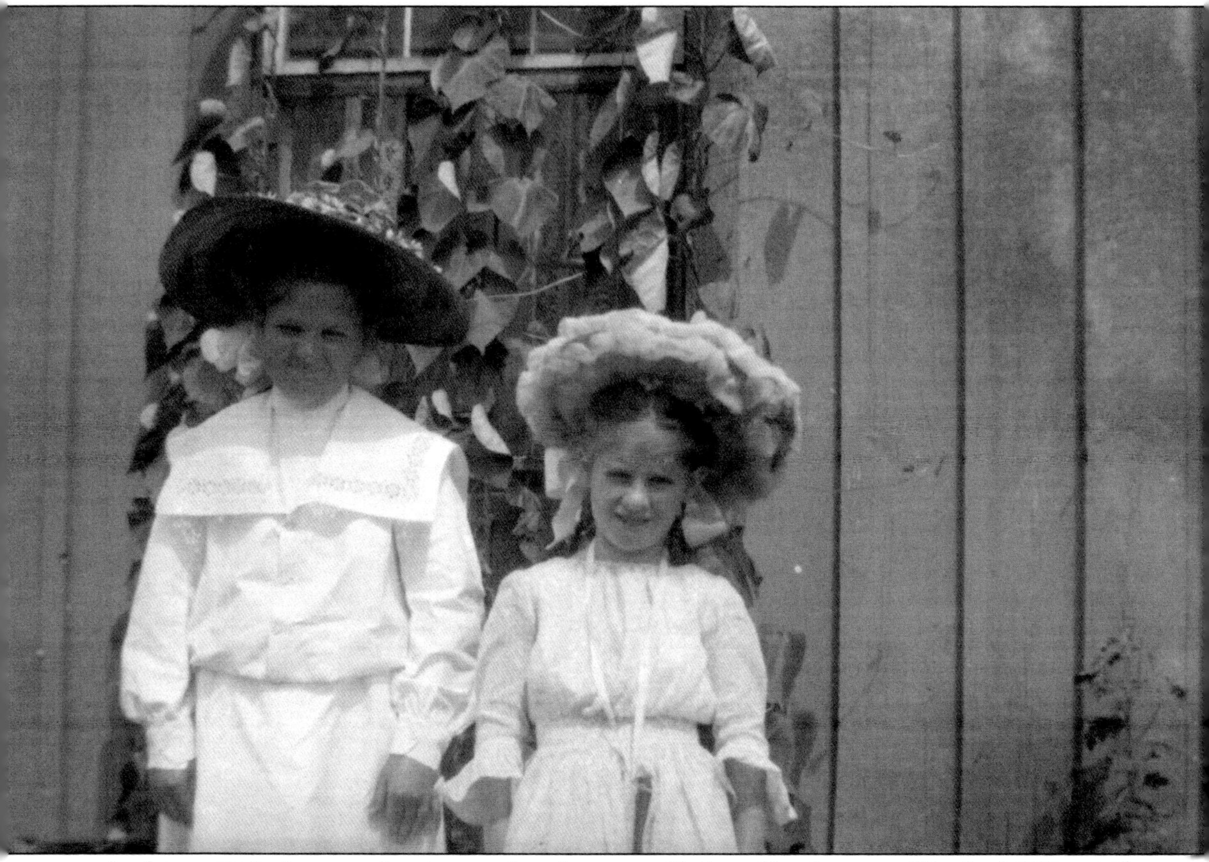

In this *c.* 1903 photograph taken at their home on Philipps Road, sisters Winifred ("Winnie") Martha (left) and Dorothy Edith (right) Philipps appear to be dressed for church or a special occasion. Edith was the youngest, and Winnie the next youngest, of nine children of Samuel Jones and Wilhelmina Williams Philipps. The older children were Mamie, Vicky, Phil, Pearl, Bertha, Susie, Tom, and Sam. Winnie married George Hottinger and lived her entire life in the Welsh Hills on property once owned by Thomas Philipps. She and George had two children, George and Sarah. Edith married Sol Markowitz and moved to Cleveland. When Sol died in 1942, Edith married a longtime friend, Pat Cummings. She had no children.

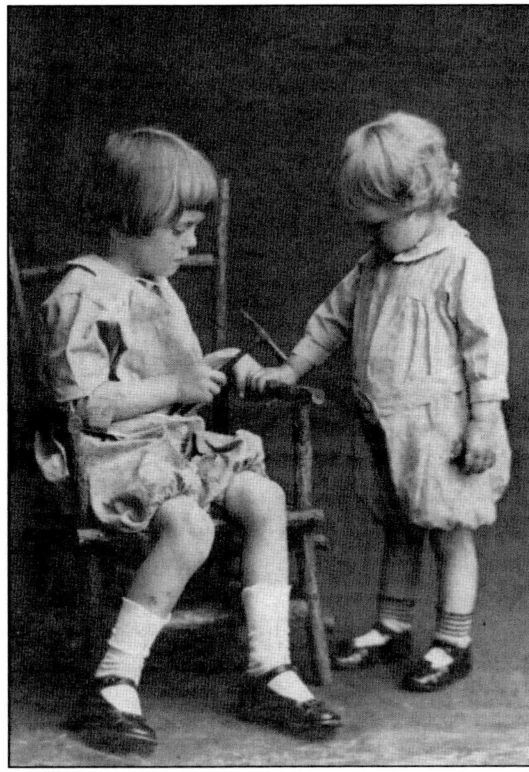

Paul David (left) and Martha Elizabeth Helm, two of Paul Vernon and Annelly White Helm's four children, pose in this photograph. Annelly was a descendant of three early settlers—Thomas Philipps, Theophilus Rees, and Samuel White Sr. A teamster for Thomas Philipps's wagon line between Beulah, Pennsylvania, and Philadelphia, Samuel White married Phillips's daughter Martha. (Courtesy of Lloyd Philipps.)

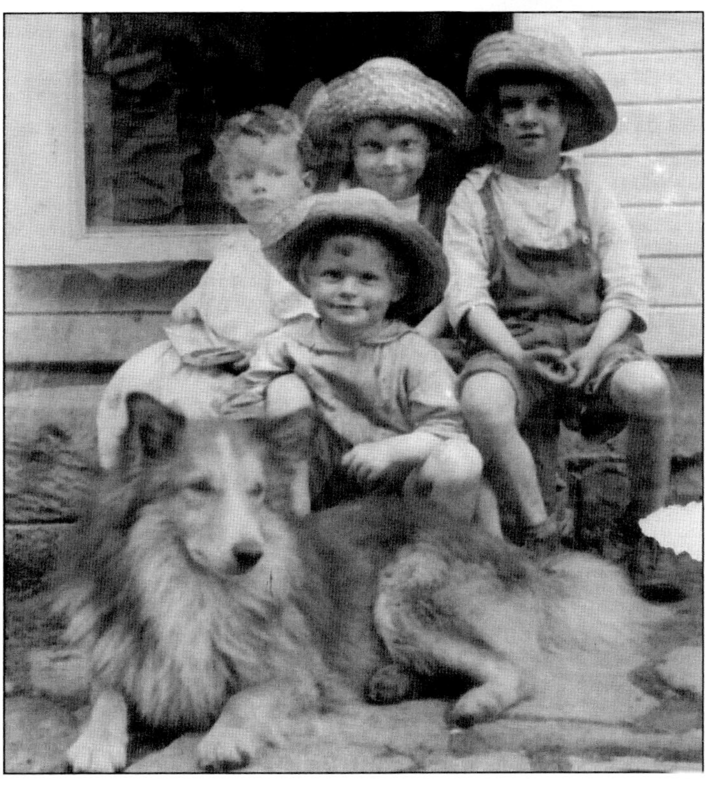

These are the children of Samuel Crane and Mary Oolaita ("Mamie") Philipps Wheeler. From left to right are (first row) John Philipps Wheeler; (second row) Samuel Crane, Oolaita Louise, and Helen Cook Wheeler. Mamie Phillips was the great-great-granddaughter of Thomas Philipps. These children grew up in New Jersey but spent many summers in Ohio. During hard times, the family moved in with Mamie's brother Phil in the Welsh Hills. As an adult, Sam Wheeler wrote about his boyhood experience in the Welsh Hills, recorded in the *Granville Sentinel* in 1980.

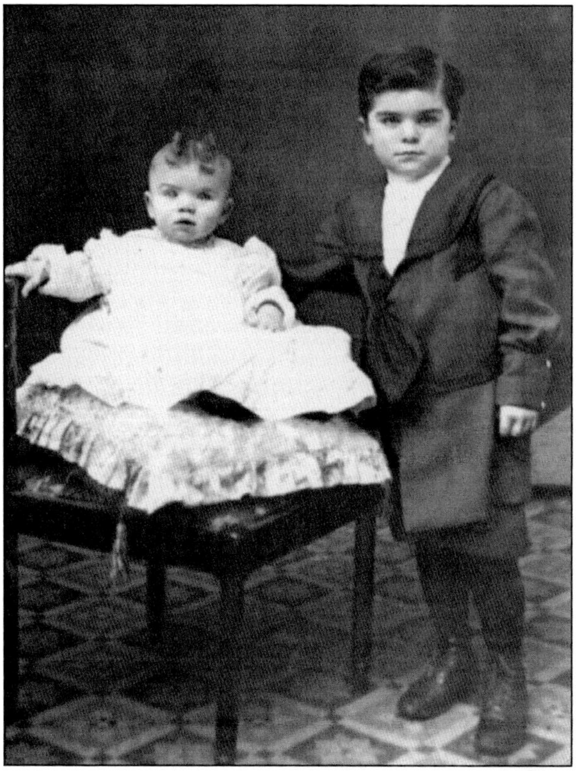

The photograph at left shows Wilbur Hankinson with his sister, Lucy. They were the children of Hayes and Mamie Eigher Hankinson. Mamie died one year after Lucy's birth. Hayes married Bertha Fleming a couple of years later, and their son, Marshall, was later added to the family. The photograph below, taken on February 28, 1916, by Thomas W. Philipps, shows Lucy with her first cousin William Hankinson, son of Archie and Mildred Jones Hankinson. Mildred died seven years after the birth of her fourth child, and Archie married Florella Wacker and added three more children to the family. Wilbur, Lucy, and William grew up on Hankinson Road.

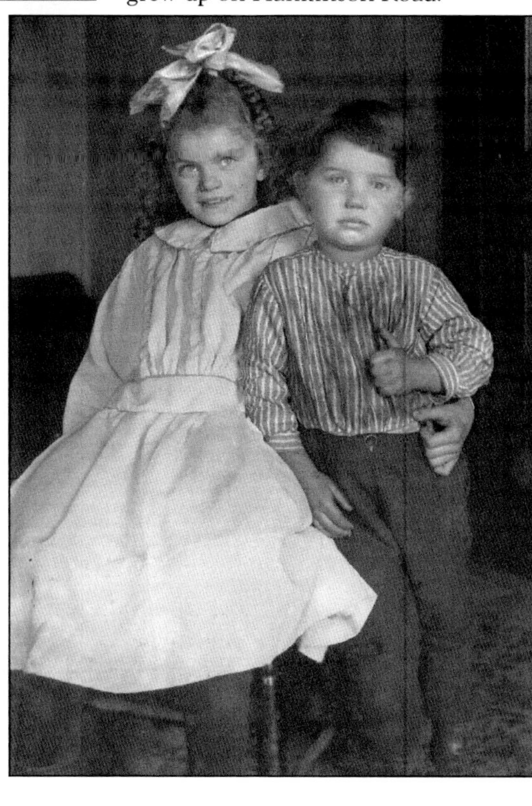

Farmwork was required of all family members regardless of age. Carrying a coal bucket, Lloyd Philipps, youngest son of Thomas Warren and Grace Philipps, appears to be happy to help. In 1928, the Philippses were living at the old Jake Frederick house on Welsh Hills Road. Lloyd now resides in the town of Granville and serves as deacon of the Welsh Hills Baptist Church.

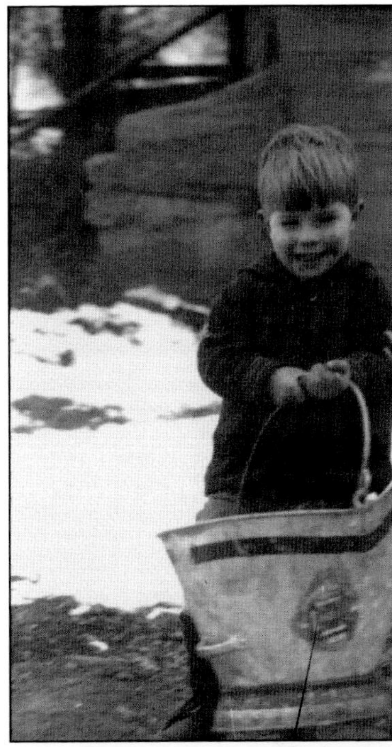

Below, Winnie Philipps (left) smiles in this playful photograph taken around 1903 at her family home. She was the sixth daughter born to Samuel and Wilhelmina Philipps. Frequent family gatherings at the Philipps house brought relatives from near and far. Winnie was always remembered for her smile.

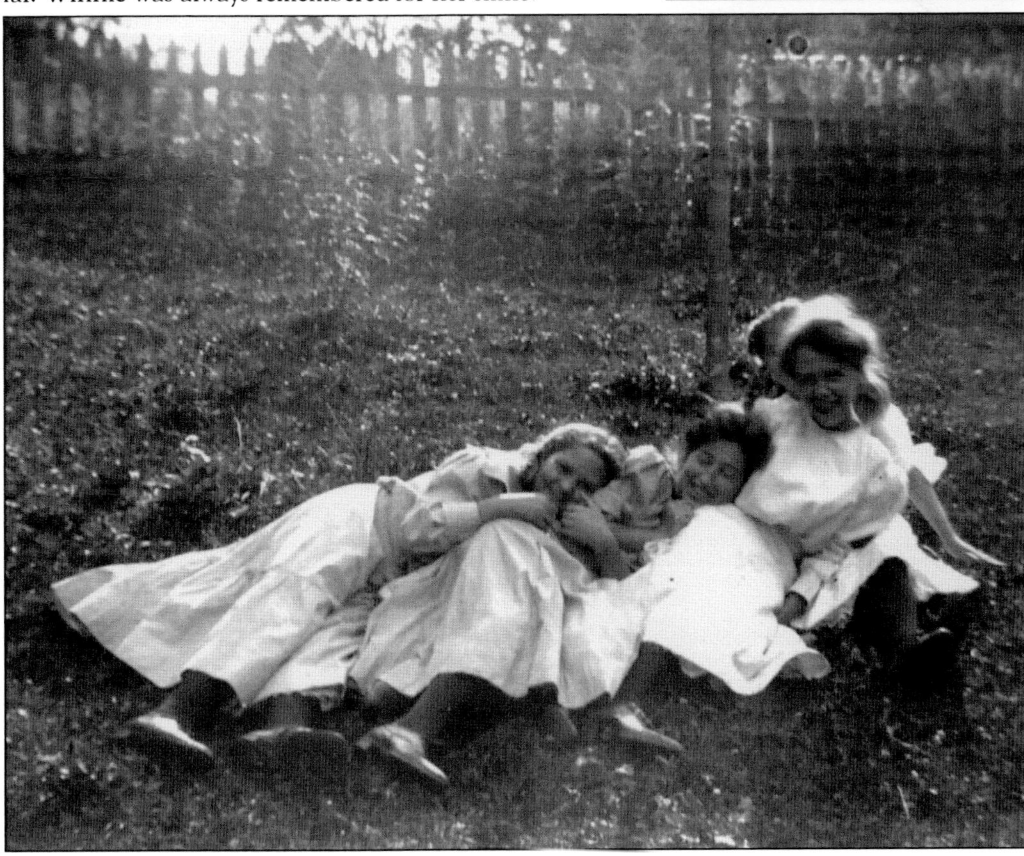

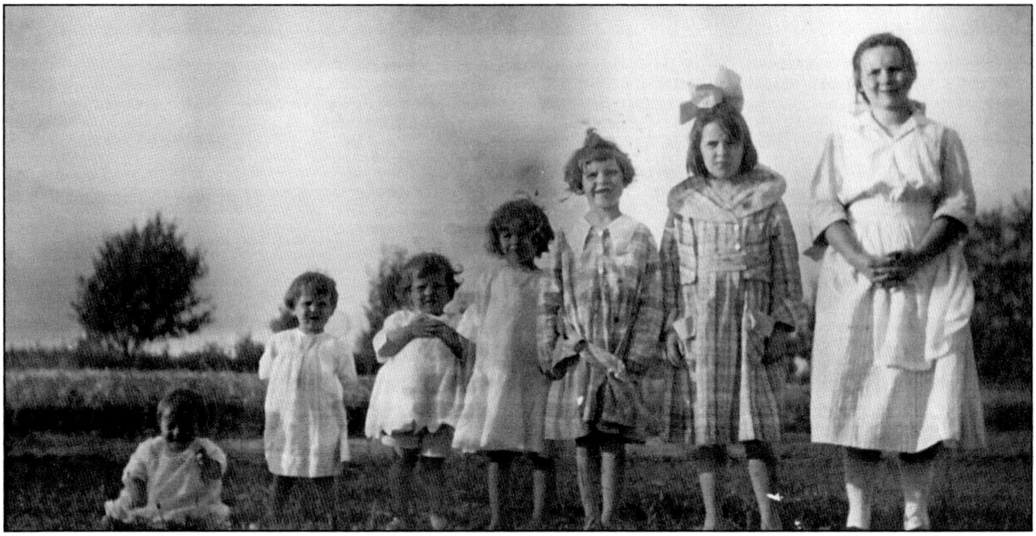

This June 22, 1919, photograph by Thomas W. Philipps shows seven of Sam and Dora Sipe's nine children. Pictured are, from left to right, David (the only son), Phyllis, Ruth, Alberta, Anna Mae, Thelma, and Adaline. The Sipes later had two more daughters, Alyce and Helen. Sam's ancestors included both David R. Jones and Thomas Philipps, who emigrated from Wales. Dora was a descendant of Simeon Hankinson, whose ancestors were English immigrants.

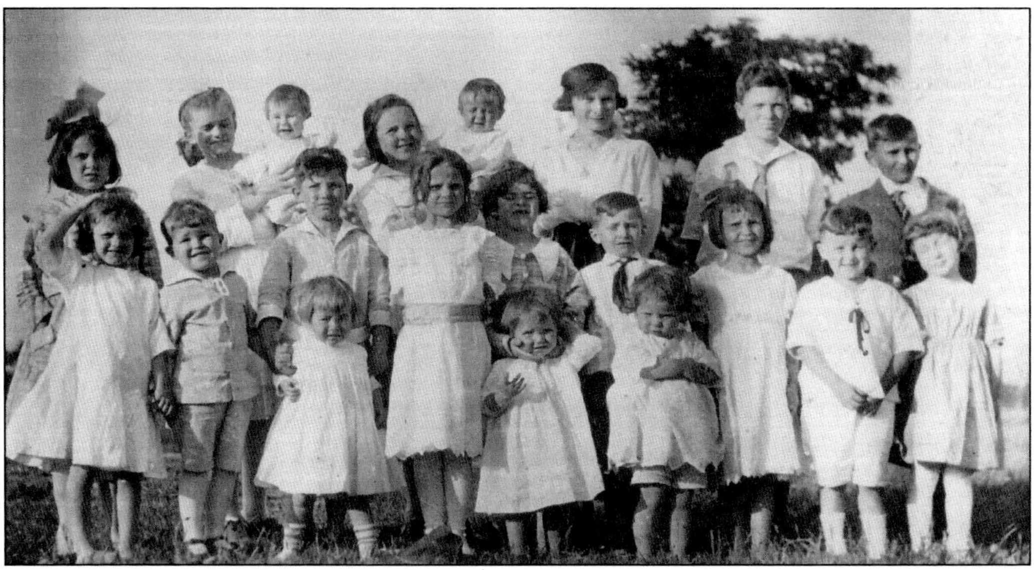

This photograph shows a gathering of cousins in 1919. They are, from left to right, (first row) unidentified girl, Phyllis Sipe, and Ruth Valentine Sipe; (second row) Alberta Sipe, Sam Philipps, unidentified boy, unidentified girl, Anna Mae Sipe, and four unidentified children; (third row) Thelma Sipe, Lucy Hankinson (holding Tommy Philipps), Adaline Sipe (holding David Sipe), Dora Hankinson Sipe, and two unidentified boys.

First cousins born two hours apart in 1918, David Sipe (left) and Thomas Philipps are about three years old in this photograph. David was born on August 31; Tom, on September 1. Their families lived one block from each other, and the doctor ran between houses during the deliveries. They are shown on one of the family farms in the Welsh Hills, where they discovered that chicken droppings are not very tasty.

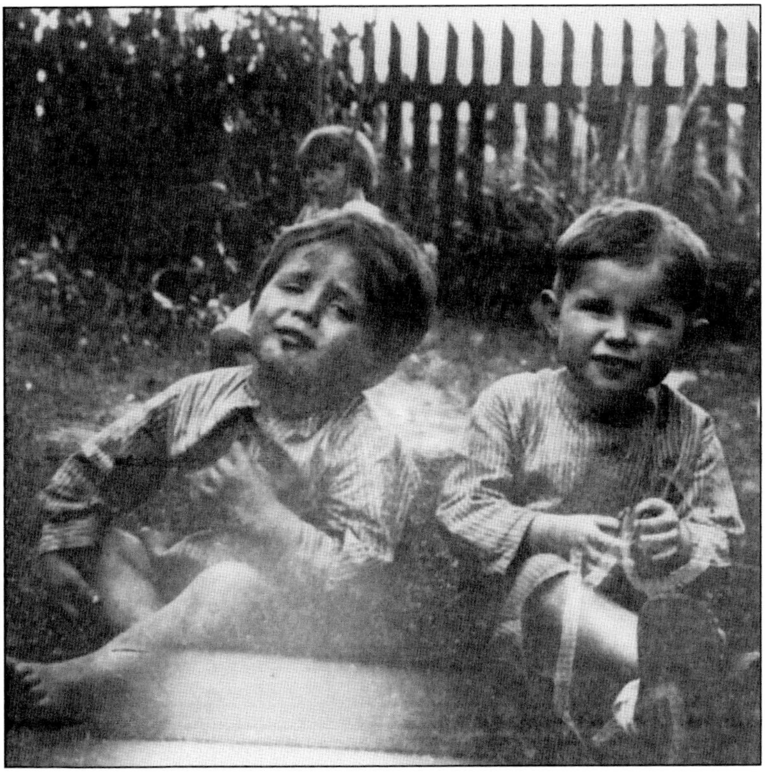

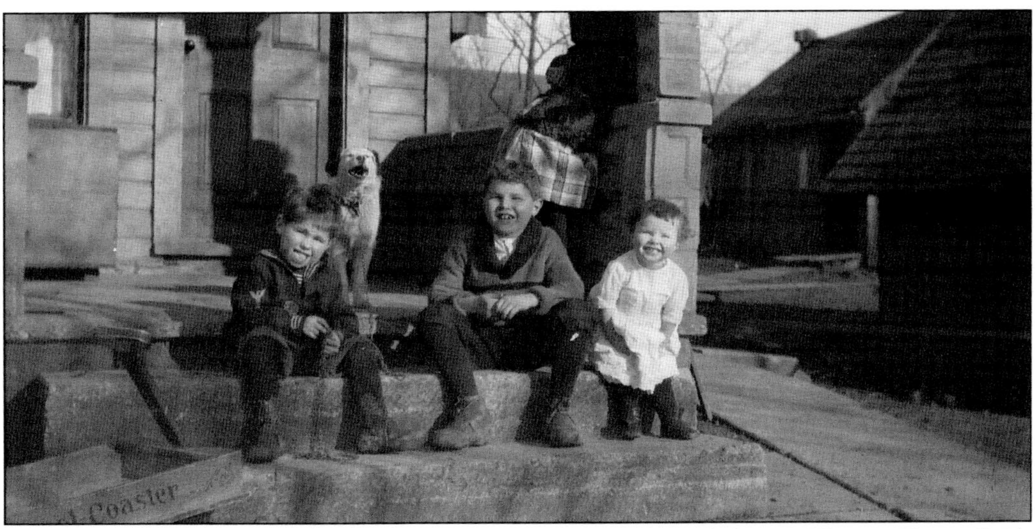


The three eldest children of Thomas Warren and Grace Evans Philipps—Thomas Evans (left), Samuel David (center), and Mary Lucille—sit on the front porch of the house built by their great-uncle Jacob G. Frederick on Welsh Hills Road. Grace's parents, Thomas and Mary Evans, owned the home and allowed her family to live there. As an adult, Sam Philipps raised his family in this house. (Courtesy of Lloyd Philipps.)

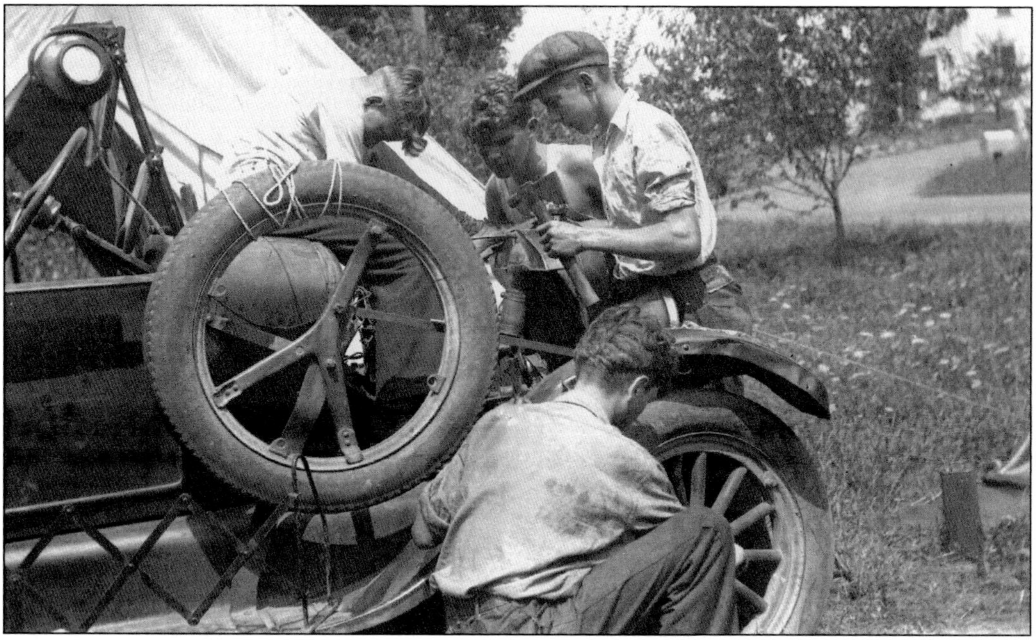

These boys occupied their summer days working on Sammy Philipps's Ford Model T. They are, from left to right, Marshall Hankinson (front), Charles Eddy, Sammy Philipps, and Larry Lloyd. This c. 1930 photograph was taken in the front yard of the old Frederick House on Welsh Hills Road where Sammy lived with his family. (Courtesy of Lloyd Philipps.)

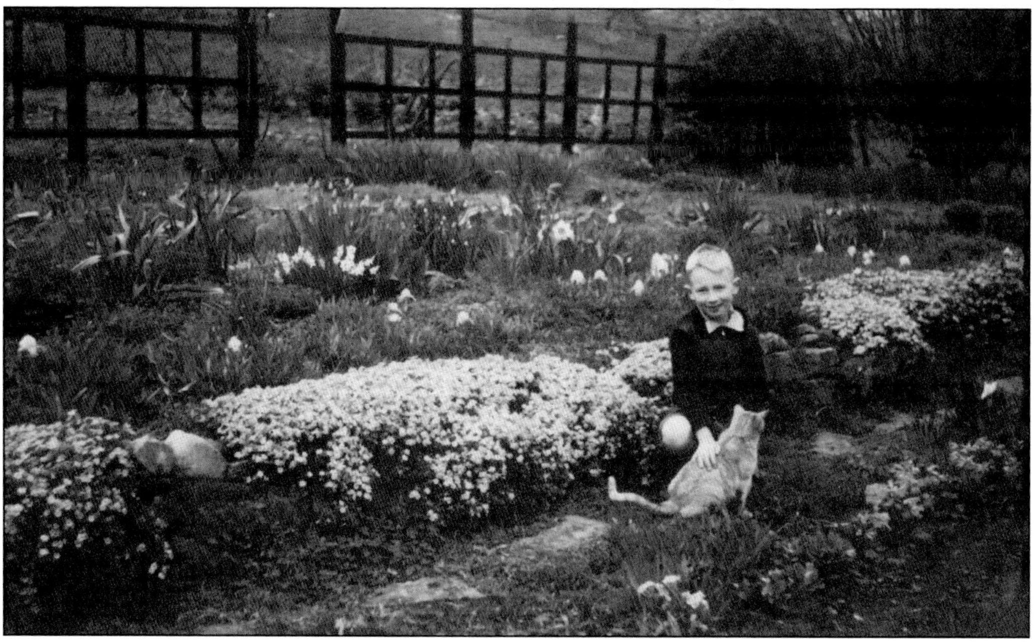

Pictured in his grandmother's garden in the early 1940s is T. David Price, the grandson of Homer and Gertrude Price and a sixth-generation descendant of Thomas Price I, born in Wales in 1754. The first Thomas Price arrived in the Welsh Hills in 1823 and purchased 87 acres from S. Turner. T. David Price inherited the Price Fruit Farm, which was later sold. T. David and his wife, Beth, now live on the old Owen farm on Burg Street. (Courtesy of T. David Price.)

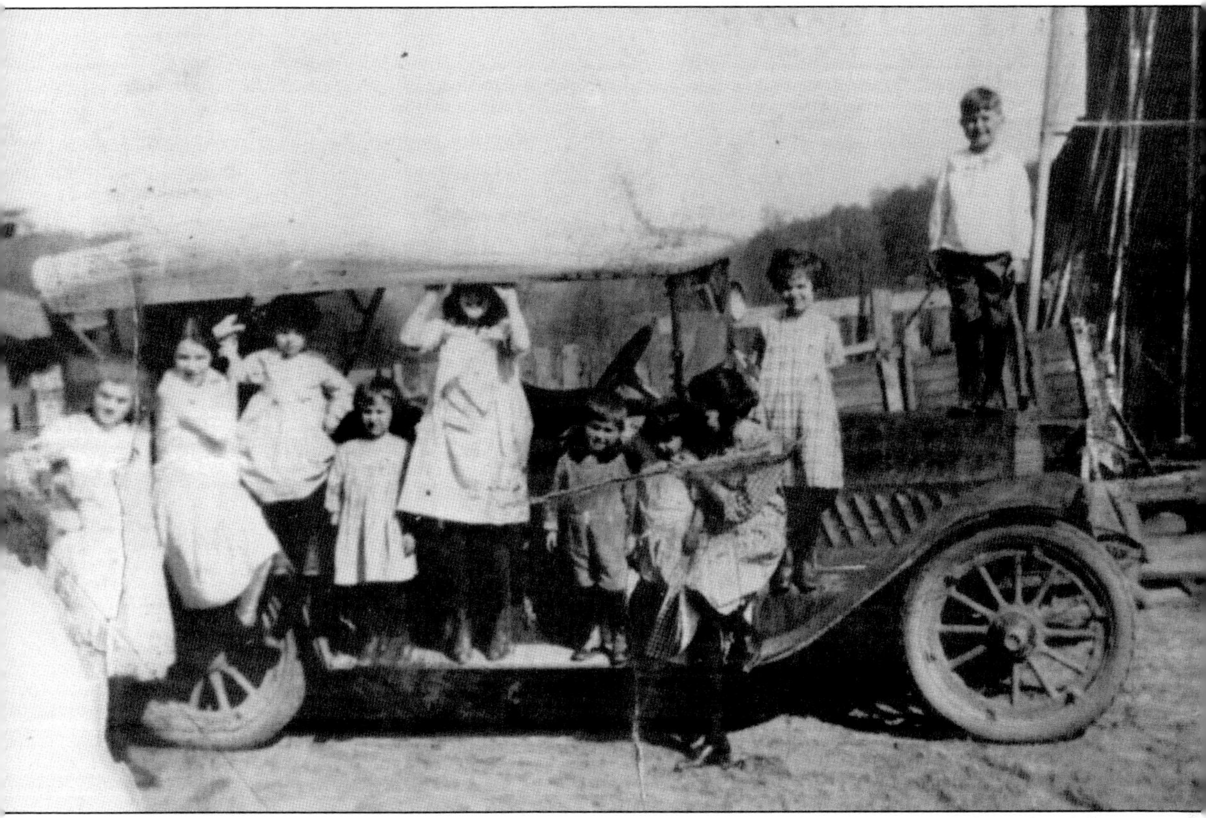

In this image from around 1922, Lucy Hankinson (young girl at far left), Tommy Philipps (middle, in darker clothes), and Sammy Philipps (on hood) pose with girls believed to be their Sipe cousins on a 1912 Chevrolet Classic 6. Most of the roads in the Welsh Hills in 1922 were still compacted dirt, and the automobile shows the evidence.

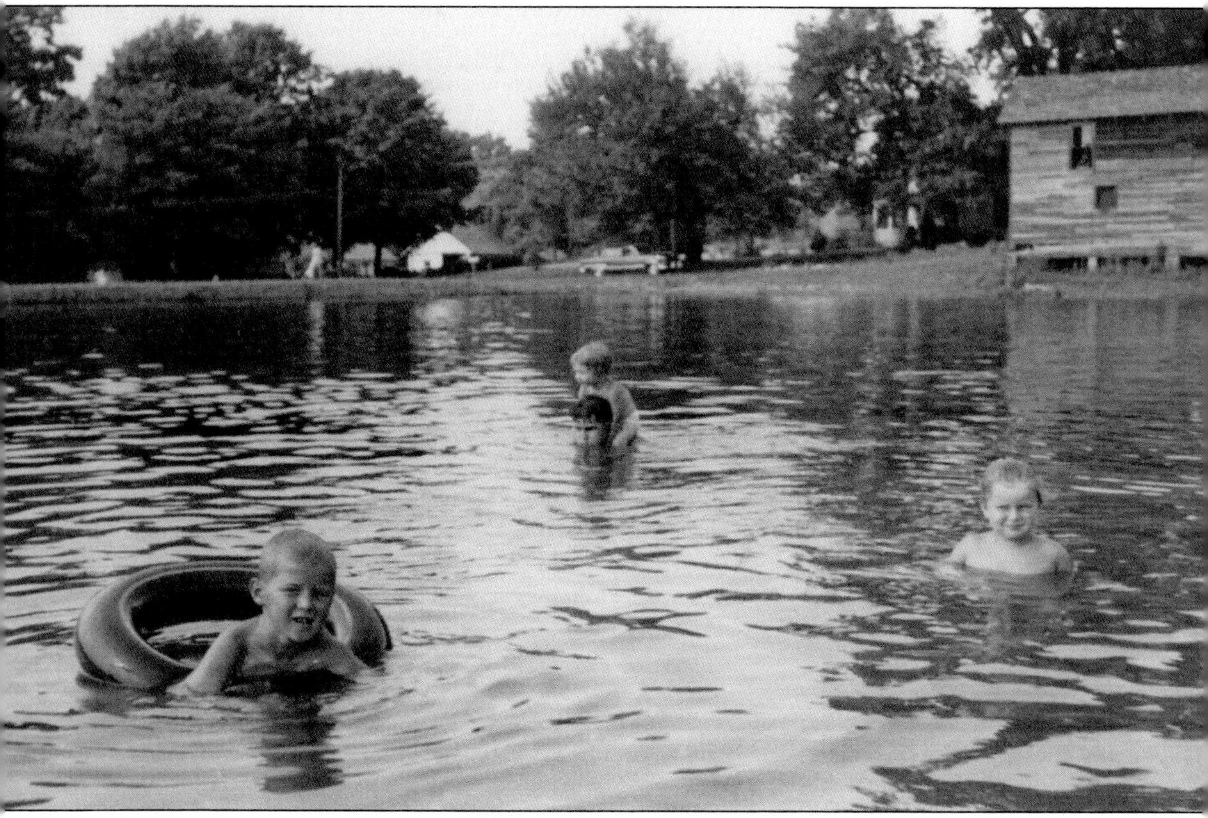

Warren Philipps (left), Thomas Philipps (with daughter Barbara on his shoulders), and Jenny Philipps are descendants of Theophilus Rees and Thomas Philipps. Warren and Jenny are the youngest of Samuel David and Helen Philipps' children, and Tom is Sam's younger brother. The pond is located on the Sam Philipps property, originally owned by his great-uncle Jacob Frederick. Constructed by Sam in the 1950s, the pond is fed by natural springs and has been a favorite swimming, fishing, and (in winter) ice-skating spot in the Welsh Hills that is still used by the current owners. The old cider mill at the pond's edge has been torn down. (Courtesy of Jennifer Philipps Welsh.)

# *Four*

# Welsh Churches

The Welsh immigrants were devoutly religious people. At the beginning, religious services were held in settlers' homes.

On February 6, 1808, Theophilus Rees donated a portion of his land for a cemetery, and, in 1809, an 18-foot-by-20-foot log church was constructed on the site. During the same period, a log meetinghouse and school was built on land belonging to Samuel Joseph Philipps, and worship was sometimes held here. On September 4, 1808, Elder James Sutton and a Mr. Steadman organized Welsh Hills Baptist Church in the cabin owned by "Big" David Thomas. The first nine members were Theophilus Rees, David Thomas Jr., Nathan Allyn Jr., David Lobdell, Joshua Lobdell, Thomas Powell, Elizabeth Rees, Elizabeth Jones, and Mary Thomas. They elected Rees as deacon and Lobdell as clerk. In 1814, Philipps deeded a portion of his property to the church for $1. Services moved here permanently when the former church building burned in 1822. When the new church burned in 1834, a frame structure was constructed on property owned by Thomas Davis in 1840. In 1908, this building became too small to handle the growing congregation, and a masonry church was constructed. The Welsh Hills Baptist Church has survived for over 200 years.

In 1832, William T. Williams, James Evans, and Robert Walter started the Welsh Hills Calvinistic Methodist Church. In 1836, a parcel of land owned by James and Mary Evans was purchased on Sharon Valley Road, and a simple frame building was constructed in 1837. This was the first Welsh Calvinistic Methodist Church in Ohio. A small cemetery was also established to serve the members of the congregation. The original elders elected in 1835 were William T. Williams, James Evans, and Alban Albans. By the early 1900s, the congregation declined, and the building ceased to be used for religious services. The Welsh Calvinistic Methodist Church was eventually absorbed into the Methodist church in Granville.

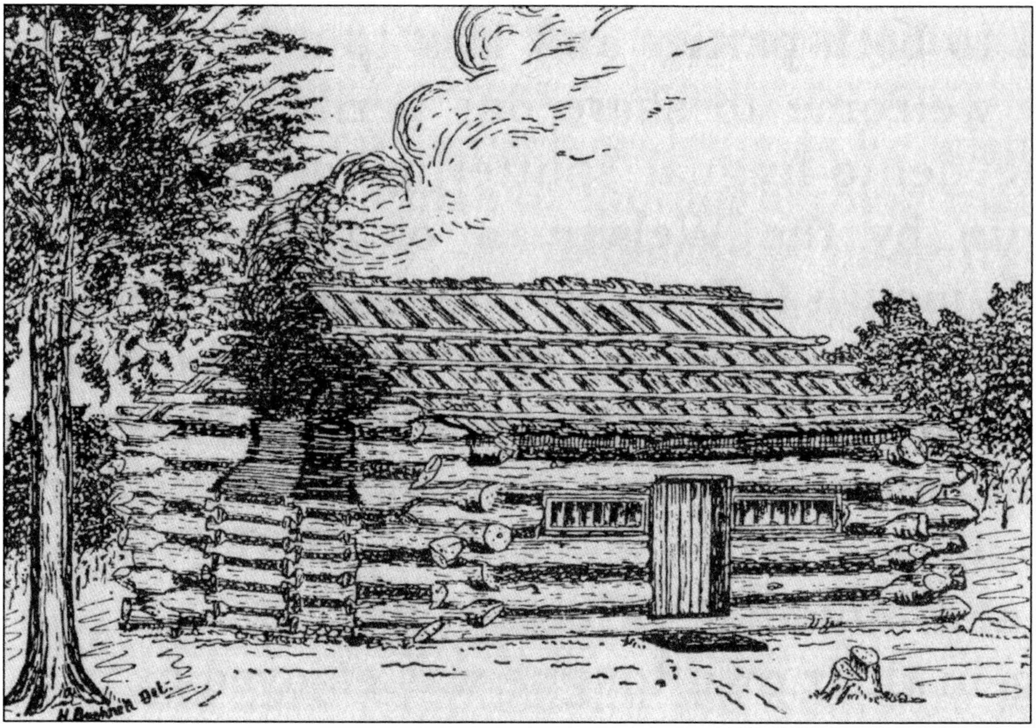

This interpretive drawing of the first log cabin used for the Welsh Hills Baptist Church was drawn by Rev. Henry Bushnell in 1889 and appeared in his book about the history of Granville. (Taken from the book reproduced by the Licking County Genealogical Society in 1976.)

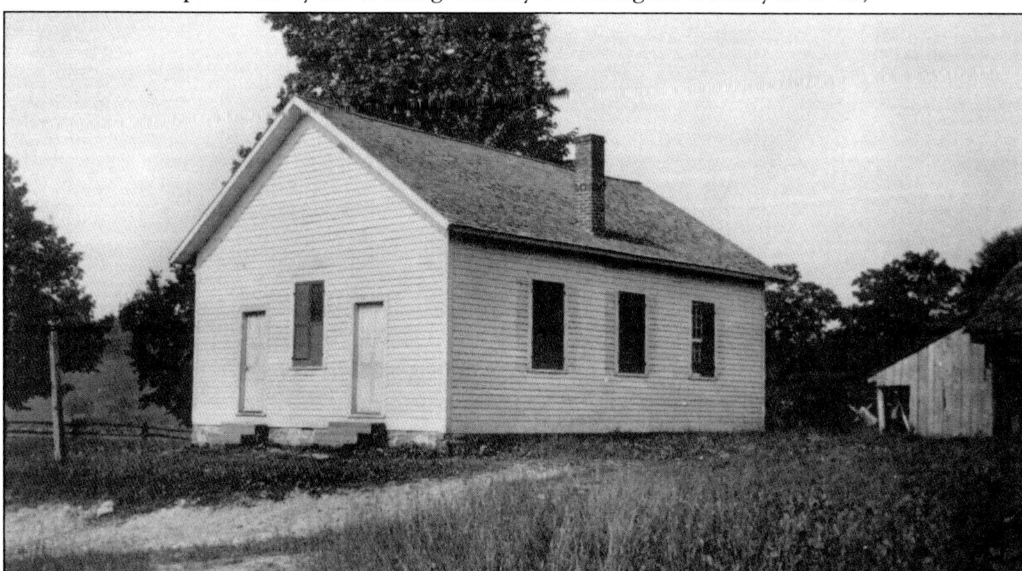

Constructed in 1840 for the Welsh Hills Baptist congregation, this building served the church for 68 years before it was replaced by a masonry structure. Evan David, Maurice Jones, and Thomas Evans constructed the 26-foot-by-36-foot building mostly of black walnut. Separate entrances served the male and female congregations. It was moved and converted to a barn when a new church was constructed.

In 1908, this masonry building replaced the wood structure. It includes a small vestibule, a sanctuary, and a back room that now contains a small kitchen. There is no indoor bathroom. The bell tower is no longer used. This photograph was taken around 1922 as the congregation entered the church for Sunday service. (Courtesy of Lloyd Philipps.)

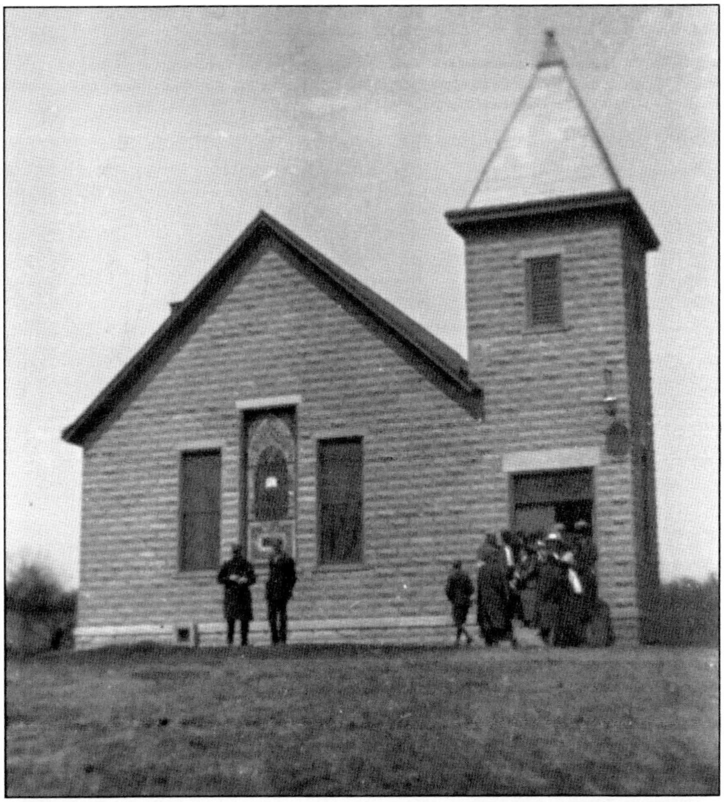

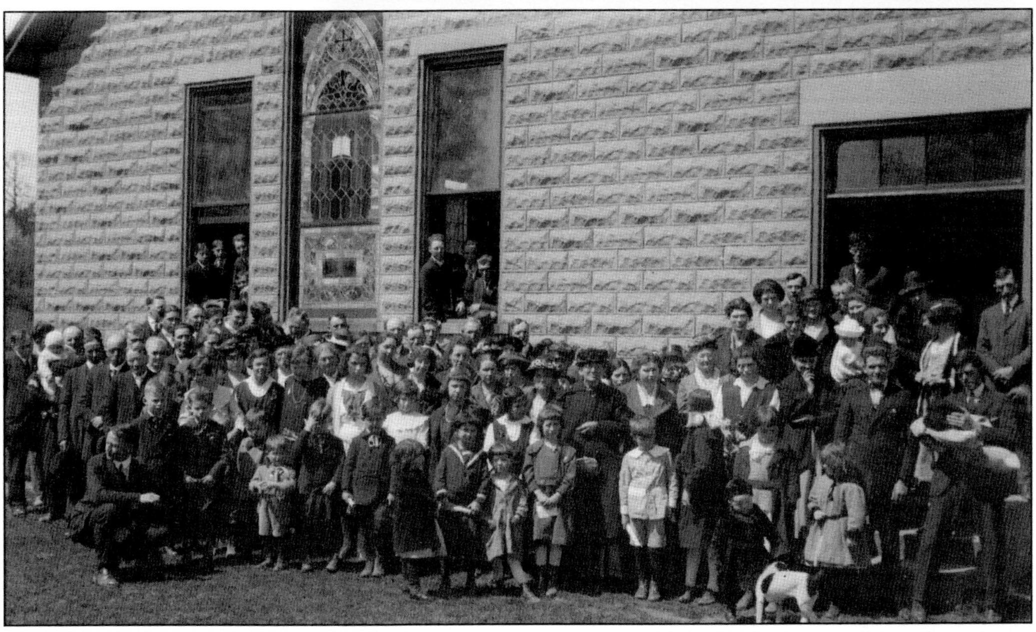

On a Sunday morning around 1922, the congregation of the Welsh Hills Baptist Church includes members of the Hankinson, Price, Evans, and Philipps families. Homer Price served as a deacon of the church for many years and is pictured in the middle of the back row, directly right of the window. (Courtesy of Lloyd Philipps.)

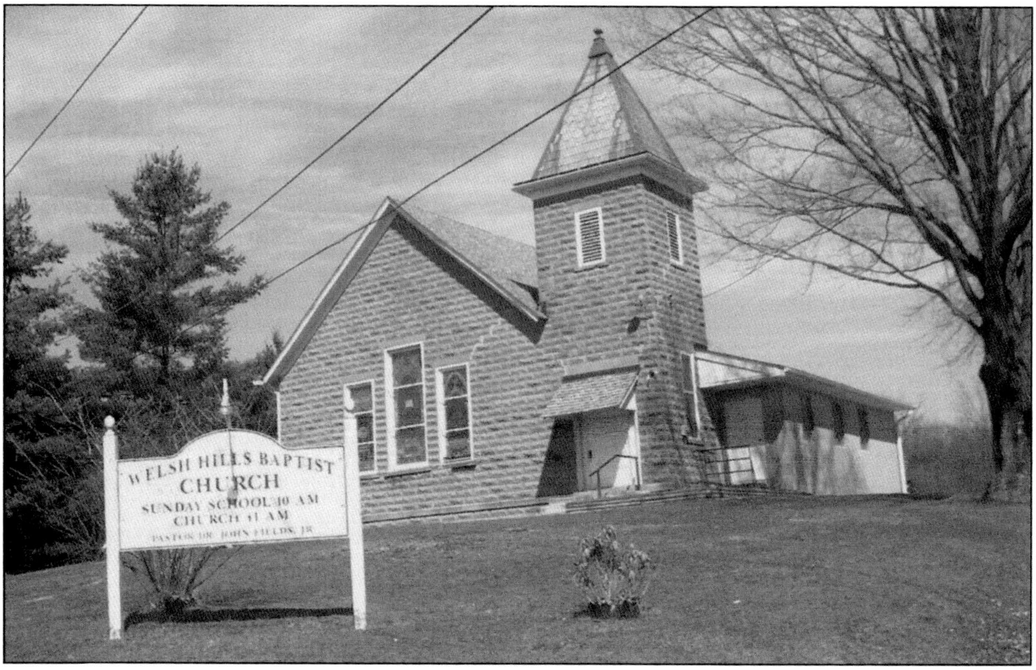


Welsh Hills Baptist Church looks very much like it did in 1908, although showing a bit of wear. The congregation has diminished greatly since 1908 and the formation of Granville Baptist Church, but many of attendees are descendants of the original Welsh families and maintain strong ties to one another. (Photograph by Janet Philipps Procida.)

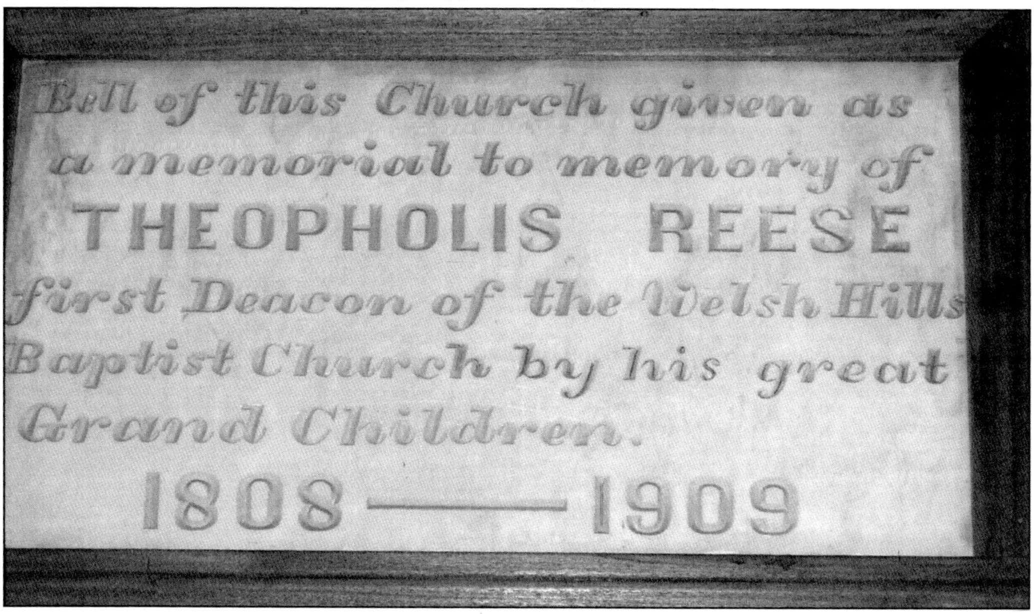


This plaque was set into the interior wall of the vestibule of the Welsh Hills Baptist Church during its construction in 1908 to commemorate the founder of the church. Unfortunately some things set in stone cannot be easily undone, like the misspelling of the name Theophilus Rees. Deacon Rees conducted the first church services upon his arrival in the Welsh Hills. (Photograph by Janet Philipps Procida.)

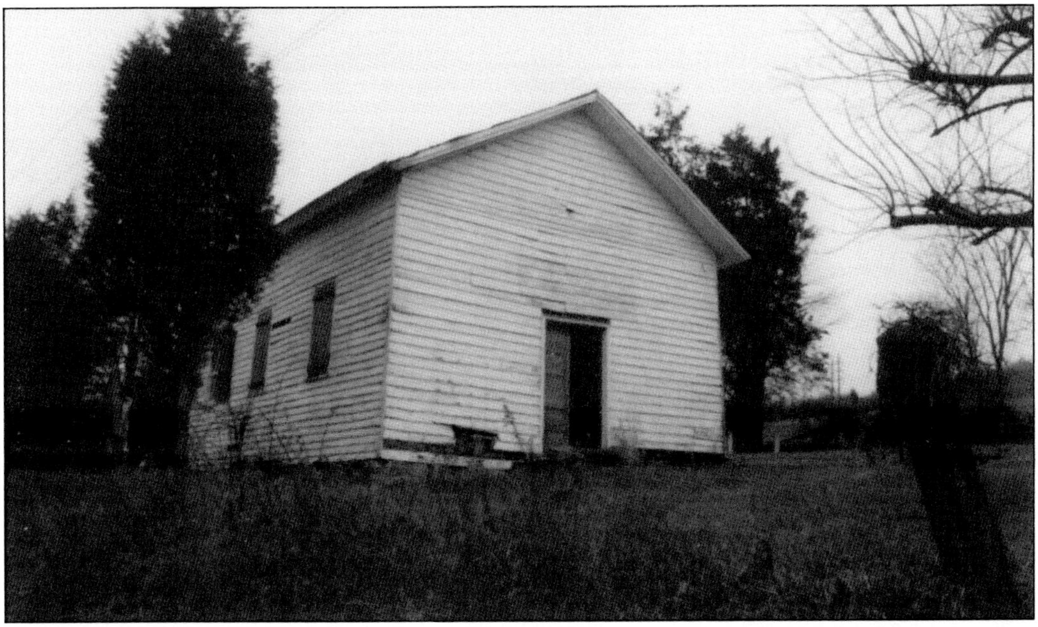

The Sharon Valley Welsh Calvinistic Methodist Church was established in 1832. The first services were conducted in the Old Stone Schoolhouse. In 1836, the trustees of the church purchased a lot in Sharon Valley containing an acre of ground for the erection of a church and a burial plot. Construction began immediately and was finished in early 1837. It was the first Welsh Calvinistic Methodist Church built in Ohio.

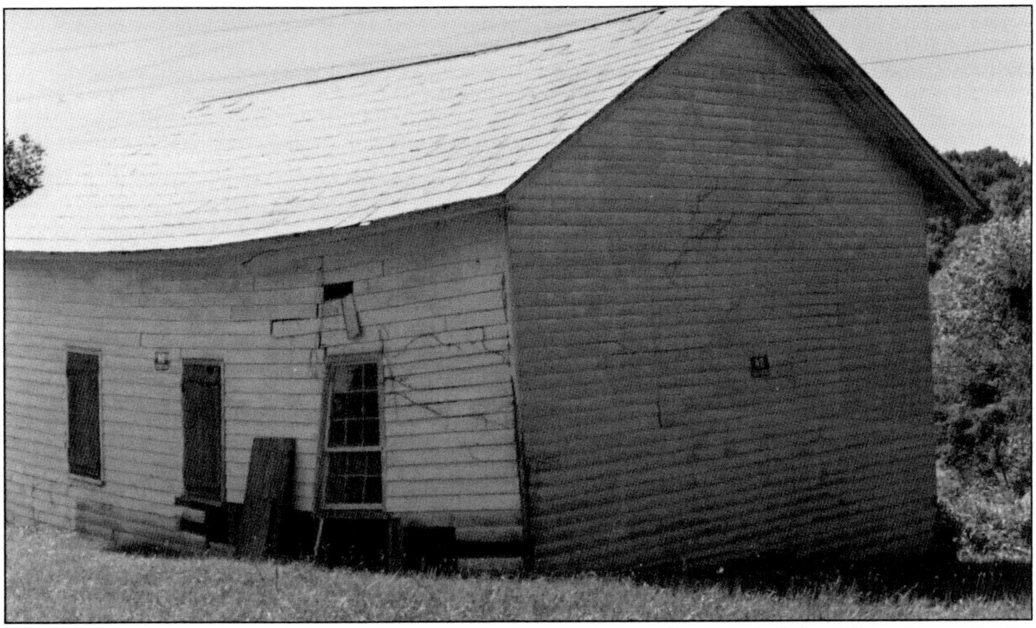

By the early 1900s, the congregation declined, since most people attended church in Granville. In 1950, the Granville Cambrian Society raised money to restore and preserve this Welsh landmark. On October 23, 1955, a rededication of the building was held with an overflow crowd of 100 people. The event was in conjunction with the Granville sesquicentennial. This photograph shows the decline of the building in the 1990s, shortly before demolition.

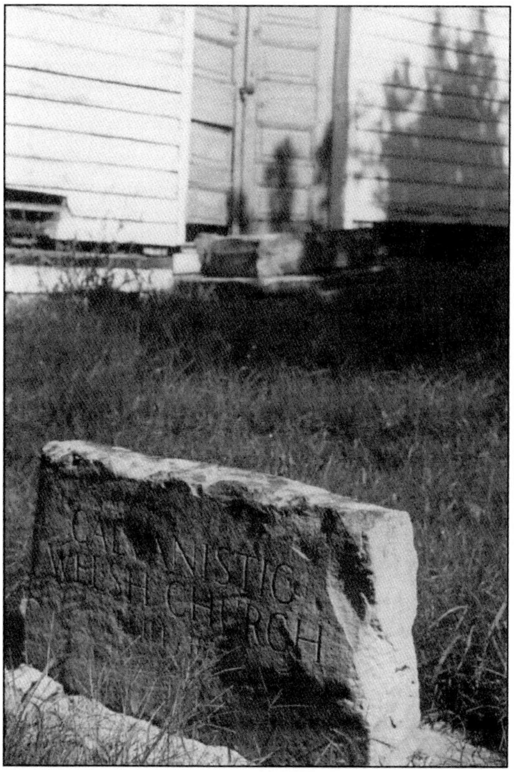


The sandstone marker was erected in the late 1800s near the entrance to the church, facing Sharon Valley Road. Unfortunately the spelling of *Calvinistic* was incorrectly set in stone to read *Calvanistic* and was never corrected. The original members of the church were Mr. and Mrs. William T. Williams, James Evans, Mrs. Evans, Alban Albans, Mrs. Albans, Miss Albans, John F. Evans, Mrs. Evans, Nathaniel Davis, Mrs. Davis, Jane Davis, William Lewis, Mrs. Lewis, Robert Walter, Jenkin Hughes, and William Parry. For many years, services in this church were conducted in the Welsh language, which offered comfort to those who had recently left their homeland. (Both photographs by Janet Philipps Procida.)

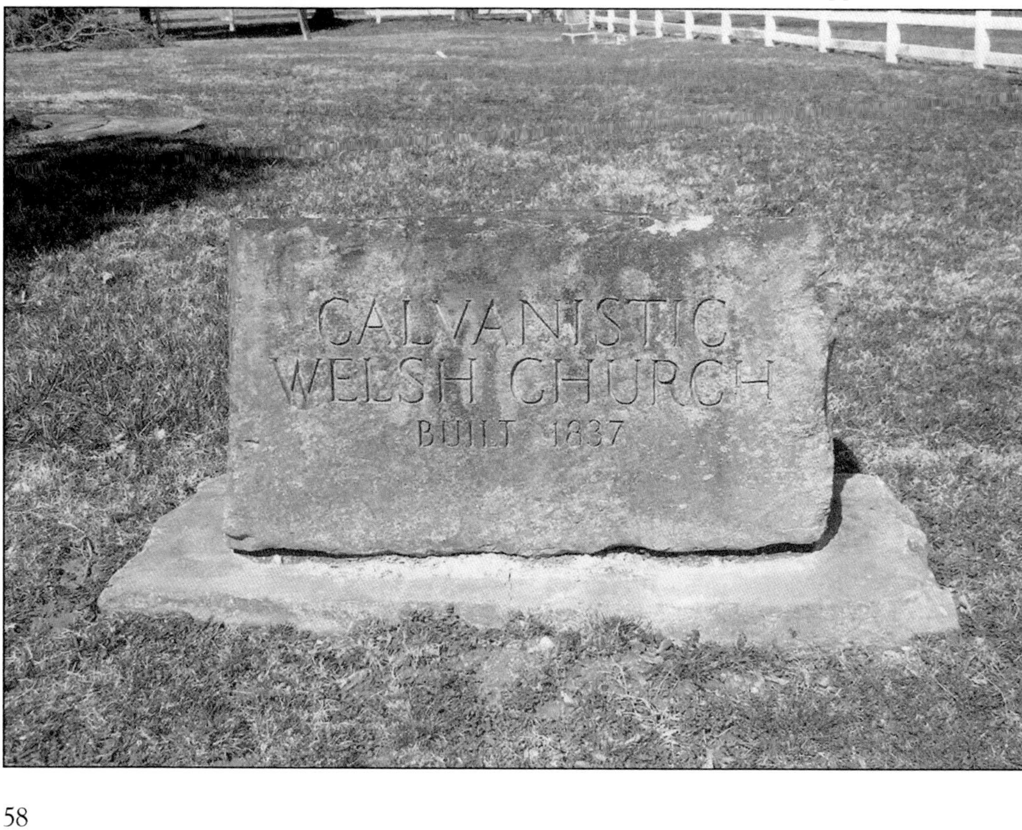

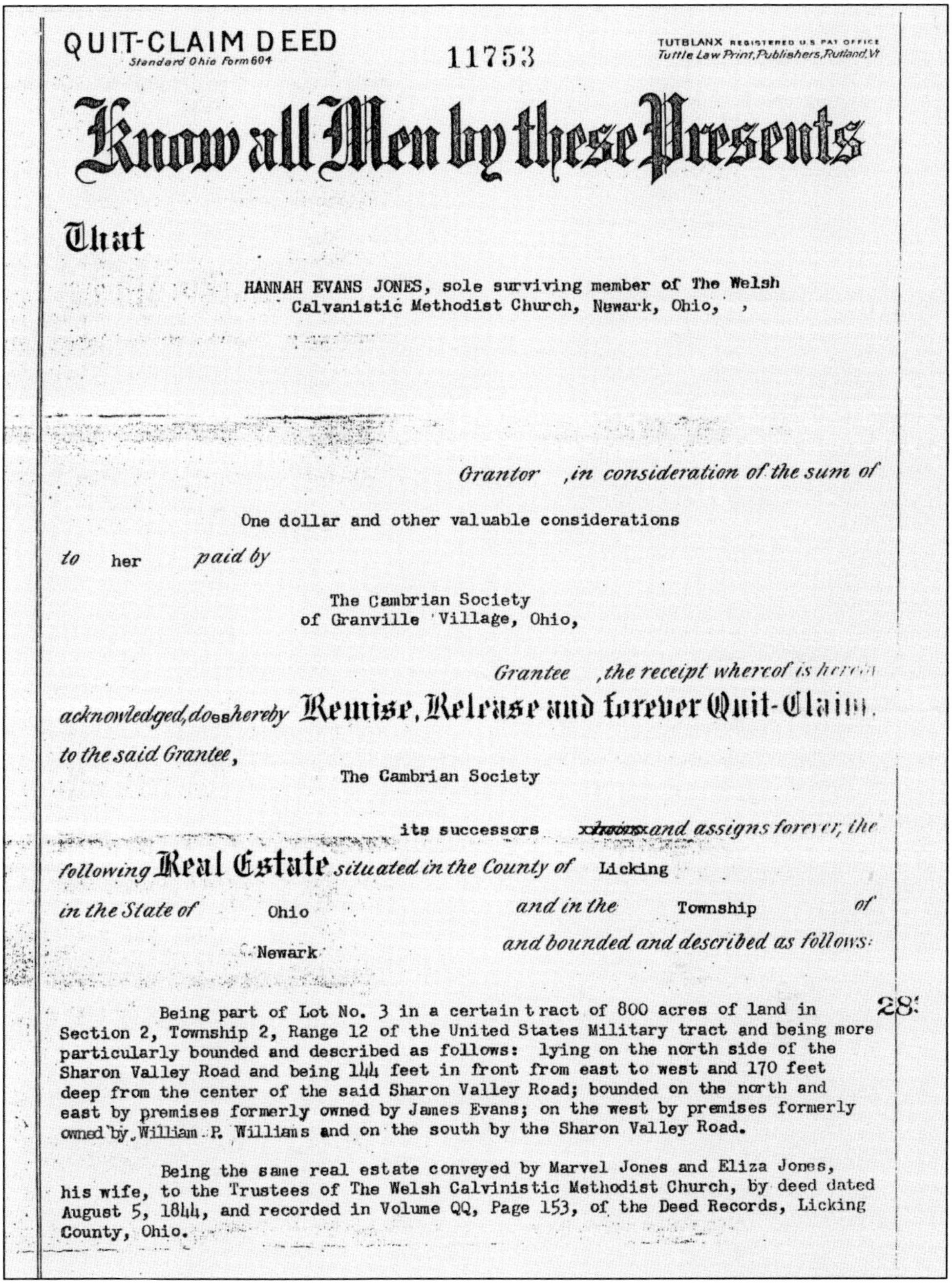

QUIT-CLAIM DEED
Standard Ohio Form 604

11753

TUTBLANX REGISTERED U.S. PAT OFFICE
Tuttle Law Print, Publishers, Rutland, Vt

**Know all Men by these Presents**

**That**

HANNAH EVANS JONES, sole surviving member of The Welsh Calvanistic Methodist Church, Newark, Ohio,

*Grantor*, *in consideration of the sum of*

One dollar and other valuable considerations

*to* her *paid by*

The Cambrian Society of Granville Village, Ohio,

*Grantee*, *the receipt whereof is hereby acknowledged, does hereby* **Remise, Release and forever Quit-Claim**

*to the said Grantee*, The Cambrian Society its successors ~~heirs~~ *and assigns forever, the following* **Real Estate** *situated in the County of* Licking *in the State of* Ohio *and in the* Township *of* Newark *and bounded and described as follows:*

28

Being part of Lot No. 3 in a certain tract of 800 acres of land in Section 2, Township 2, Range 12 of the United States Military tract and being more particularly bounded and described as follows: lying on the north side of the Sharon Valley Road and being 144 feet in front from east to west and 170 feet deep from the center of the said Sharon Valley Road; bounded on the north and east by premises formerly owned by James Evans; on the west by premises formerly owned by William P. Williams and on the south by the Sharon Valley Road.

Being the same real estate conveyed by Marvel Jones and Eliza Jones, his wife, to the Trustees of The Welsh Calvinistic Methodist Church, by deed dated August 5, 1844, and recorded in Volume QQ, Page 153, of the Deed Records, Licking County, Ohio.

In 1950, the Granville Cambrian Society began to take an active interest in the restoration and preservation of this Welsh landmark. Following an encouraging survey of the church structure and grounds, work began. Further support came in the form of a quitclaim deed for the property, drawn to the society by Hannah Evans Jones of Granville, the sole living communicant member of the Welsh Calvinistic Methodist Church as originally organized. Under the leadership of Jeanette Evans, an outpouring of money and labor came forth for the needed structural repairs and refinishing and refurbishing of the sanctuary. By October 23, 1955, the church was ready and a service of rededication was held with an overflow group of 100 people in attendance.

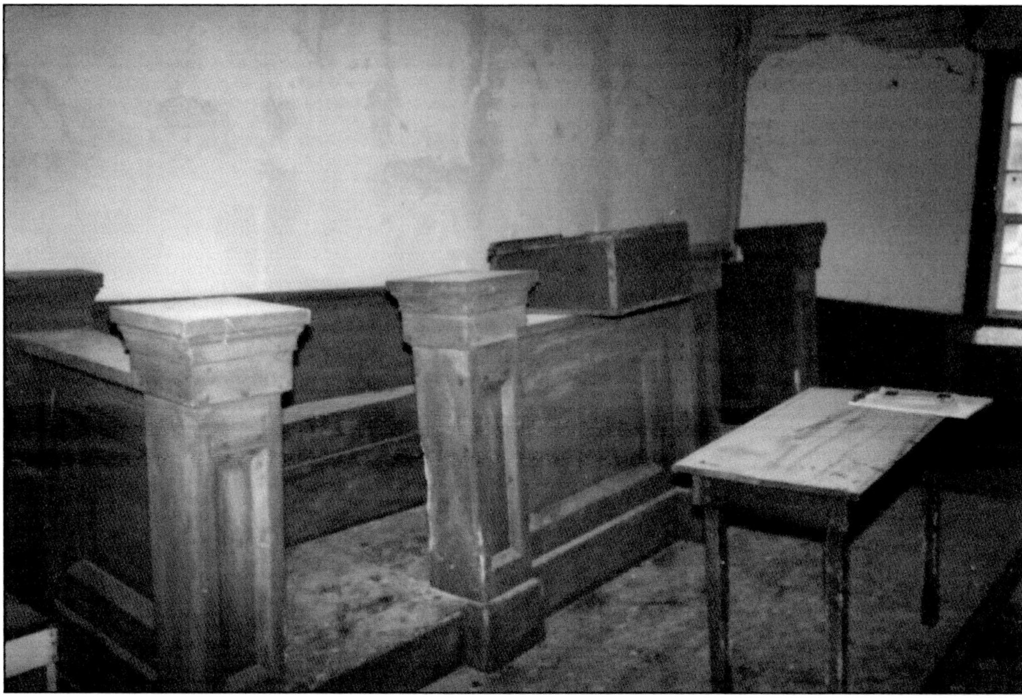

The original building was 21 feet by 30 feet and cost $321.89 to construct, with gratuitous labor performed by friends of the church. The pulpit, chancel, and mourners' benches were constructed of cherry, and the wainscoting was walnut. Wooden pegs were set in the walls for hanging wraps. For evening services, light was provided by oil lamps set in reflector brackets on the walls. A stove provided the necessary heat. These photographs show the interior furnishings provided in 1955 for the restoration. The pulpit and pews now reside in the Old Academy Building in Granville.

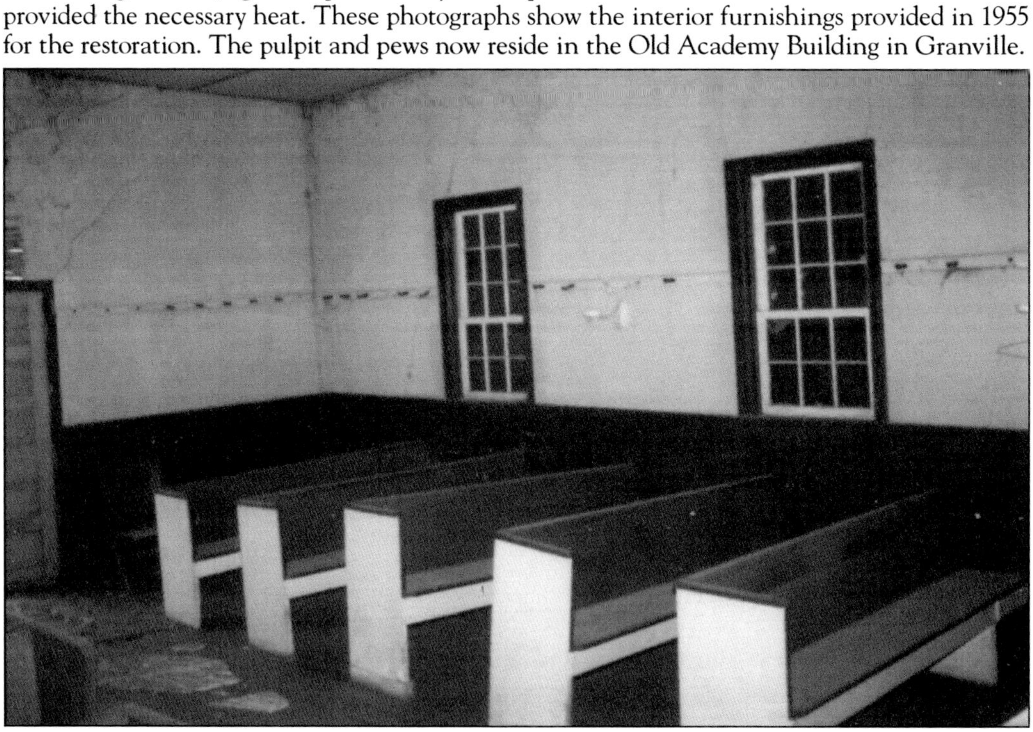

# *Five*

# Welsh Schools

Education was important to the Welsh settlers. In 1809, they set about building a log structure on property donated by Theophilus Rees for the Welsh Hills Baptist Church, at the site of the current Welsh Hills Cemetery. The early church, meetinghouse, and school was employed many years before being replaced by a wooden structure, constructed on property donated by Samuel Joseph Philipps, son of Thomas Philipps. This building was also used as a church, meetinghouse, and school, with additional property set aside for a cemetery, known today as the Philipps Cemetery on Philipps Road. Destroyed by fire in 1822, it was succeeded in 1823 by another frame building that was destroyed by fire in 1834. In 1825, local Welsh masons constructed a school from locally quarried stone. Located on Welsh Hills Road, south of Sharon Valley Road, the Old Stone Schoolhouse was also a meetinghouse and was later used by the Welsh Hills Baptist congregation in 1834 when their frame church was destroyed. It was also used by the Welsh Calvinistic Methodist congregation between 1832 and 1837. The newly established Welsh Hills Agriculture and Historical Society utilized this building. In 1858, the Old Stone Schoolhouse was abandoned, but its remains stood for many years. The stone schoolhouse was replaced by a frame structure constructed on property sold to Granville Township by Edward Price. This frame school served until 1899, when a brick structure was erected. The 1825 capstone from the Old Stone Schoolhouse was set into this brick building, which became the school for Granville Township Subdistrict 9 and was called the Welsh Hills School. The brick school was also used as a meeting place for the local Grange, which purchased it at auction in 1924, when there ceased to be any schools located in "the Hills." This building was finally demolished in 1981. The author recalls attending many Rees family reunions in this building as a child.

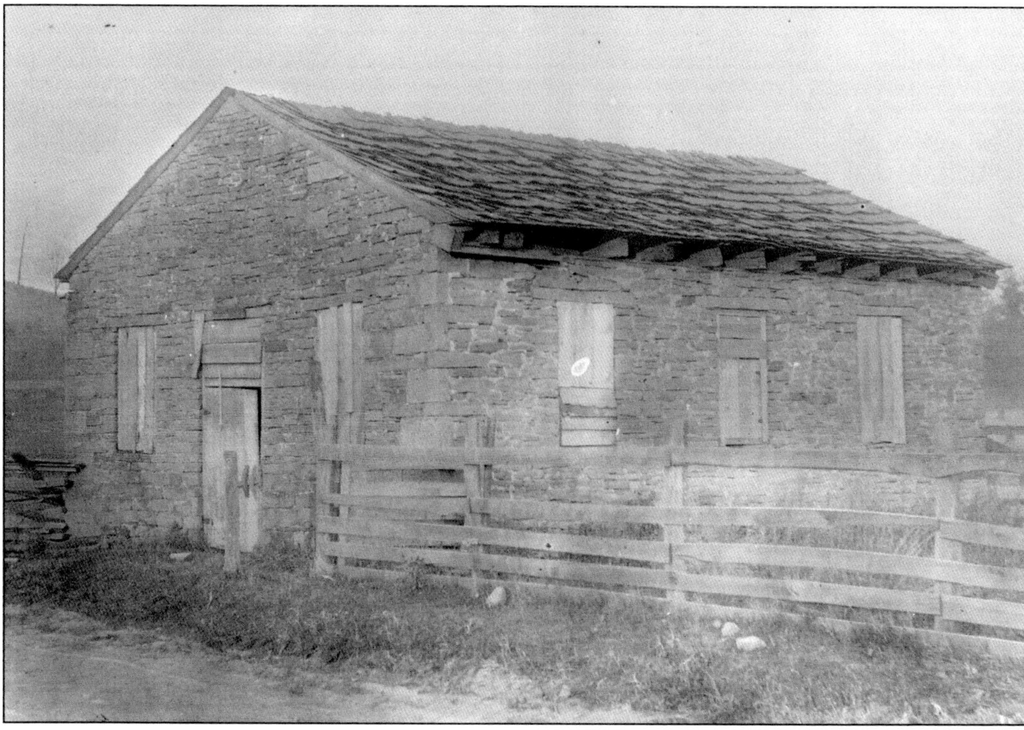

These two photographs show the Old Stone Schoolhouse during its declining years. The construction of this school was a community effort. The cost was divided into shares of $5 each, obtained by subscription. Each subscriber took as many shares as he could handle, most being paid in work. Davis Thomas, Nicodemus Griffiths, Gershom Griffiths, and Samuel Thomas quarried nearby stone in the fall of 1823. John Thomas laid the first stone, and Elder Thomas Hughes and Joseph Evans constructed the walls. Hughes plastered the walls; Samuel Griffith Phillipps made shingles for the roof; Gershom Griffiths and Alexander King laid the floor; Elijah Russell made the door; and Edward Price bought the stove and windows.

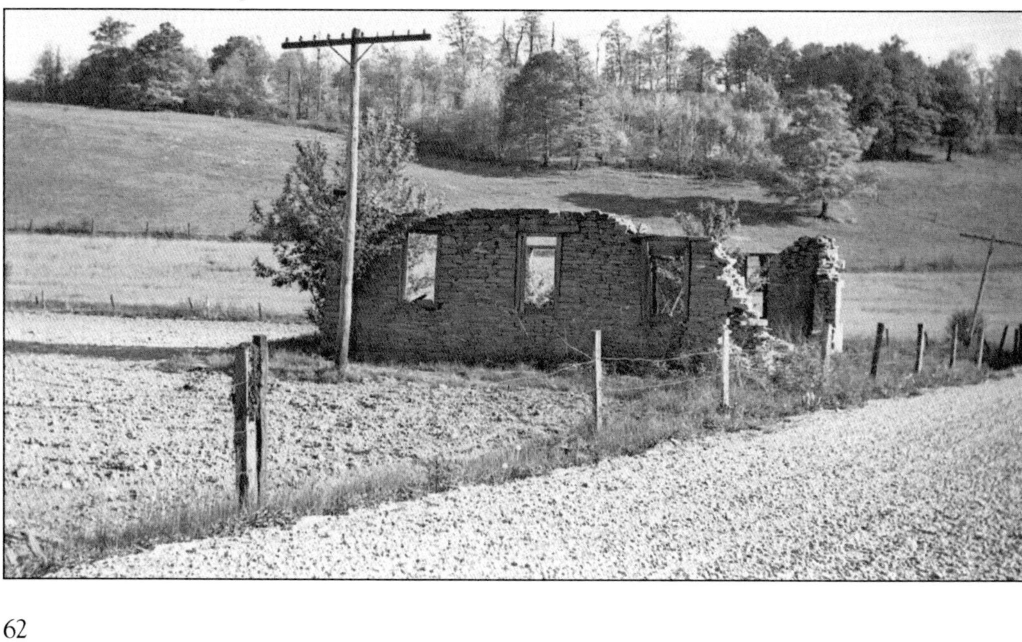

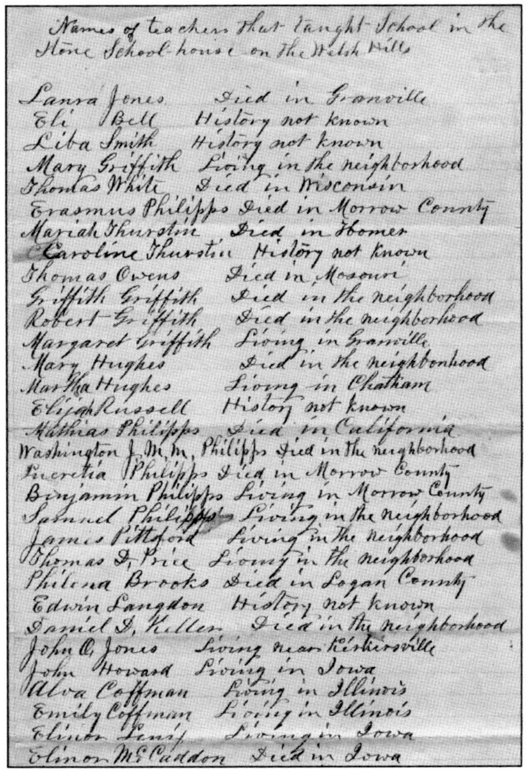

Names of teachers that taught School in the
Stone School-house on the Welsh Hills

Laura Jones Died in Granville
Eli Bell History not known
Liba Smith History not known
Mary Griffith Living in the neighborhood
Thomas White Died in Wisconsin
Erasmus Philipps Died in Morrow County
Mariah Thurstin Died in Homer
Caroline Thurstin History not known
Thomas Owens Died in Missouri
Griffith Griffith Died in the neighborhood
Robert Griffith Died in the neighborhood
Margaret Griffith Living in Granville
Mary Hughes Died in the neighborhood
Martha Hughes Living in Chatham
Elijah Russell History not known
Mathias Philipps Died in California
Washington J. M. M. Philipps Died in the neighborhood
Lucretia Philipps Died in Morrow County
Benjamin Philipps Living in Morrow County
Samuel Philipps Living in the neighborhood
James Pittsford Living in the neighborhood
Thomas D. Price Living in the neighborhood
Philena Brooks Died in Logan County
Edwin Langdon History not known
Daniel D. Keller Died in the neighborhood
John O. Jones Living near Kirkersville
John Howard Living in Iowa
Alva Coffman Living in Illinois
Emily Coffman Living in Illinois
Elinor Lewis Living in Iowa
Elinor McCaddon Died in Iowa

These handwritten notes from the late 1800s were part of meeting minutes recorded that listed the names of teachers who taught at the Old Stone Schoolhouse between 1825 and 1858. The list states the whereabouts of the former teachers at the time of this meeting. The end recognizes that 19 of the teachers named were Welsh. It also acknowledges several people in attendance at this meeting who assisted with the construction of the stone schoolhouse. Edward Price donated jthe stove; and T.J. Thomas, grandson of Theophilus Rees, and James Pittsford donated the table. (Courtesy of Ruth Valentine Sipe.)

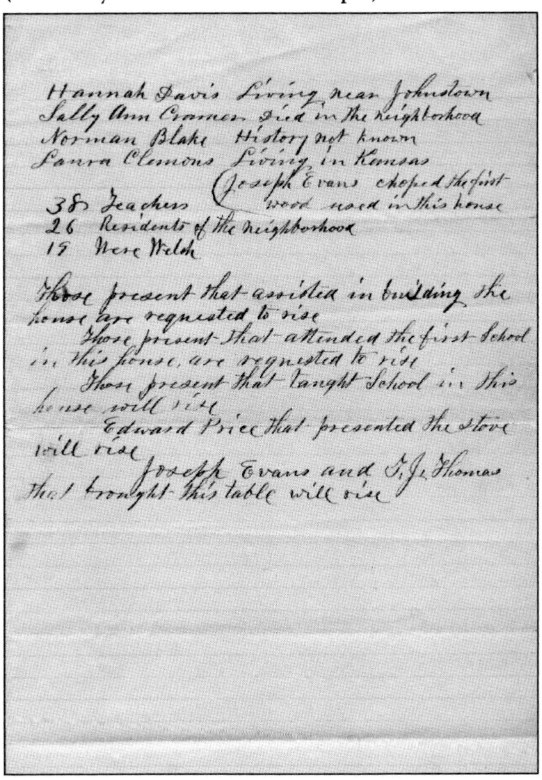

Hannah Davis Living near Johnstown
Sally Ann Cramer Died in the neighborhood
Norman Blake History not known
Laura Clemons Living in Kansas
Joseph Evans choped the first wood used in this house
38 Teachers
26 Residents of the neighborhood
19 Were Welsh

Those present that assisted in building the house are requested to rise
Those present that attended the first school in this house, are requested to rise
Those present that taught School in this house will rise
Edward Price that presented the stove will rise
Joseph Evans and T. J. Thomas that brought this table will rise

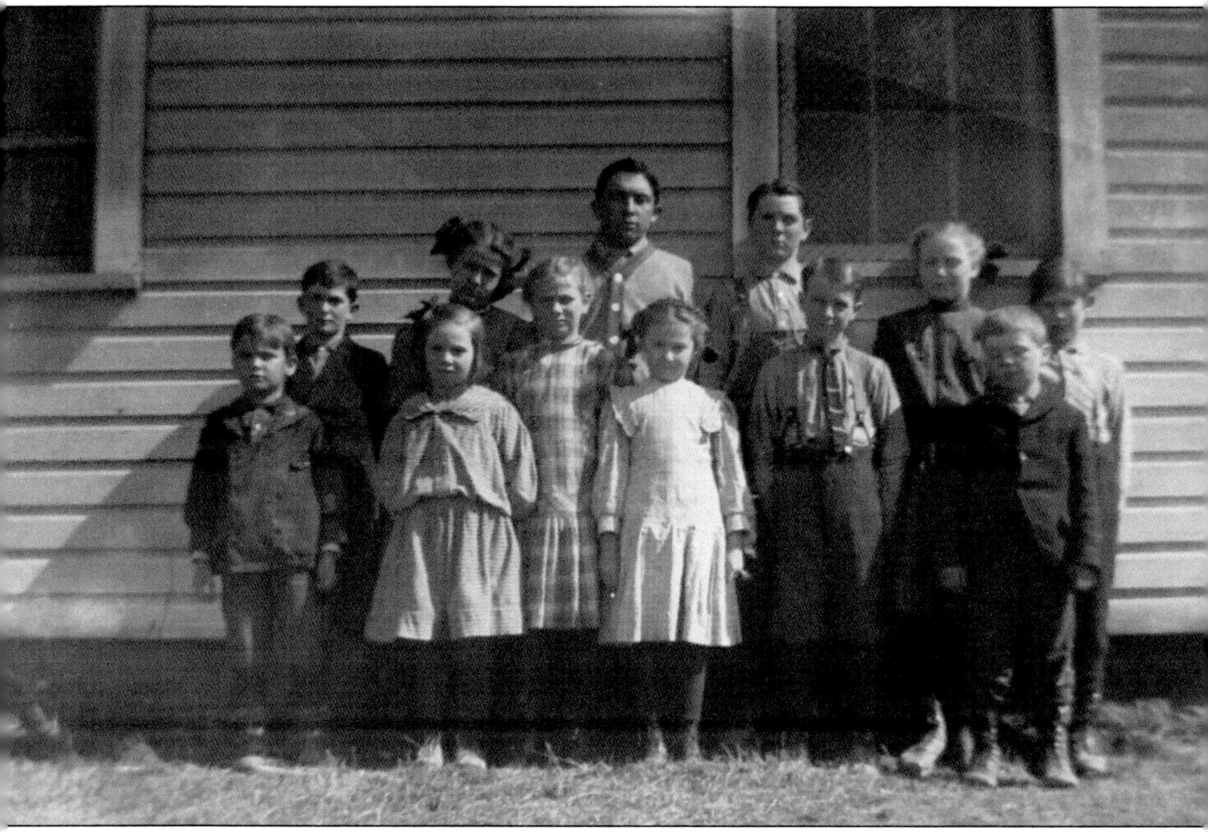

Thomas Warren Philipps (second row, far right) was approximately nine years old when this photograph was taken outside the Welsh Hills School around 1898. Tom's father, Samuel J., and grandfather Samuel G. served as teachers at the school, and he was later to become a teacher as well. His great-great uncle John H. was one of the first teachers in the Welsh Hills. One of nine one-room schoolhouses that served Granville Township during this time period, this school was designated as School No. 9 and called the Welsh Hills School. Other children living in the Welsh Hills attended North Street School, also known as School No. 8. Country schools typically consisted of a single room with a central stove for heating. This wooden schoolhouse was constructed in 1858 to replace the Old Stone Schoolhouse.

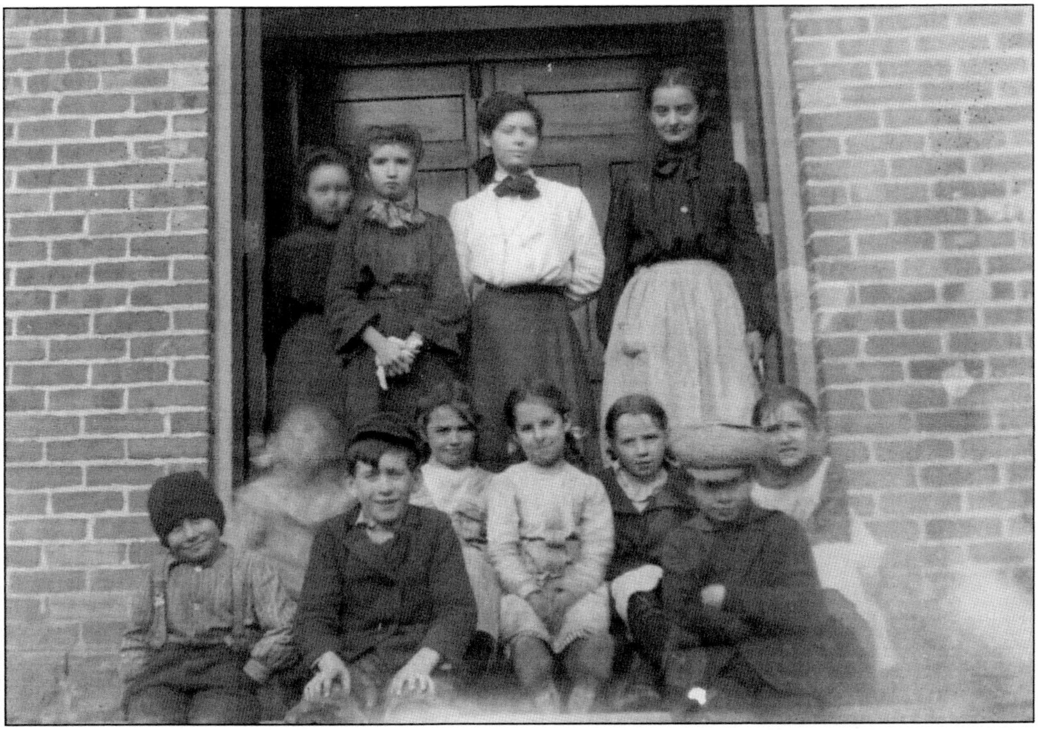

This picture was taken at the entrance of the Welsh Hills brick school. This building replaced the frame structure in 1899. Set in the gable of this brick structure was a stone with the date 1825, taken from the Old Stone Schoolhouse and likely cut by Elder Thomas Hughes.

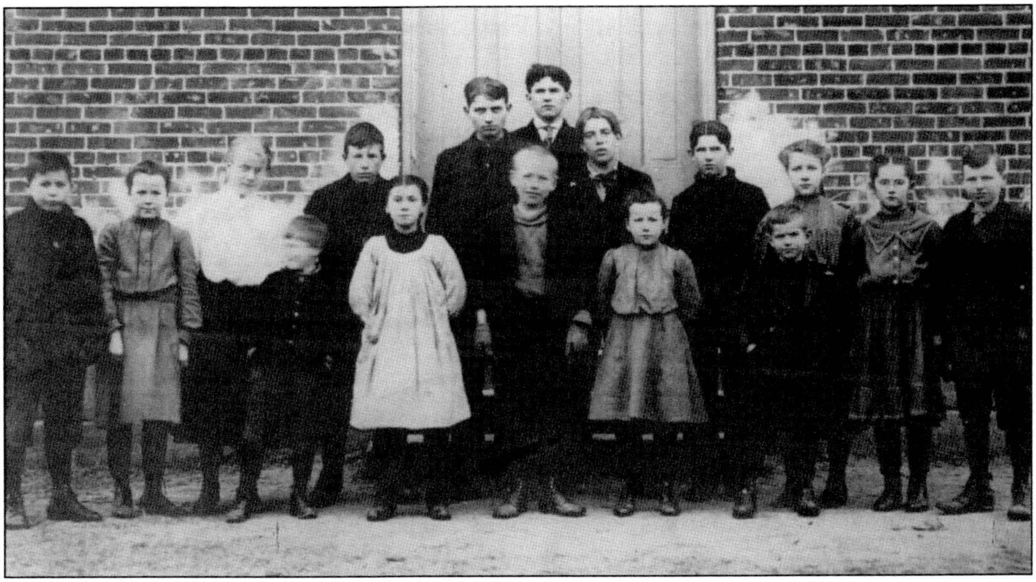

Identified in this *c.* 1905 photograph in front of the Welsh Hills School are brothers Thomas Warren Philipps (center of picture, in back) and Samuel John Philipps (second row, fourth from left). Their father, Samuel Jones Philipps, taught at this school; and their grandfather Samuel Griffith Philipps taught at the Old Stone Schoolhouse. Tom and Sam would also become schoolteachers during their adult life.

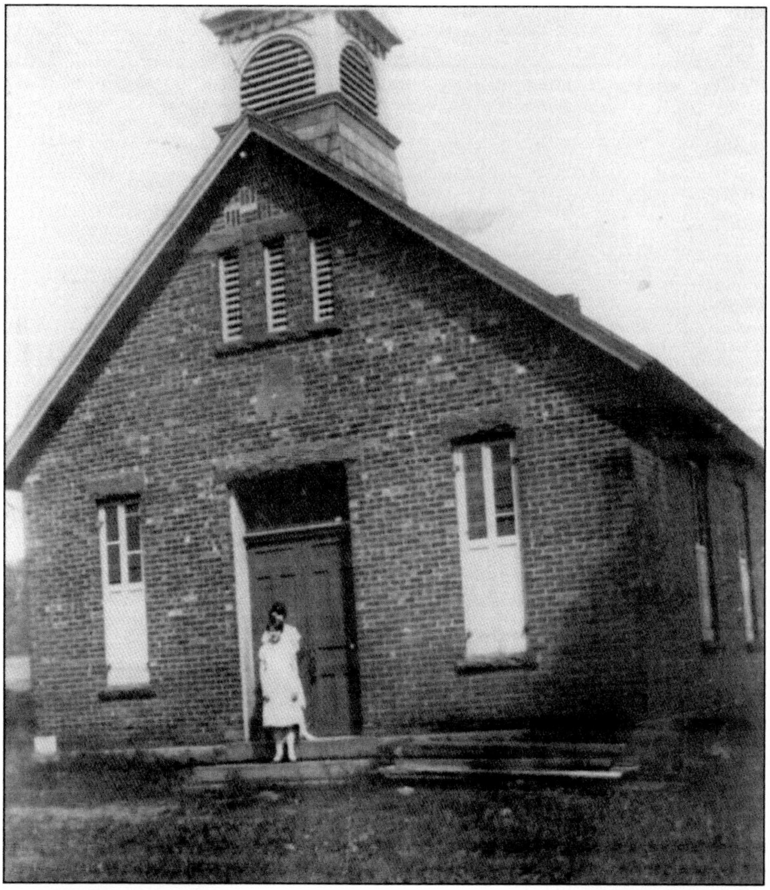

The brick Welsh Hills School (left and below) served the community from 1899 to 1924. Located on Welsh Hills Road near the border between Granville and Newark Townships, it was also used as a meeting place for the Welsh Hills Grange. In 1924, the school was sold to the grange at auction for $770. The property originally belonged to Edward Price, a Welsh native, who sold the land to the Granville Township around 1858 for the construction of a frame school building. The photograph below clearly shows the outhouses used at the time.

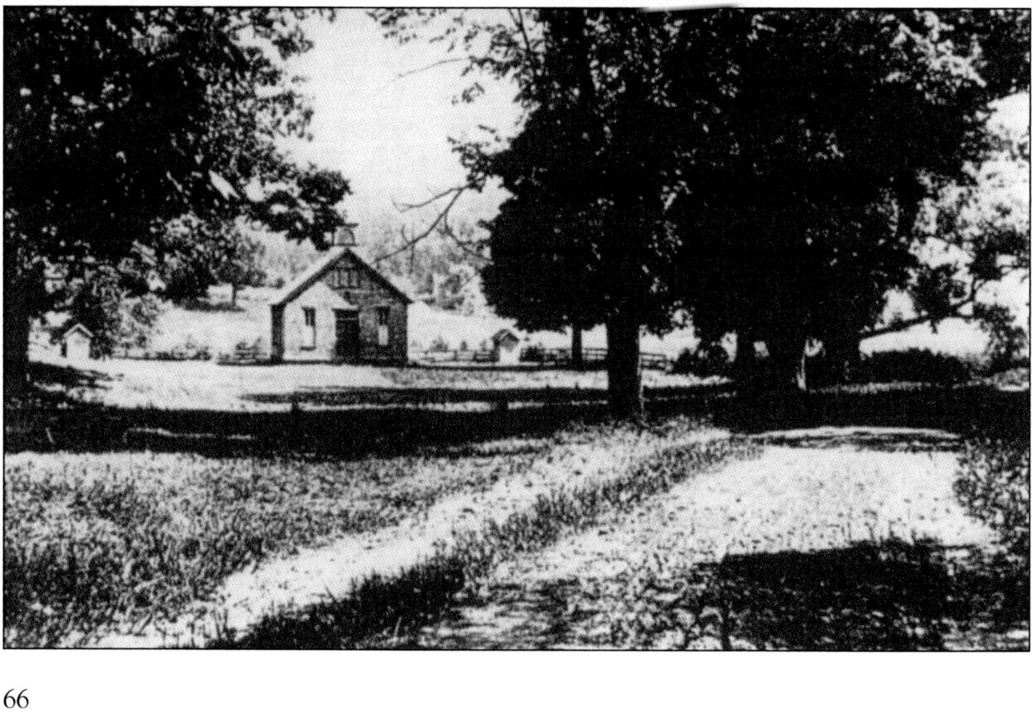

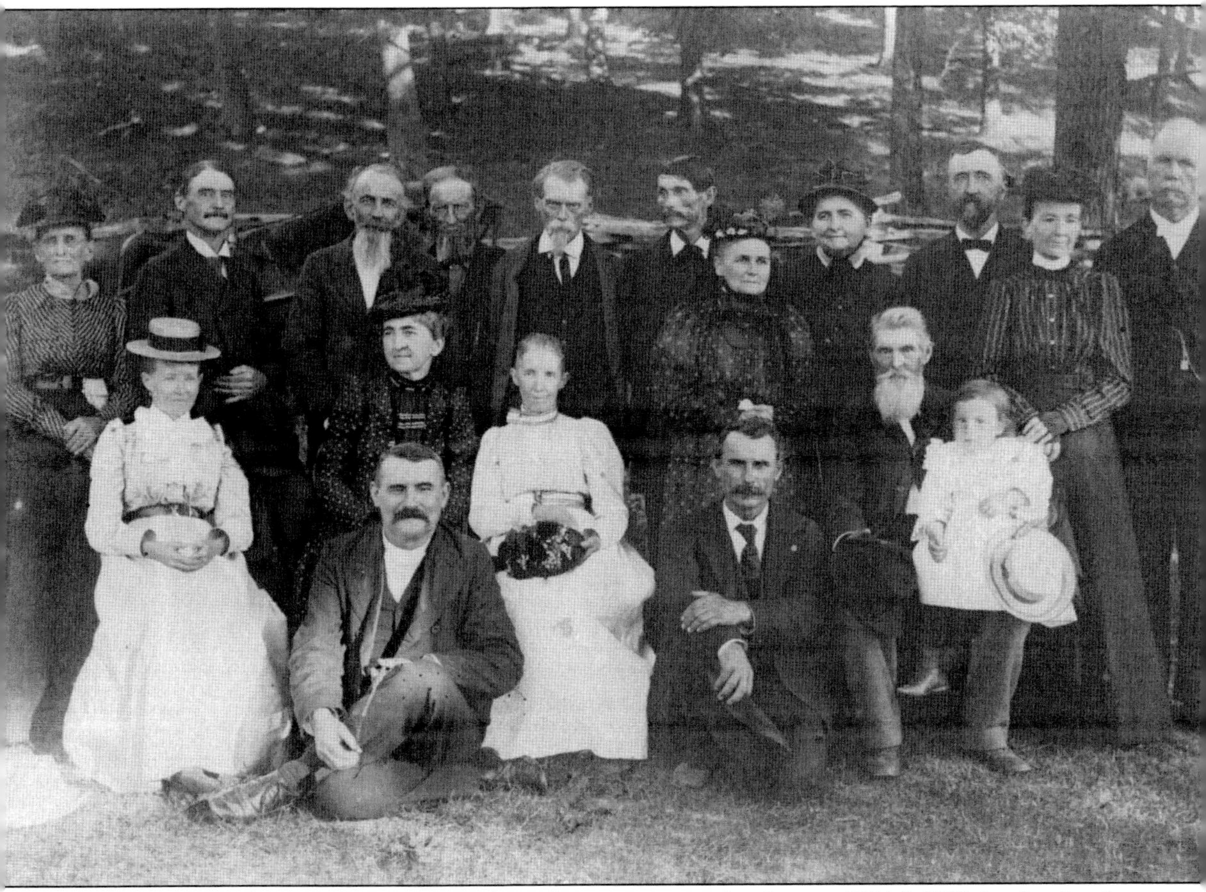

This photograph was taken in 1899 when the cornerstone for the new Welsh Hills brick school was laid. The people in this image had been students in the previous frame building and served as teachers in both schoolhouses. They are, from left to right, (first row, seated on ground) brothers Thomas Wendell Philipps and Samuel Jones Philipps; (second row, seated) Belle Bishop, Susan Pittsford, Mrs. Case, and Elias Evans, holding Will Williams; (third row) Mrs. David Hankinson, Isaac Evans, Ben King, William David Evans, George Evans, Cyrus Evans, Nellie Frederick (sister of Tom and Sam Philipps), Mary Pittsford Hillbrant (sister of Susan Pittsford), David Pittsford, Amelia Williams, and Rev. William Miller. Thomas Wendell Philipps served as prosecuting attorney for Licking County. Parents of some of these people were also teachers from the Old Stone Schoolhouse, including Samuel G. Philipps, James Pittsford, and Thomas D. Price. (Courtesy of the Granville Historical Society and Ernest King.)

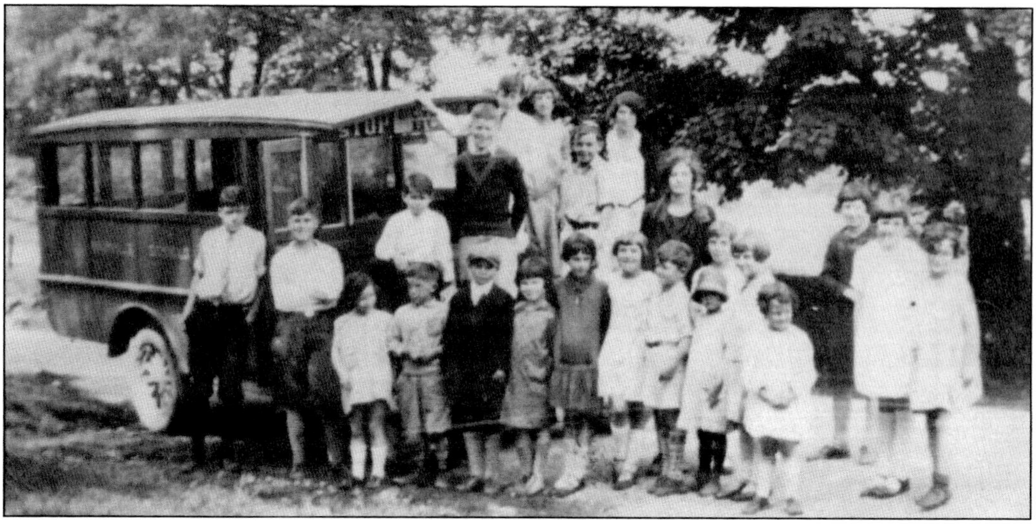

After the closing of the last Welsh Hills School in 1924, children living in the area were transported to the Union School, located on Granger Street in Granville. Modes of transportation included horseback, buggy, bus, and walking. This photograph shows the bus used to pick up children in the Welsh Hills during the 1930s. (Courtesy of Jennifer Philipps Welsh.)

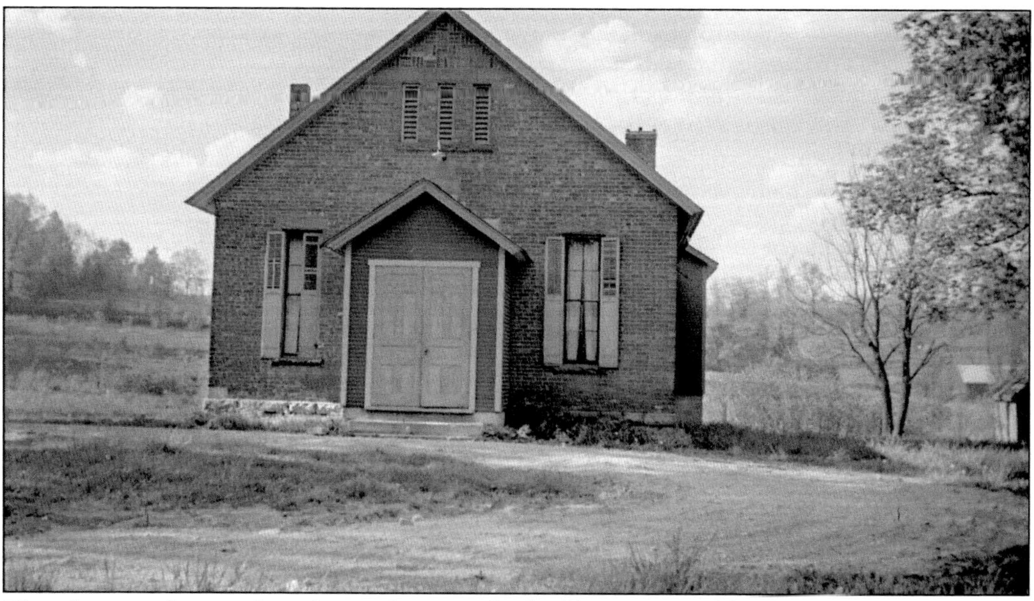

This photograph was taken during the time the building was used by the Welsh Hills Grange. The bell tower was removed and an extended vestibule added. The interior included a small stage at the rear of the main room that was used for plays and special events. The brick school was to become a residence before being demolished in 1981.

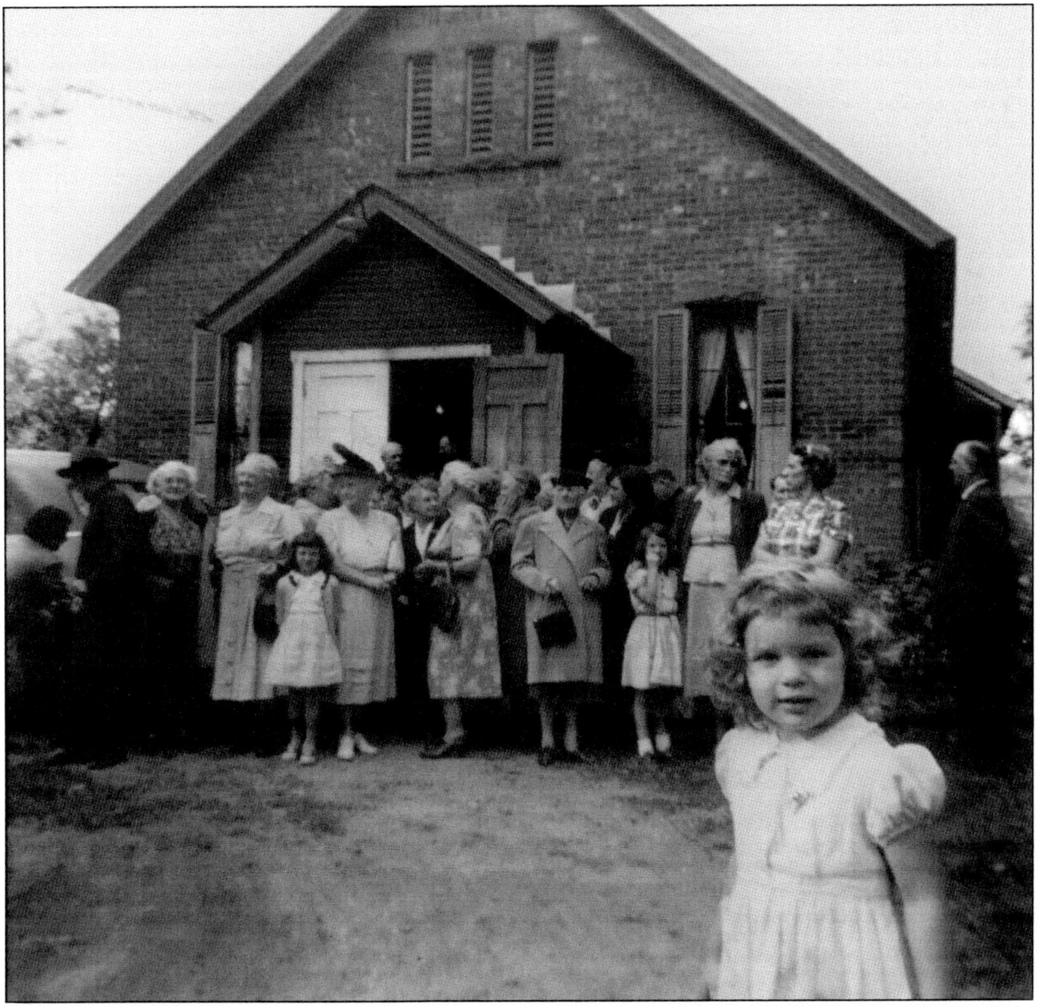

The community used the Welsh Hills Grange building. This photograph, taken around 1951, shows a gathering of former students of the Welsh Hills School No. 9. The young girl in the foreground is Patty Wheeler, whose grandmother, Mamie Philipps Wheeler (seventh from left), attended the school. Others identified in this image are Mamie's sister Winnie (ninth from left) and Grace Evans Philipps (directly in front of the window), wife of Thomas Warren Philipps and sister-in-law to Mamie and Winnie. Grace is standing with her granddaughter Karen Humphrey. (Courtesy of Patty Wheeler Andrews.)

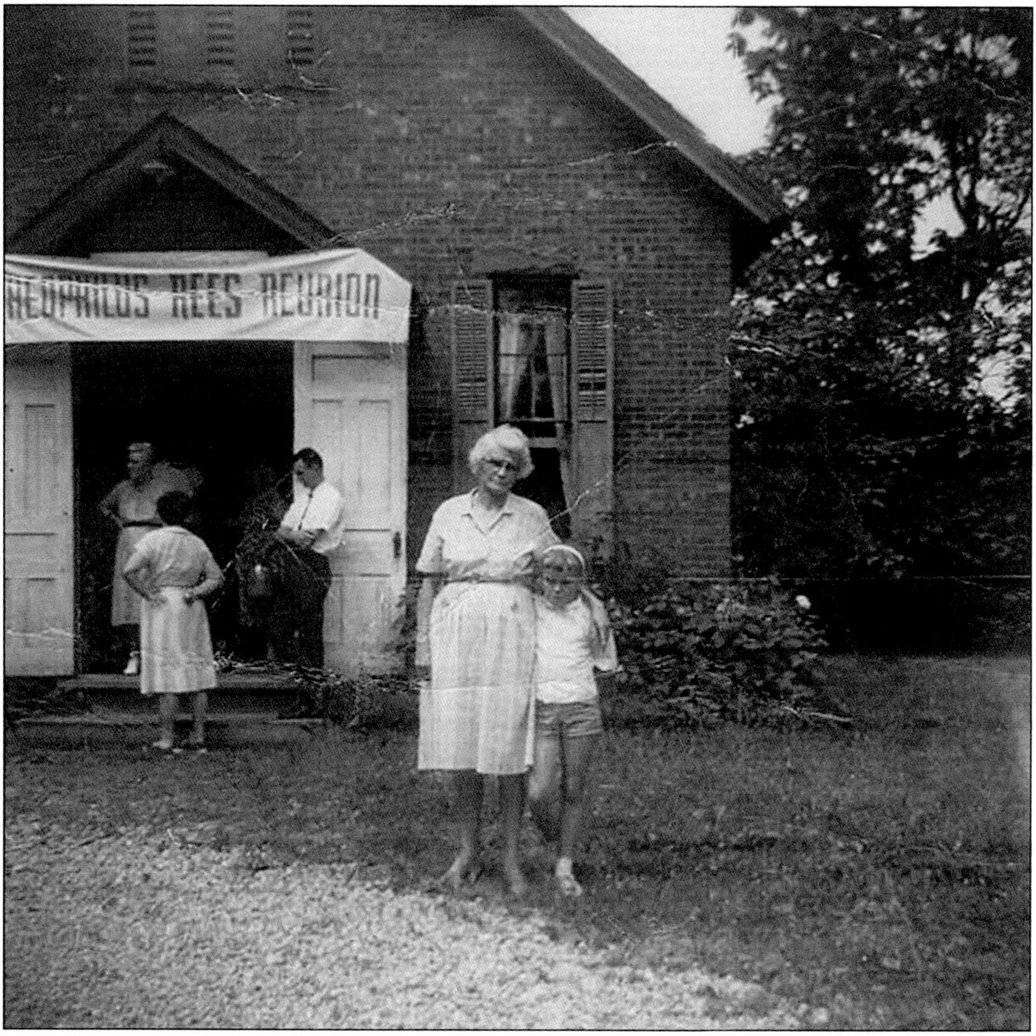


This photograph shows descendants of Theophilus Rees at their annual family reunion in August 1961. In the foreground is Reah Grace Evans Philipps, great-great-great-granddaughter of Theophilus Rees, with her granddaughter Bobbi Roberts. Grace married Thomas Warren Philipps, a direct descendant of Thomas Philipps. The author was present at this reunion with her parents, two sisters, and countless cousins. (Courtesy of Karen Harden.)

# *Six*

# Homes and Farms

The first cabin to be constructed in the Welsh Hills was built in 1801 by John Rees, as instructed by his father, Theophilus. John was also charged with clearing some land and planting wheat in preparation for the arrival of the first families. In 1802, Theophilus Rees, David Lewis, and David Thomas arrived with their families, along with Simon James. Each family erected its own cabin in the Hills. Both Theophilus Rees and Thomas Philipps divided their lands among their sons and daughters. Jimmy Johnson also received 100 acres from Rees. In 1820, sturdy frame houses began to replace the log cabins. Wood was plentiful and the most appropriate building material. Upon his arrival in 1837, David R. Jones noted that 33 farms existed in the Welsh Hills upon which stood 77 dwellings of all descriptions. Samuel Joseph Philipps constructed one of the first brick homes in the area with bricks fired on the site. A member of the Evans family constructed the single notable stone house on Jones Road. Many of the original homes are still located in the Hills, and most have been greatly modified to accommodate modern standards.

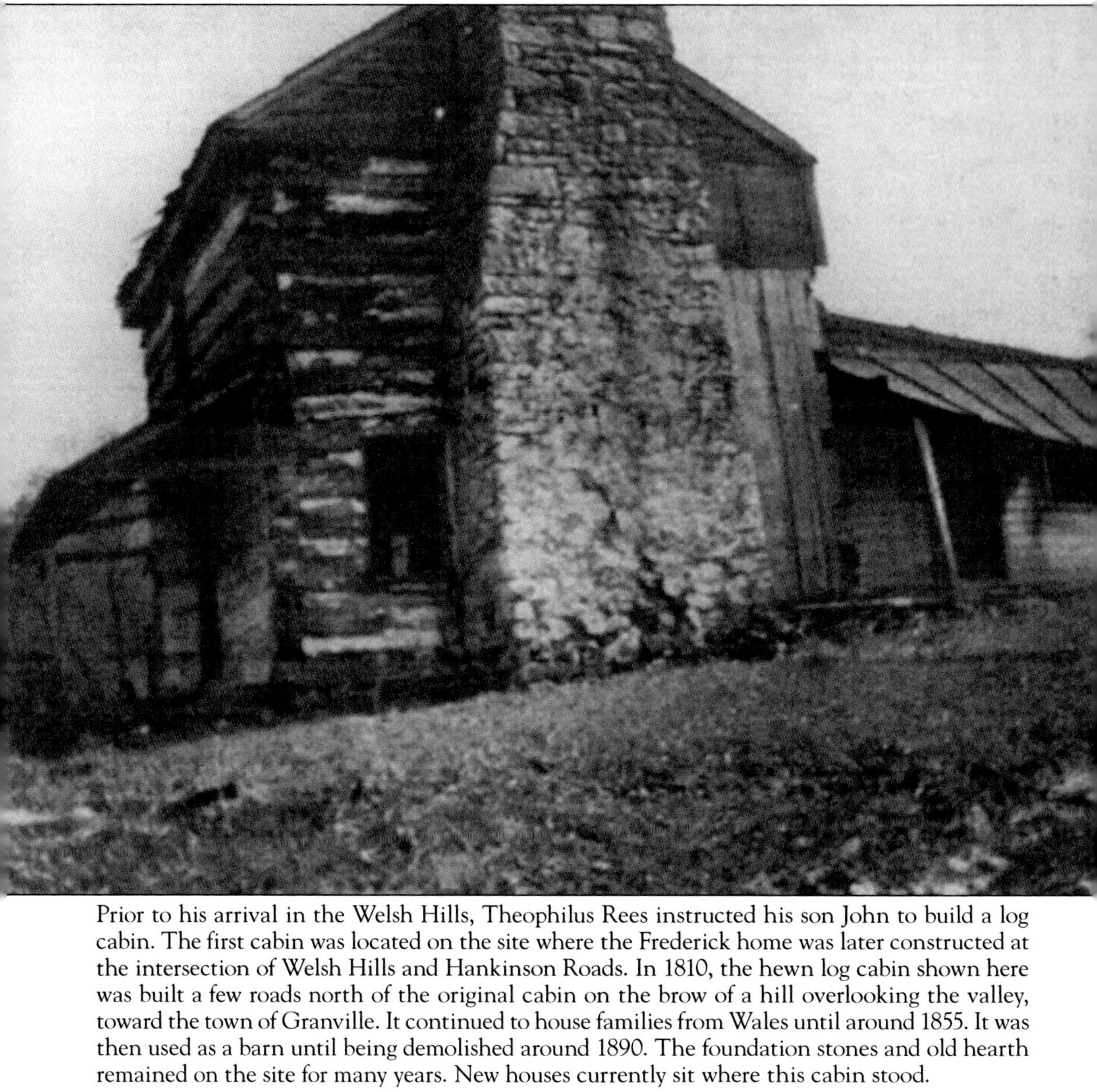

Prior to his arrival in the Welsh Hills, Theophilus Rees instructed his son John to build a log cabin. The first cabin was located on the site where the Frederick home was later constructed at the intersection of Welsh Hills and Hankinson Roads. In 1810, the hewn log cabin shown here was built a few roads north of the original cabin on the brow of a hill overlooking the valley, toward the town of Granville. It continued to house families from Wales until around 1855. It was then used as a barn until being demolished around 1890. The foundation stones and old hearth remained on the site for many years. New houses currently sit where this cabin stood.

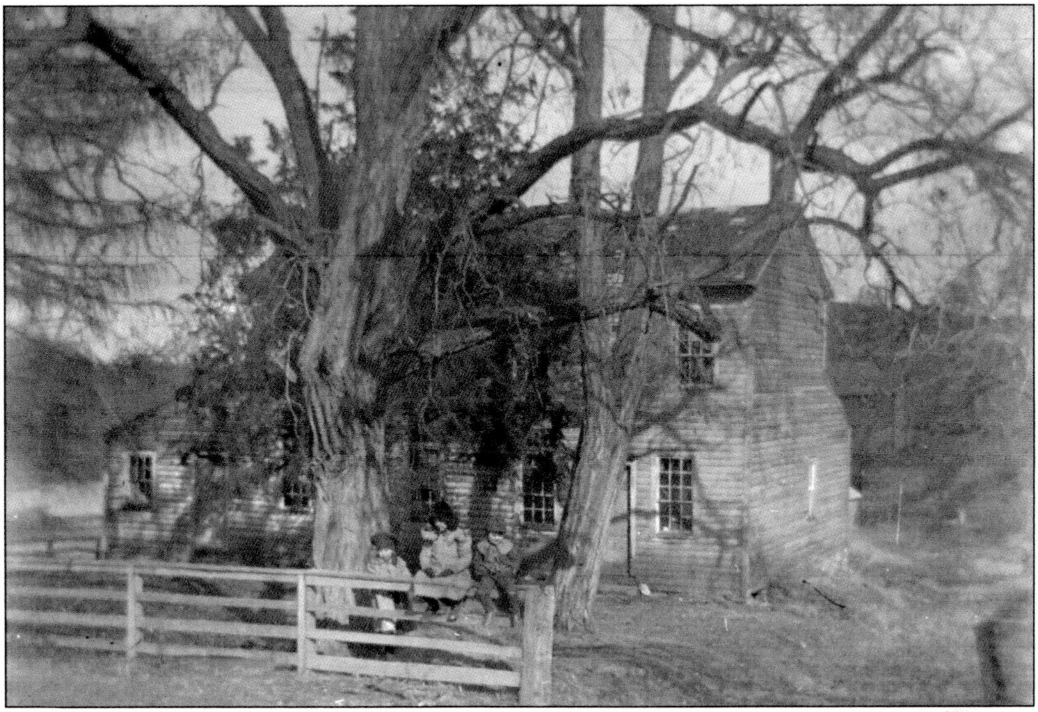

William and Thomas Cramer constructed this house around 1820. It was called the Big Spring Farm, because it was located adjacent to the Big Spring, one of the larger natural soft water springs in the Hills. David R. Jones and family occupied the home upon their arrival from New York. When the Joneses moved, Rebecca Cramer and William Hankinson purchased it for their family.

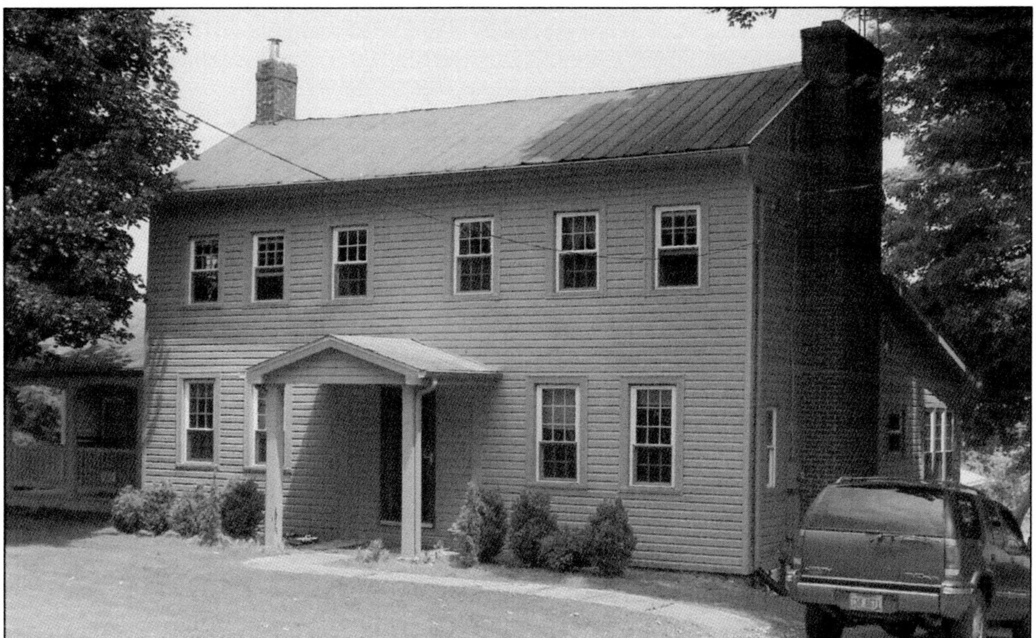

The home is still occupied by a descendant of Simeon Hankinson and Thomas Cramer. Rick Foster is their great-great great-grandson.

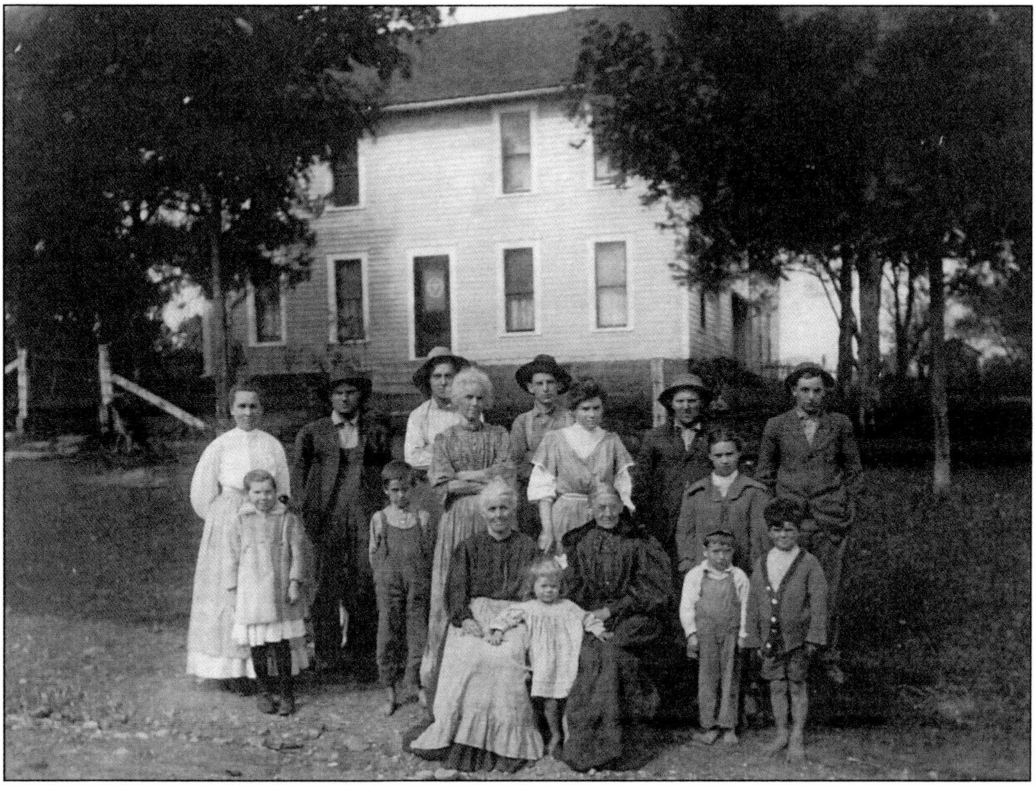

William Cramer built this house on Hankinson Road and gave it to his daughter Mary when she married Thomas Evans. In this photograph are, from left to right, (first row) Rebecca Cramer, Lucy Hankinson, Margaret Hankinson, Bill Cramer, and Wilbur Hankinson; (second row) Addie Cramer, Gene Evans, Mary Hankinson Evans, Grace Evans, and May Cramer; (third row) Maggie Cramer, Philip Philipps, Albert Hankinson, Hayes Hankinson, Will Cramer, and Tom Cramer.

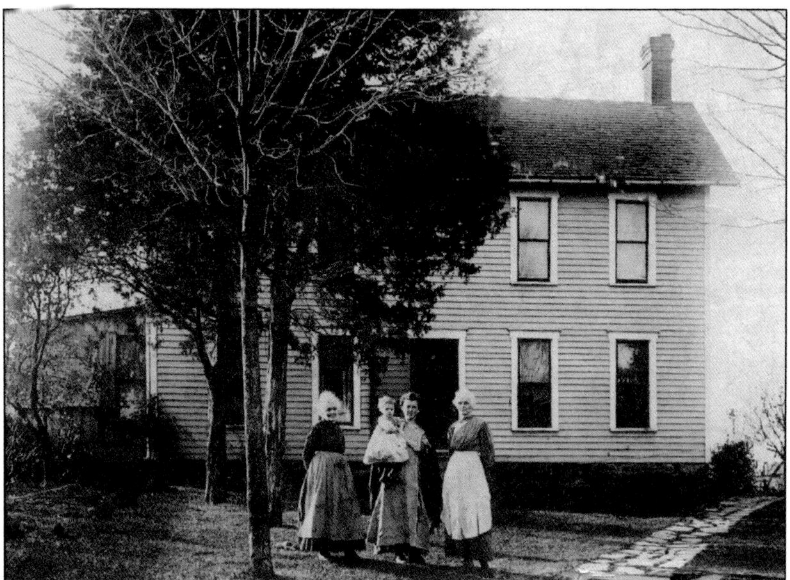

Pictured in front of the William Hankinson home are his wife and daughter, Rebecca Cramer Hankinson (left) and Mary Hankinson Evans (far right). Mary was the wife of Thomas Evans. Many members of the Hankinson family were born, raised, and died in this house, now owned by Norm Kennedy.

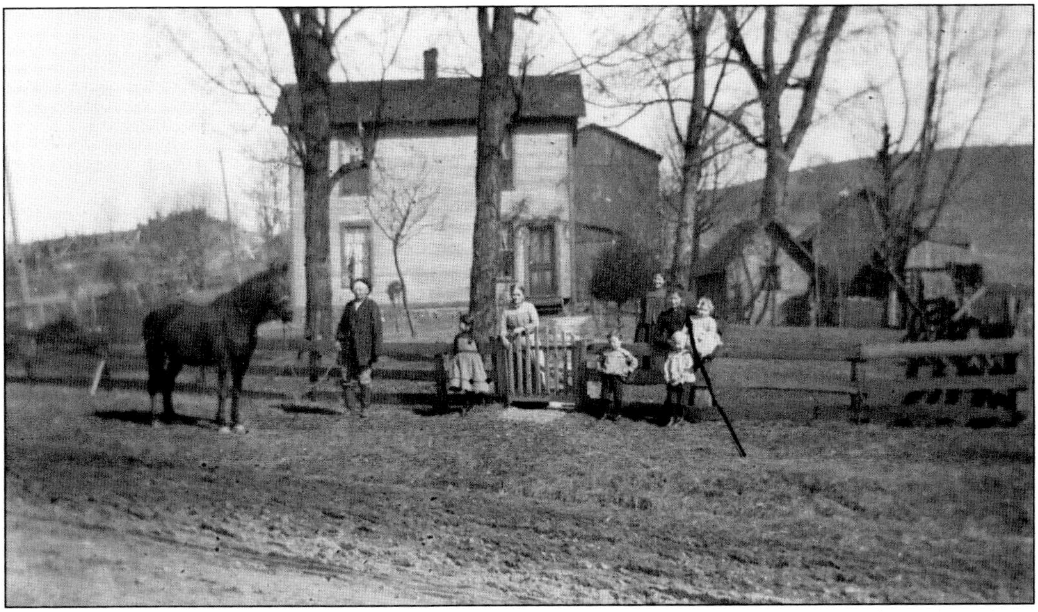

Jacob Frederick constructed this house on Welsh Hills Road in the late 1870s upon his return from serving in the Union army. It was around this time that he married Nellie Philipps, daughter of Samuel Griffith Philipps. Jake is pictured in this photograph holding the horse's reins. His wife, Nellie, is standing behind the wooden gate. Jake and Nellie had three children who survived into adulthood—Arthur, Ada, and Nellie.

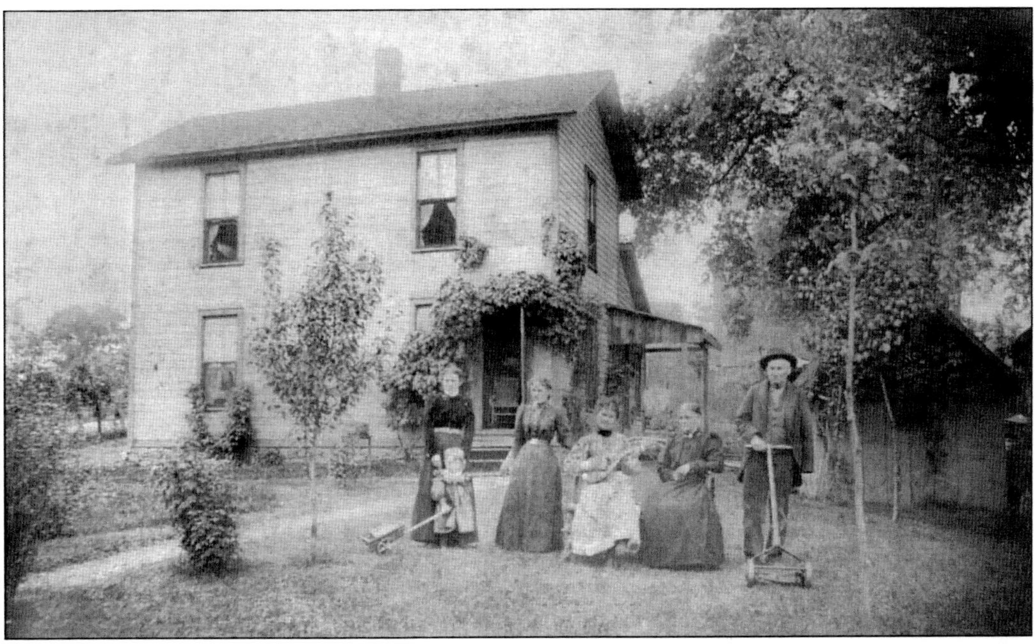

The Fredericks posed for this photograph around 1899. They are, from left to right, Nellie Frederick Briggs (daughter of Nellie and Jake), her son Leonard, Ada Frederick (daughter of Nellie and Jake), Mary "Mamie" Philipps (niece of Nellie and Jake), Ellen (Nellie Philipps) Frederick, and Jacob (Jake) Frederick. Jake lost his left arm on November 23, 1863, at the Battle of Missionary Ridge. It is amusing to note that Jake posed with his lawn mower. Mamie sits as if playing the mandolin.

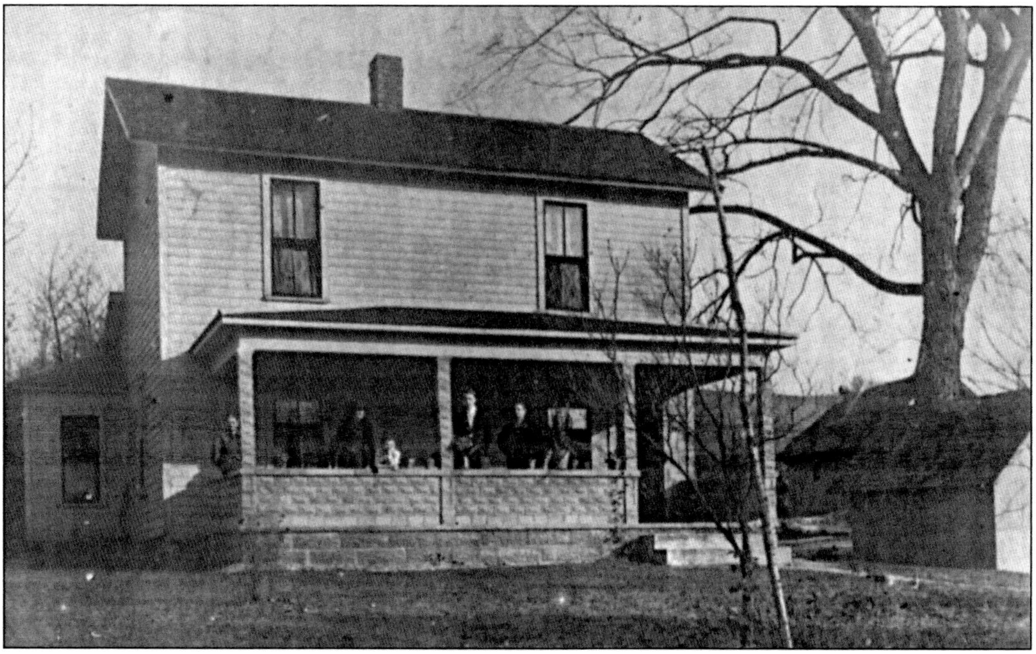

This photograph was taken sometime after 1909, the year that Jake Frederick added the front porch. Nellie is at the far left, and Jake is directly to her right. Tom and Mary Evans bought the house and allowed their daughter Grace Philipps and her family to live there for several years until they had enough money to buy a home in Granville.

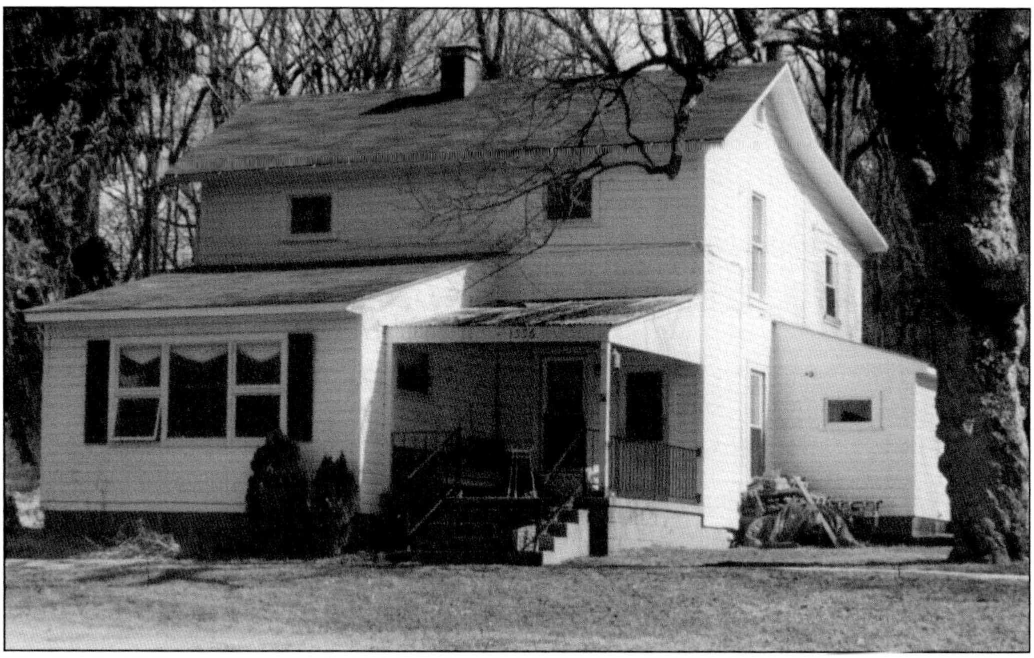

The Frederick house continued to change in appearance as different families occupied it. This is how it looked when Samuel (Sam) David Philipps lived here with his wife and four children. Sam, grandnephew of Jake and Nellie, lived in this house when he was a boy. His parents were Thomas and Grace Philipps.

This photograph was taken in the 1920s by Thomas Warren Philipps during the time that Tom and Grace lived in the Frederick house on Welsh Hills Road. A tornado had lifted the recently built chicken house and carried it about 100 feet from its original location. It landed near this duck, which never abandoned its nest. Tommy Philipps, their son, recalls seeing the chicken house in the air, upside down and illuminated by lightning.

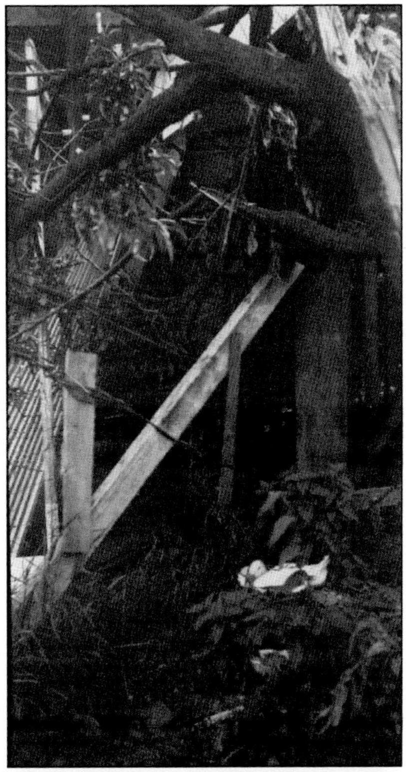

Samuel David Philipps built this pond when he owned the Frederick home. The old cider mill is visible at the left. The pond, fed by several natural springs, was always stocked with fish. It was also a favorite place for relatives to go swimming in the summer and ice-skating in the winter. Sam received government funding to construct the pond as a water reservoir. (Courtesy of Jennifer Philipps Welsh.)

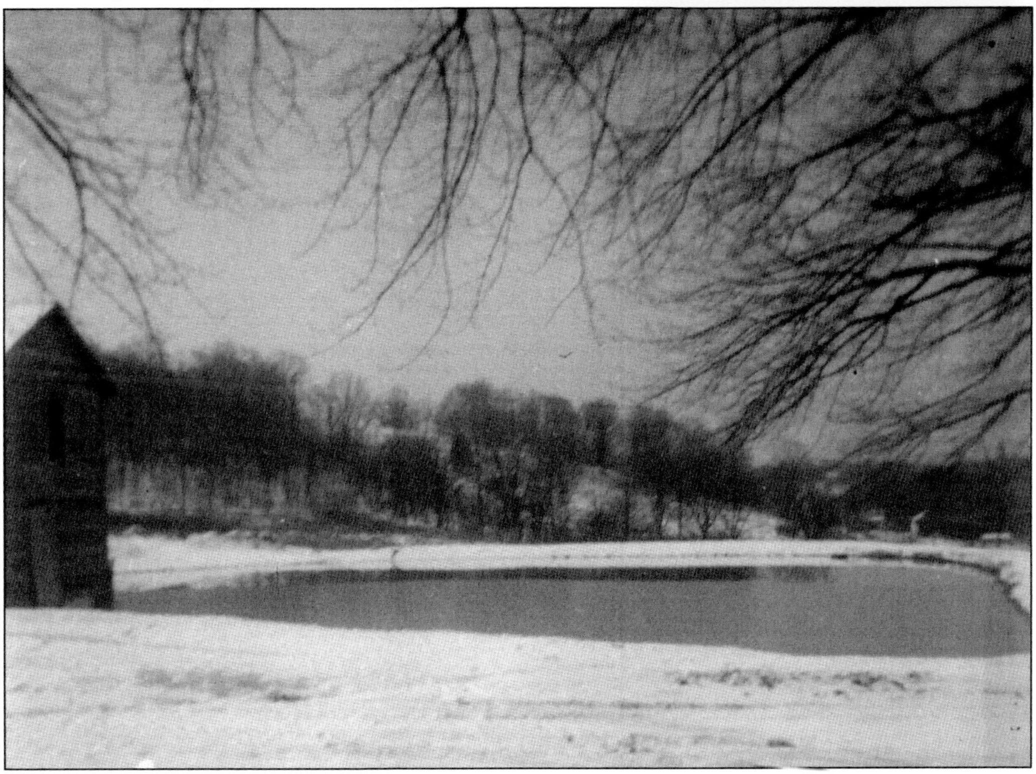

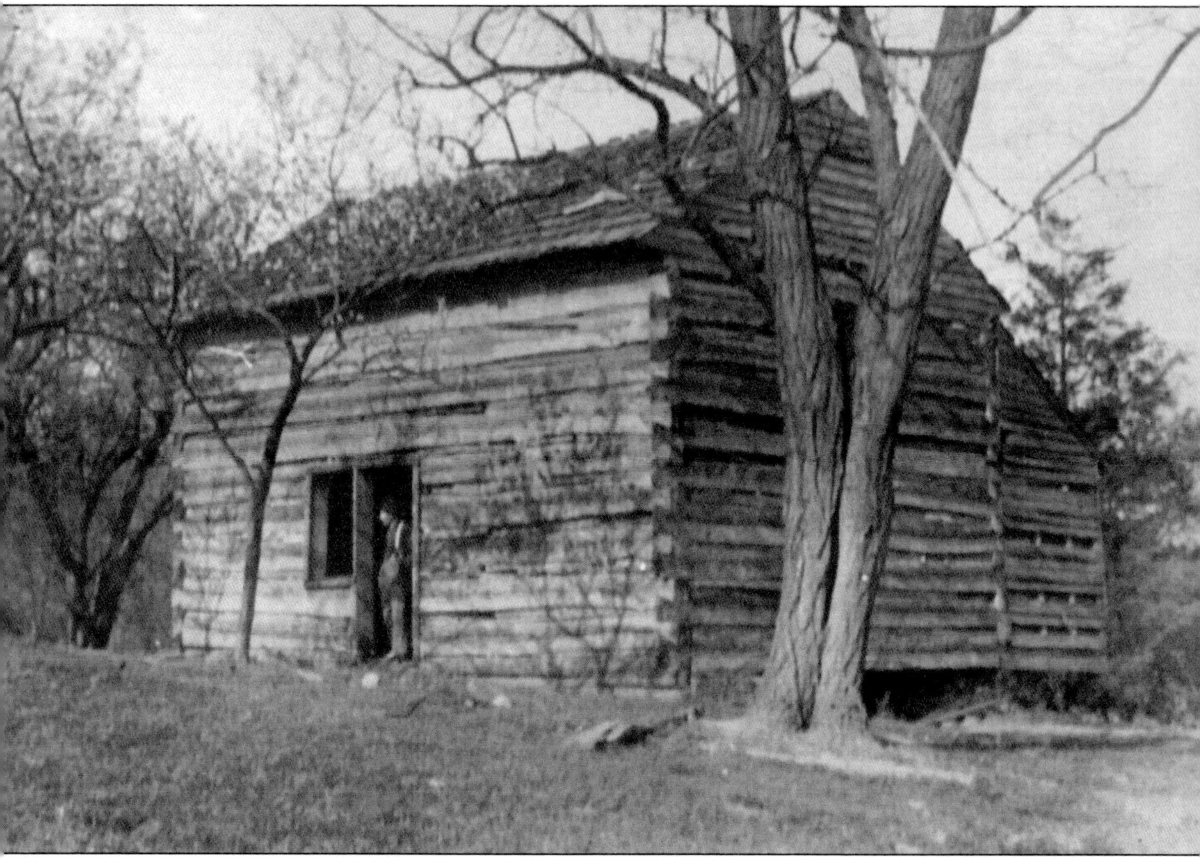

This is the Henry Williams cabin that is presumed to have been located on the site where the Williams house now stands on Welsh Hills Road. Standing in the doorway is Herbert Griffith, son of Howard Effingham Griffith. Henry Williams was the grandson of William and Isabella Pugh Williams, who came to America from Wales in 1820 with their three children and lived in Delaware County, Ohio, prior to moving to the Welsh Hills. Henry Williams's parents were William Paul Williams and Mary Hughes.

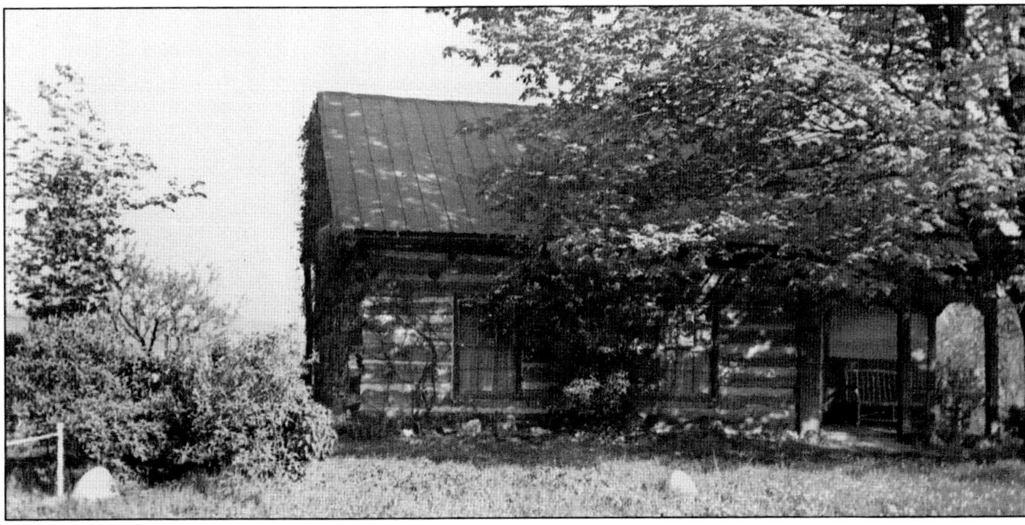

This is the last remaining log cabin located in the Welsh Hills. It was the home of George and Mary Williams and their sons until the early 1900s. The cabin remained a summer dwelling for descendants of the Williams family for many years. It is now deteriorating but stands as a reminder of the area's early architecture. As noted on the map of Granville from the 1866 Atlas of Licking County (see page 13), the property where this cabin is located was previously owned by John Pittsford, who had a sheep farm. Directly across Welsh Hills Road was the Mt. Pleasant farm owned by David Williams. (Below photograph by Janet Philipps Procida.)

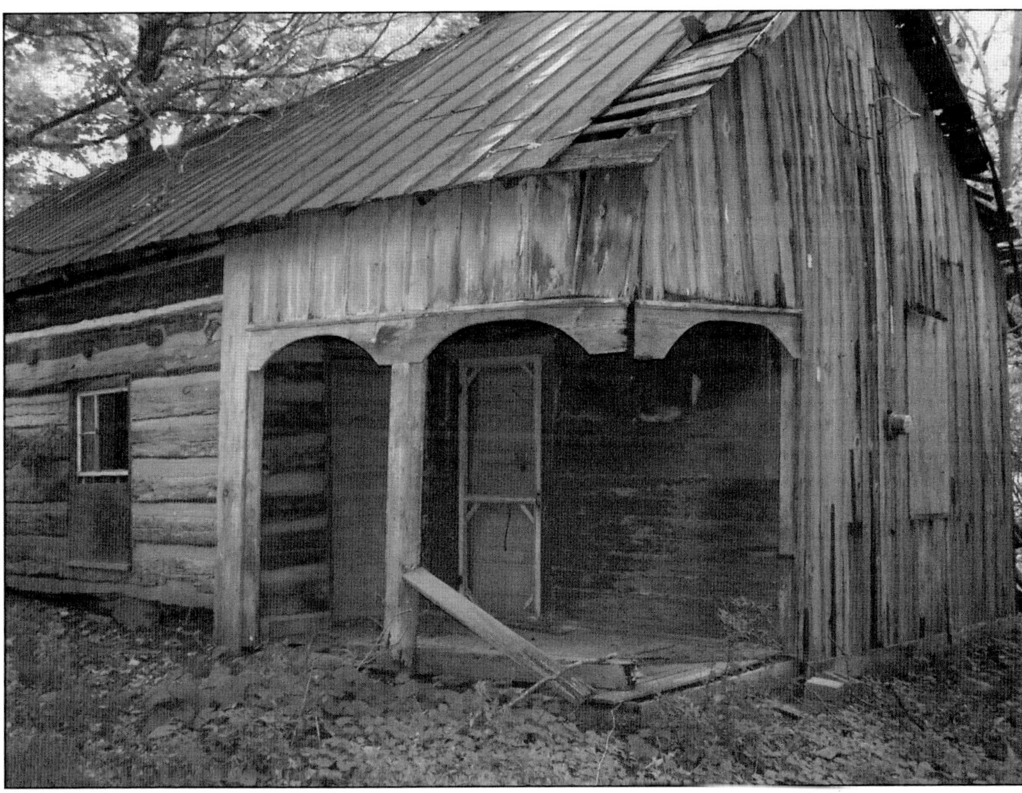

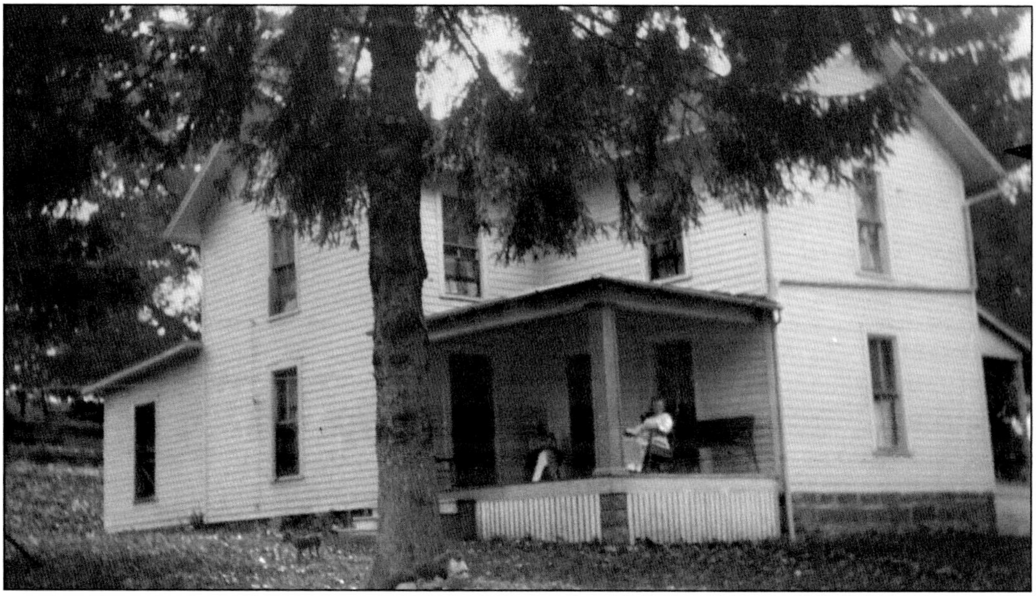

A little farther north on Welsh Hills Road is property that was owned by John W. Williams, an immigrant from Brecon, Wales, who was married to Esther Jones, from Cardiganshire, Wales. John and Esther raised five boys and six girls in this home. The farm consisted of 54 acres, where John had a flock of 20 sheep that provided wool to supply the family with clothing and blankets. Around 1900, David Elijah Williams wrote about his father, "He had learned to do about everything under the sun." John made shoes for his family and mended shoes for other members of the community. He was also trained as a mason. The current photograph (below) shows that little has changed on this house in 100 years, including the pine tree in the front yard. (Below photograph by Janet Philipps Procida.)

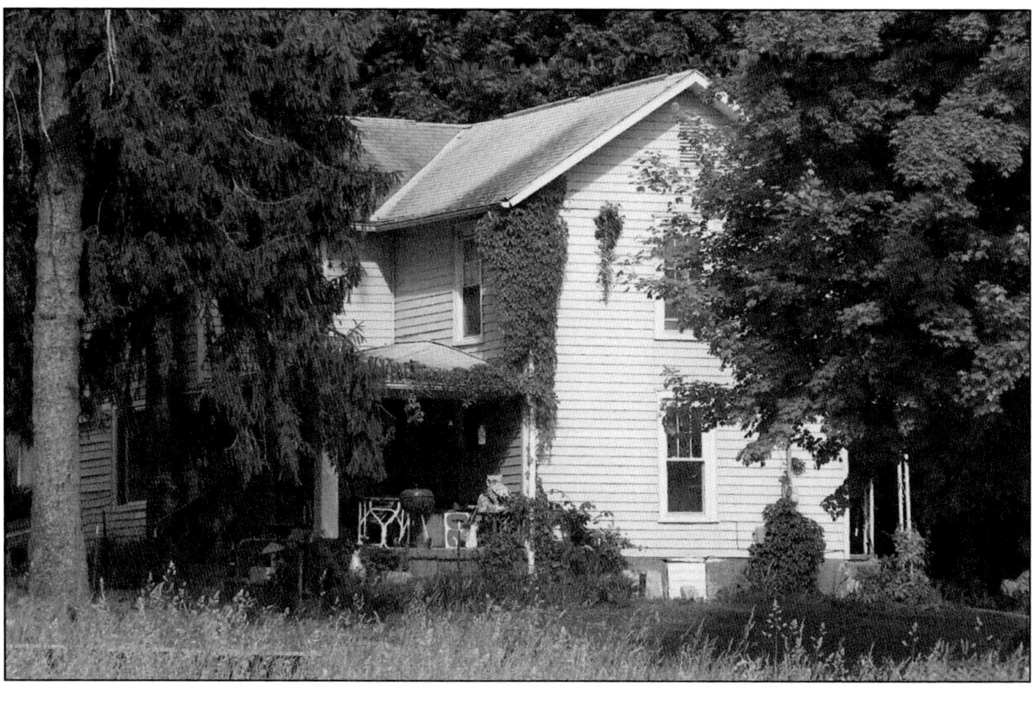

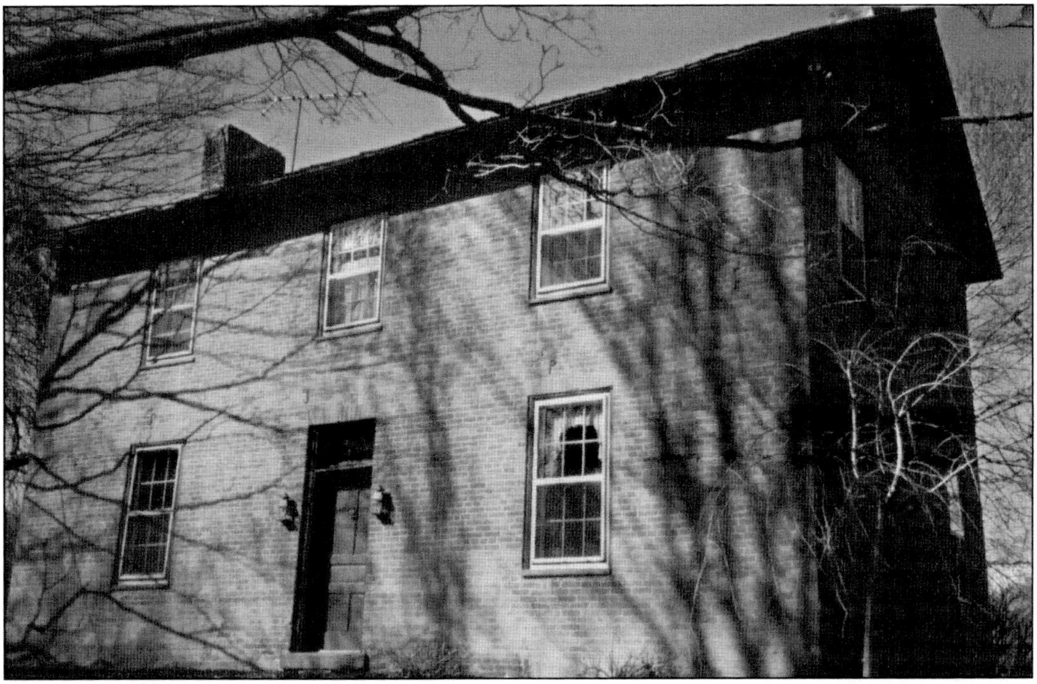

Samuel Joseph Philipps constructed a brick home around 1835 on the 100 acres conveyed to him in 1810 by his father, Thomas Philipps. The "Philipps Brick" is considered the oldest brick house constructed in the Welsh Hills. This house replaced the original log cabin located northeast of the current structure. It is recorded that the bricks were fired on the site. Some of the brick ties spell out the name P-H-I-L-I-P-P-S around all four sides of the house. There are two rooms on each floor, and each room has its own fireplace. Large, deep closets flank the chimneys that rise within the building walls. The Hobbs family, also well known in the Welsh Hills, later occupied the dwelling.

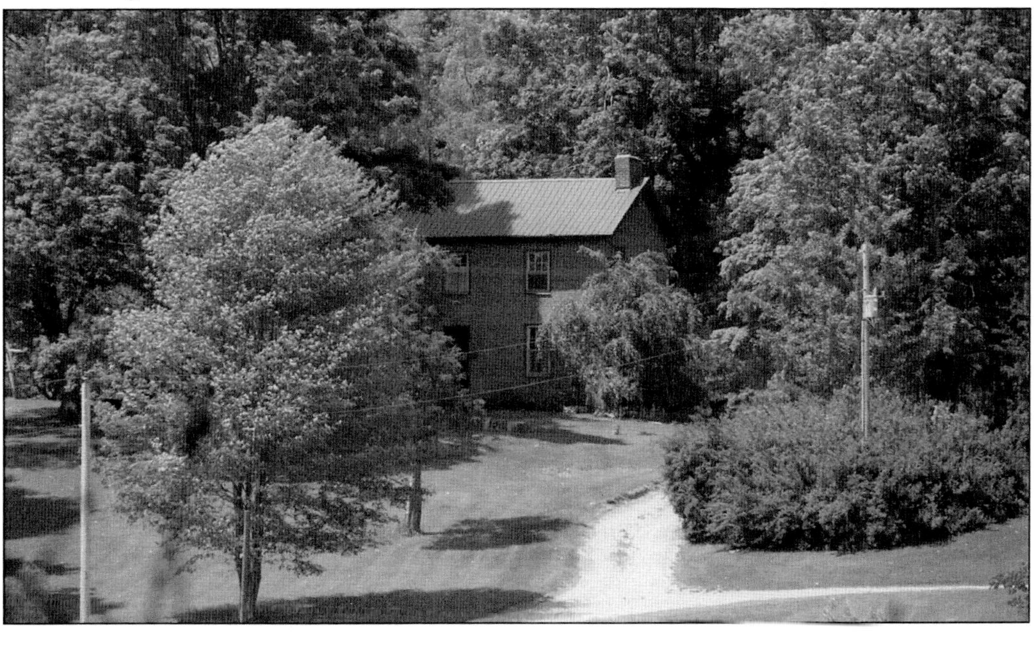

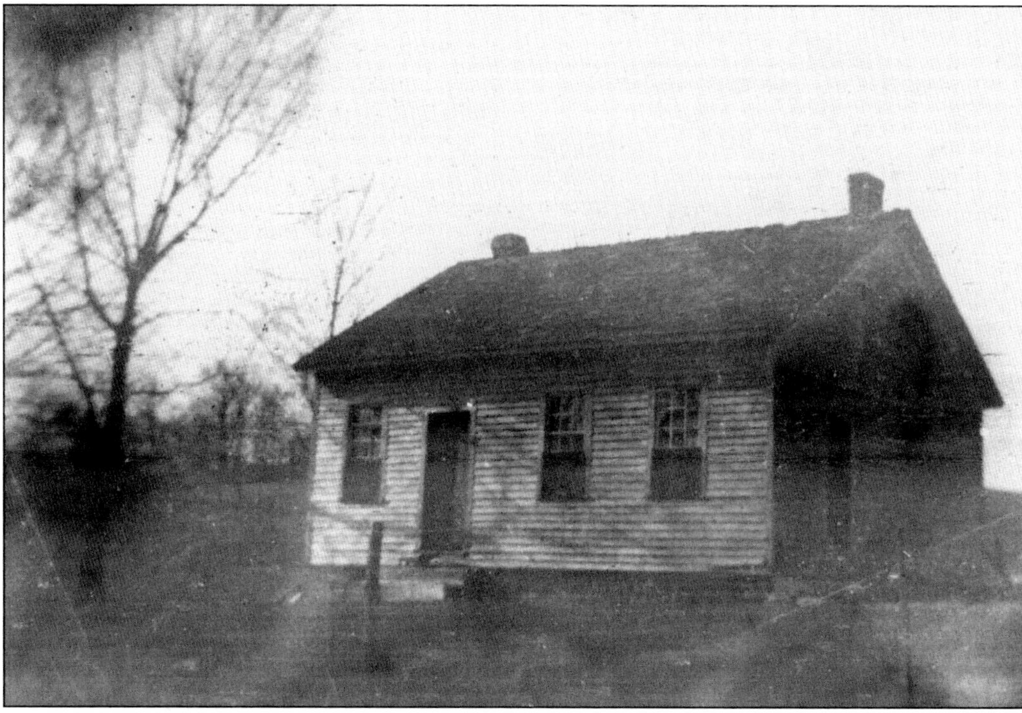

Samuel Griffith Philipps built this frame house for his family. He was the son of Samuel Joseph Philipps and grandson of Thomas Philipps. His father built the Philipps Brick house located a short distance away. Samuel and Susannah raised nine children in this house.

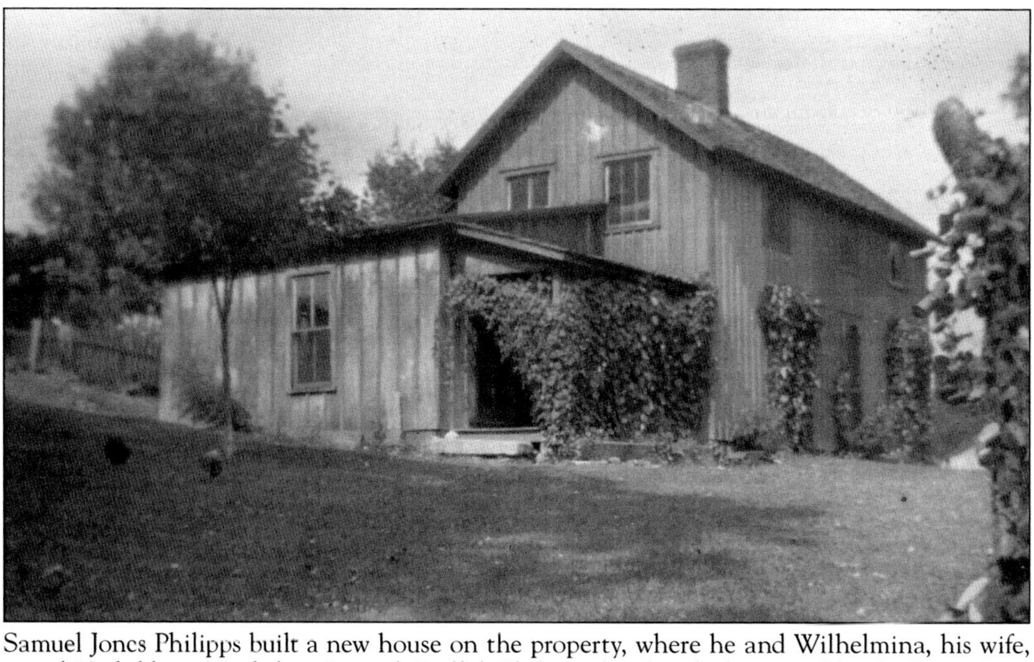

Samuel Jones Philipps built a new house on the property, where he and Wilhelmina, his wife, raised 10 children. His father, Samuel Griffith Philipps, lived with them until he died in 1899 at age 93. This home was destroyed by fire in 1914 and replaced by another, which also burned. The current house, owned by Kenneth (Sam) Philipps, is the third on this site.

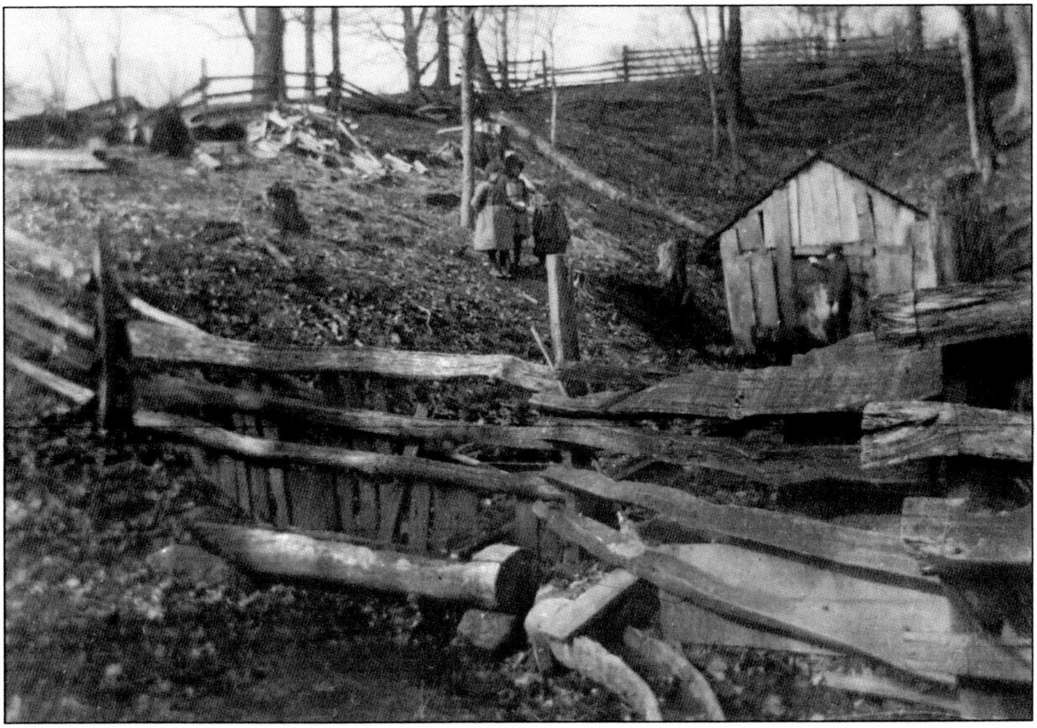

The springhouse on the Philipps farm housed the cream separator. Sam Wheeler, a descendant of Thomas Philipps, lived at the farm during part of his childhood and wrote about the spring. He states that the soft water spring was located deep in a ravine south of the house. The water welled up into a cement casement near the spring, and a pipe carried it to the springhouse and into a water jacket around the cream separator. Surplus water was carried out to a trough used by livestock.

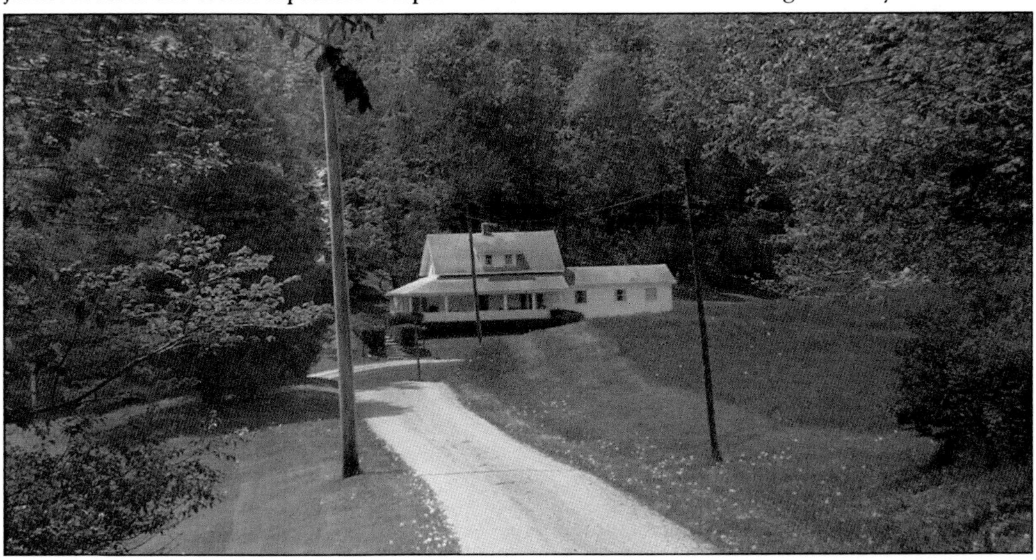

The first and second frame houses on the Philipps property were ultimately replaced by the current structure by Philip Philipps. His father, Samuel Jones Philipps, died in 1910, leaving the property to his eldest son. Phil's son Kenneth (Sam) is the current owner. A Philipps has continuously occupied this site since 1804. (Courtesy of Carol Philipps.)

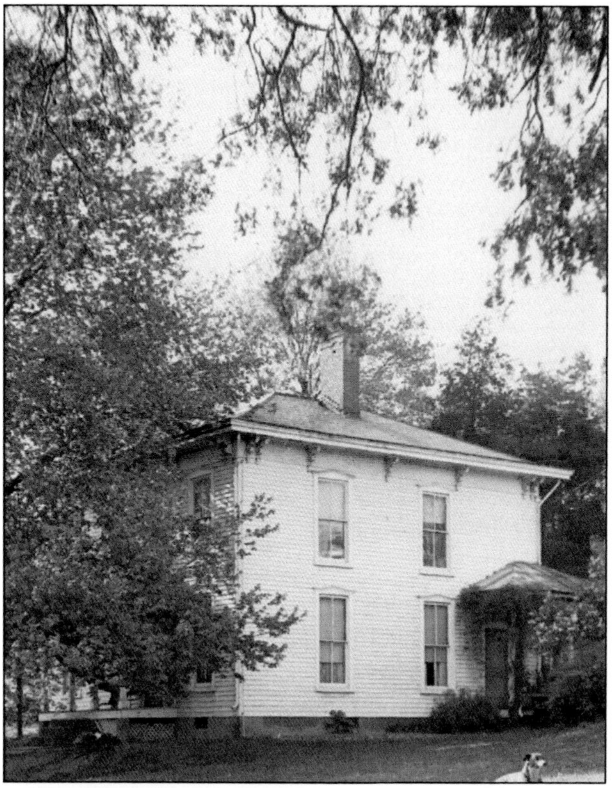

Thomas Evans built this home in the early 1850s on property purchased from Samuel Joseph Philipps. Thomas was the son of Joseph and Ann Evans, who left Carmarthenshire, Wales, on January 12, 1801. Joseph and Ann lived in Beulah, Pennsylvania, before relocating to the Welsh Hills. Thomas Evans married Eliza Thomas, granddaughter of Theophilus Rees, in 1825. They raised seven children in this home and were faithful members of the Welsh Hills Baptist Church, where Thomas served as deacon for seven years and clerk for 25 years. Thomas died at his home in 1857 after a brief illness; he was 54. His son Elias and daughter-in-law, Martha, received the property and house. Eliza lived out her life and passed away in 1875. Elias's son Carey Evans and daughter-in-law, Esther Palmer, later inherited the home and property. Jim Kennedy now owns it.

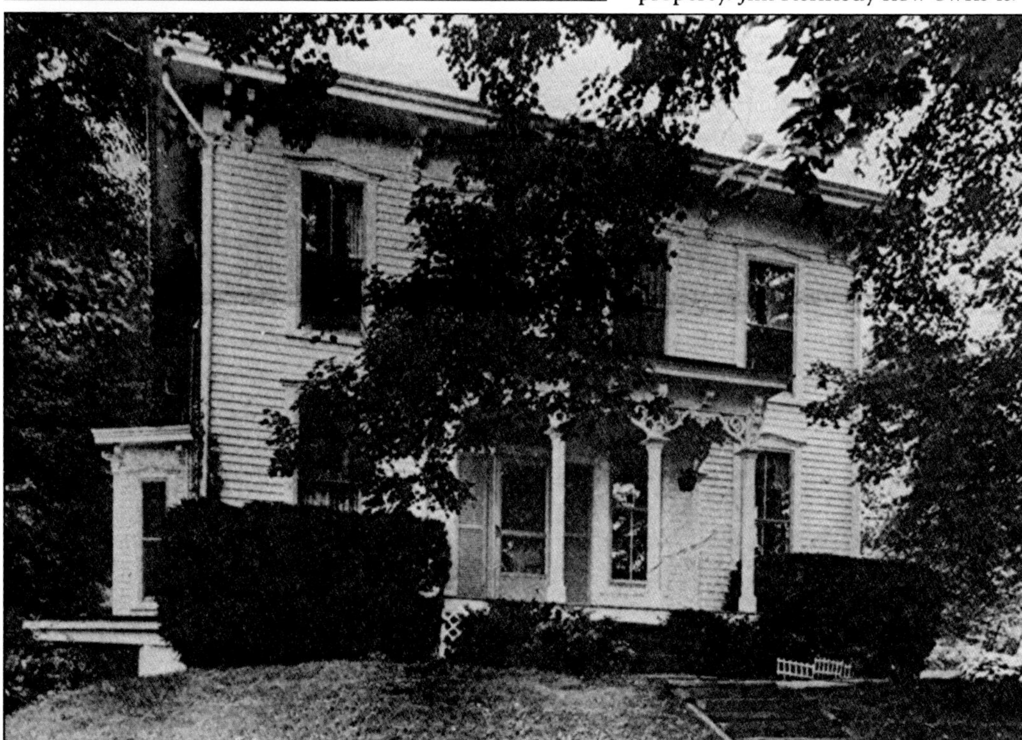

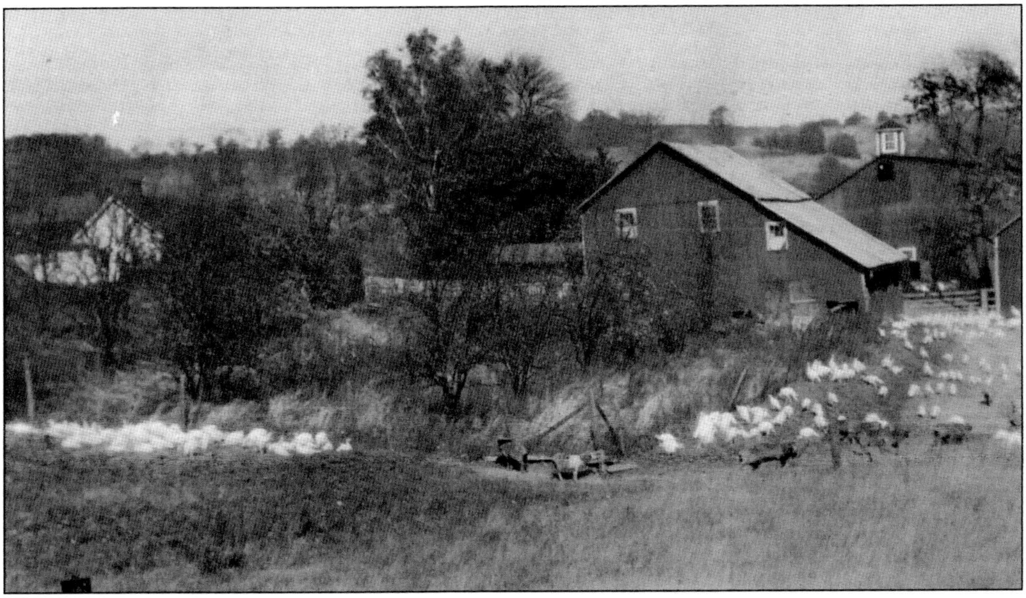

Thomas Price I, an immigrant from Wales, established the Price farm. Price left Wales in 1821 and resided for two years in Steubenville, Ohio. He then purchased 87 acres in the Welsh Hills from S. Turner. Thomas Price was a weaver by trade but established the first orchard on the property that would later become a successful business. The farm and 87 acres was deeded to his son Edward and wife, Mary Pittsford Price, in 1832 for $800. The farm passed on to Thomas Davis Price and wife, Sarah Jones Price, then to their son Homer Charles Price and wife, Gertrude Harlan Price. Homer Price became dean of the College of Agriculture and Domestic Science at Ohio State University. He was a renowned authority on growing fruit trees, and the Price Fruit Farm prospered under his guidance. The photograph below shows the White Holland turkeys raised by Gertrude Price. (Courtesy of T. David Price.)

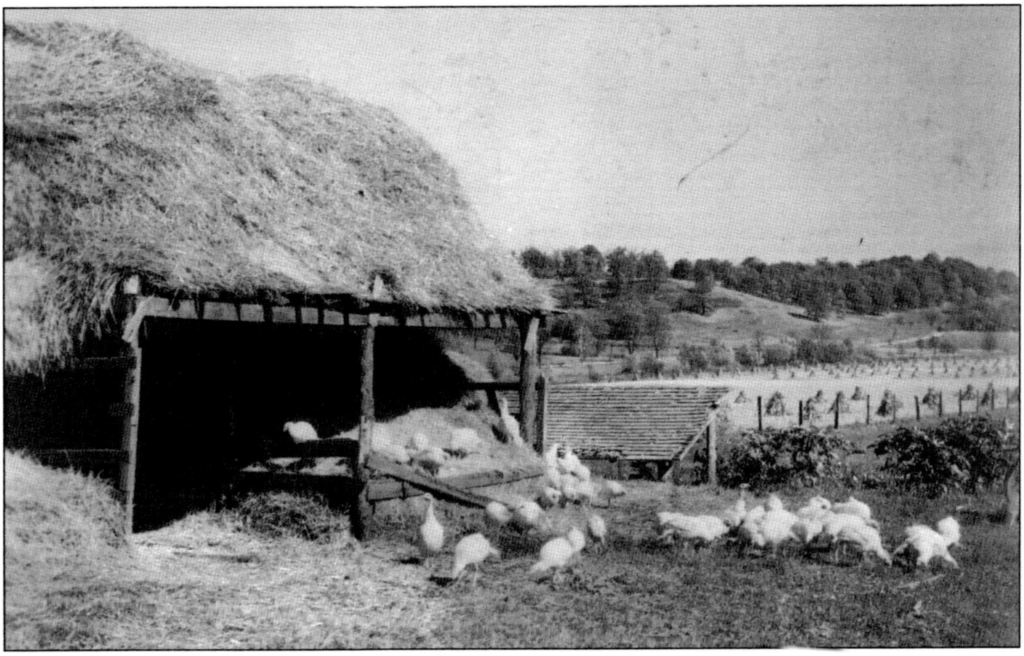

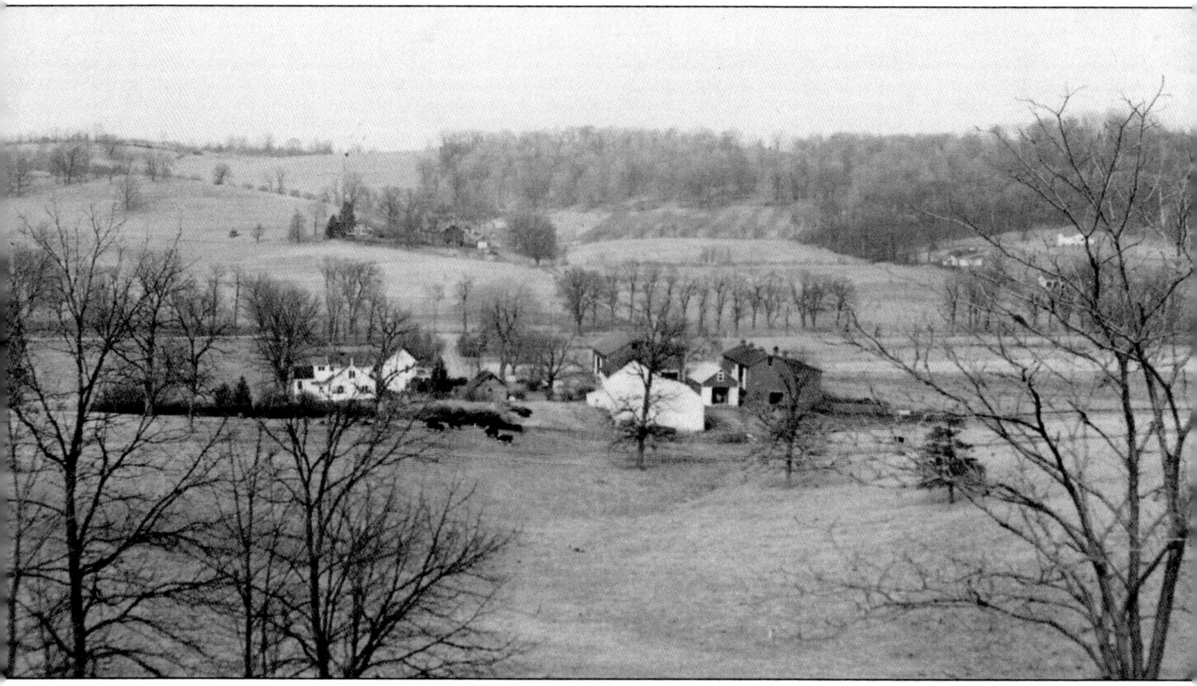

This photograph taken in 1954 is a view from the hill overlooking the Price family farm in the foreground and the King family farm on the distant hill. Both the Price and King families developed orchards on their property and supplied the surrounding area with an abundance of fresh fruit. The road separating the two farms is called Price Road. Both farms were located in the Newark Township portion of the Welsh Hills. At the right of the King farm, on the distant hill, the neat rows of the orchard can be seen. It was noted by David D. Jones in 1905 that during the early days the only well in the Welsh Hills was on the Edward Price farm and was a great curiosity. A local land developer purchased both farms. (Courtesy of T. David Price.)

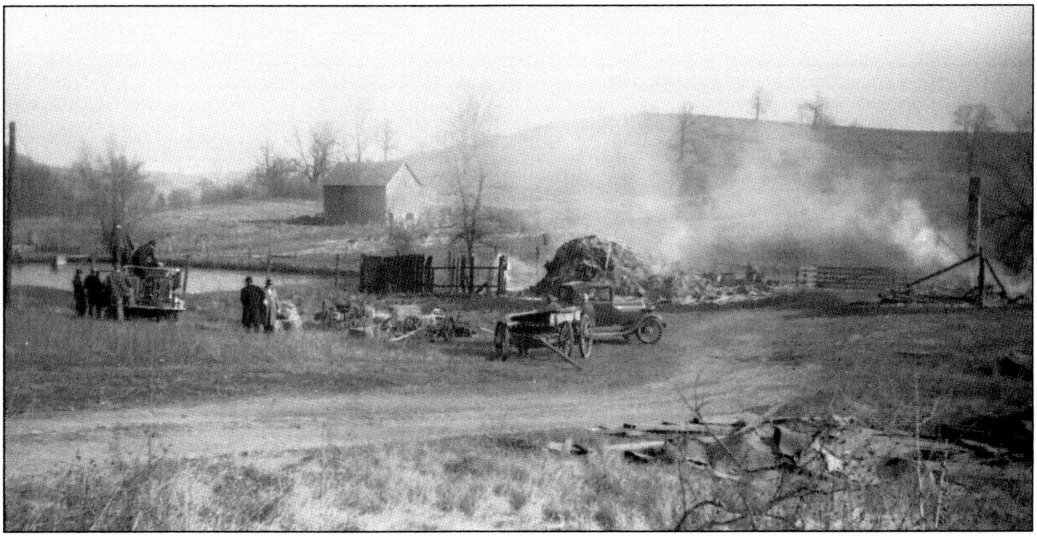

This photograph above shows the aftermath of the fire that completely destroyed the Peterman home. The house was located on Hankinson Road just south of the Big Spring Farm. The pond seen at the left in both photographs was a fish hatchery operated by Licking County. The photograph below shows this same view today. Nothing remains of the fish hatchery except a large puddle still fed by one of the natural springs. (Courtesy of Thomas E. Philipps.)

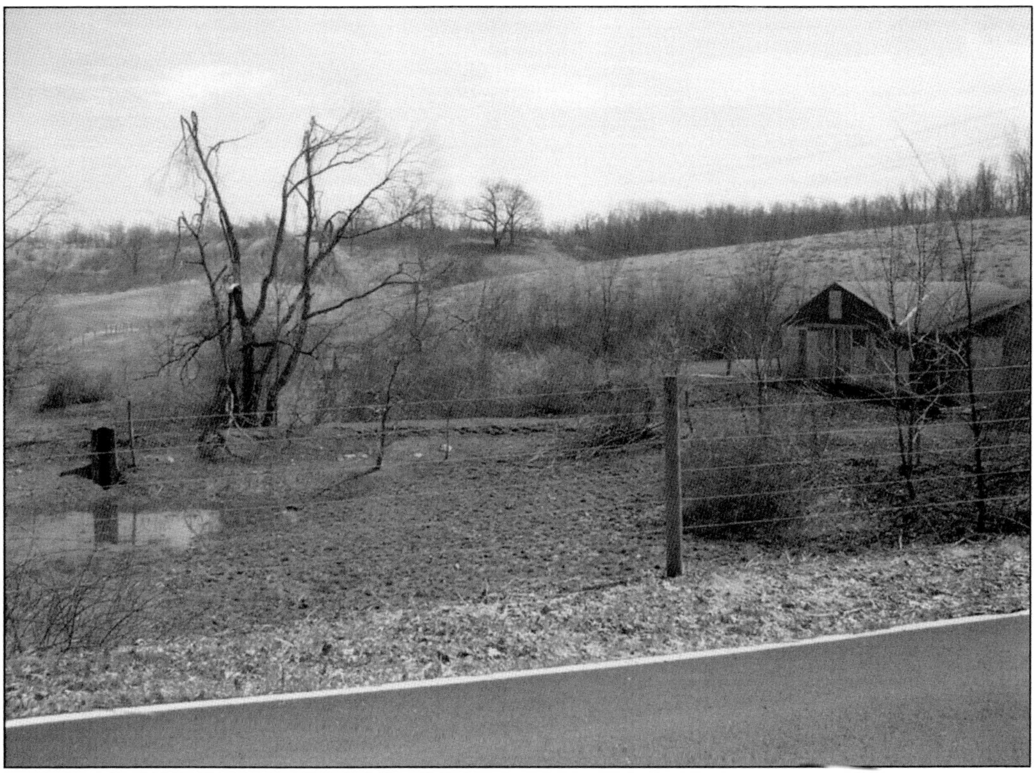

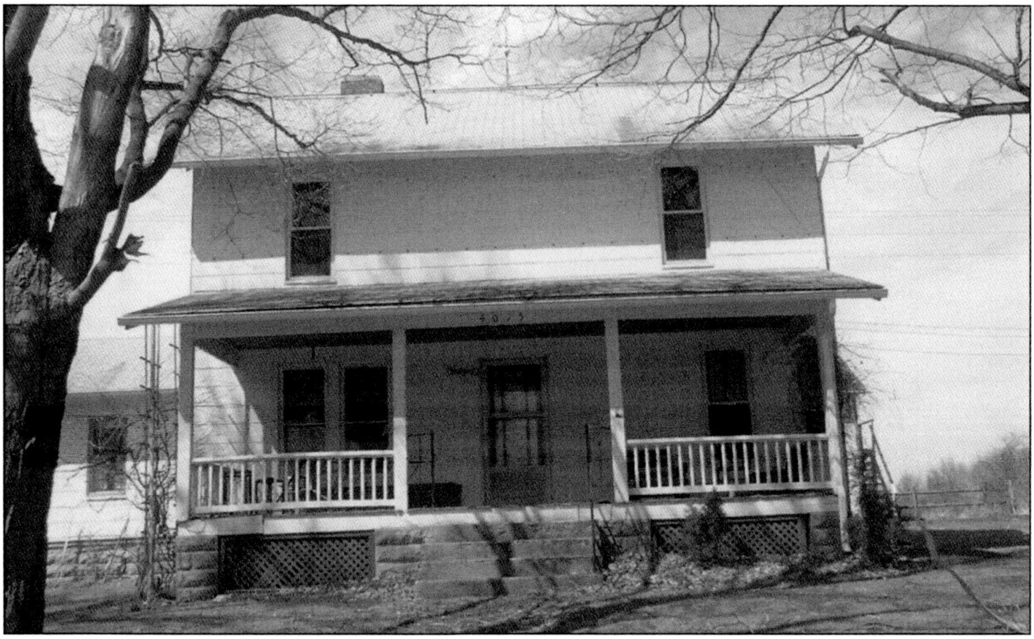

Daniel Griffith and his wife, Anne, were from Pembrokeshire, Wales, and sailed aboard the ship *Amphion* with Theophilus Rees and Thomas Philipps. Daniel settled in Beulah, Pennsylvania, at the same time that many of the other Welsh Hills families lived there and moved to the Welsh Hills in 1810. The original Griffith homestead was located in Brushy Fork Valley along Dry Creek Road. The house pictured is located at the top of the hill, south of the original homesite, and is owned by Don Griffith, a descendant of Daniel and Anne. (Photograph by Janet Philipps Procida.)

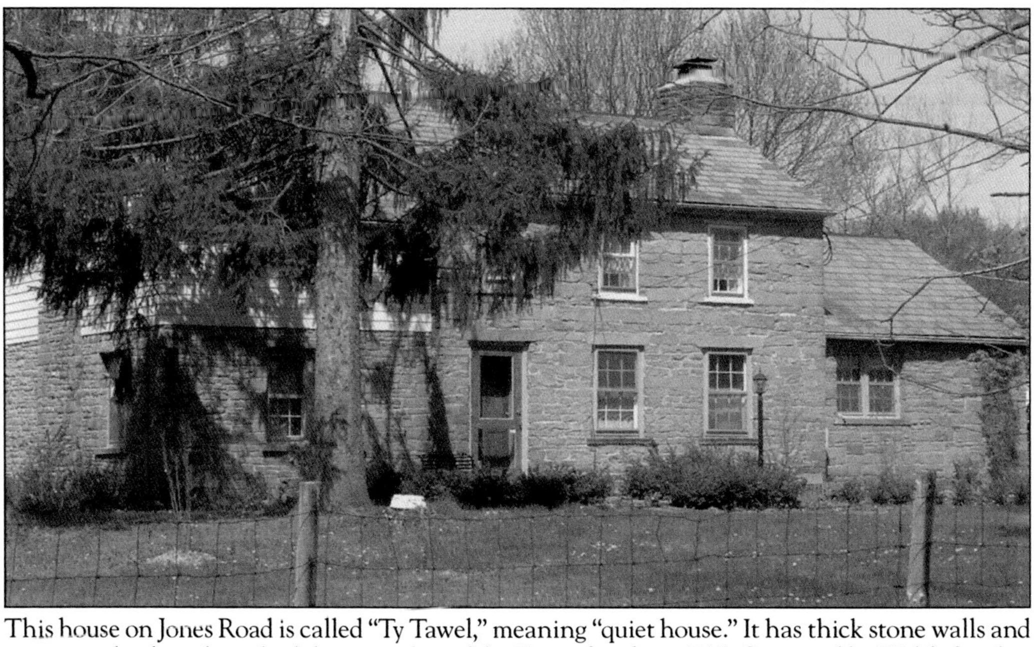

This house on Jones Road is called "Ty Tawel," meaning "quiet house." It has thick stone walls and is supposed to have been built by a member of the Evans family in 1815. Occupied by Welsh families for over 150 years, the home was restored in the 1960s by Raymond J. Lewis and is thought to be the oldest surviving Welsh house in Licking County. (Photograph by Janet Philipps Procida.)

# *Seven*

# Welsh Cemeteries

On February 6, 1808, Theophilus Rees donated land, for the purpose of a cemetery, named Welsh Hills Cemetery. It was located near the "Big" David Thomas cabin used as a church by the Welsh Baptists. On that same day, the first person was interred in these hallowed grounds. He was Rees Thomas, son of David Thomas and grandson of Theophilus Rees. Rees Thomas was not quite eight years old. When the church moved to another site, the cemetery expanded to its current size. Theophilus Rees and his wife, Elizabeth, are buried here along with the sculptor Tom Jones and many members of notable founding families of the Welsh Hills.

In 1814, Samuel Joseph Philipps set aside a portion of his land and sold it to the township for $1. The Philipps Cemetery was established on this site. Most of the founding pioneers from the Philipps family, including Thomas Philipps and Samuel Joseph Philipps, are interred here.

Four years after the formation of the Welsh Calvinistic Methodist Church in 1832, the trustees of the church purchased a lot in Sharon Valley containing an acre for a church building and burial ground. The original church members were William R. and Mrs. Williams, James and Mrs. Evans, Alban Albans, Mrs. and Miss Albans, John J. and Mrs. Evans, Nathaniel Davis, Mrs. and Miss Jane Davis, William and Mrs. Lewis, Robert Walter, Jenkin Hughes, and William Parry. Many of these people can be found in the burial grounds. The church building has been demolished, but the cemetery can still be seen along Sharon Valley Road.

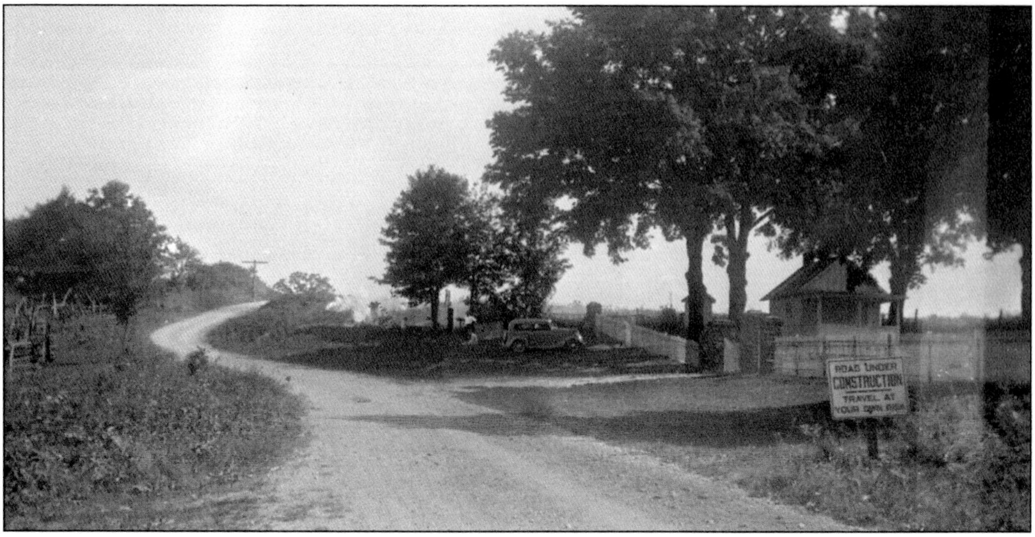


These photographs compare the Welsh Hills Cemetery in the late 1930s and the present day. With the exception of more trees in the current photograph (below), little has changed. The same two trees stand between the building and the fence. The early photograph (above) was taken around the time that construction was beginning to widen and pave Welsh Hills Road. A sign in the foreground states, "Road under Construction. Travel at your own risk." (Below photograph by Janet Philipps Procida.)

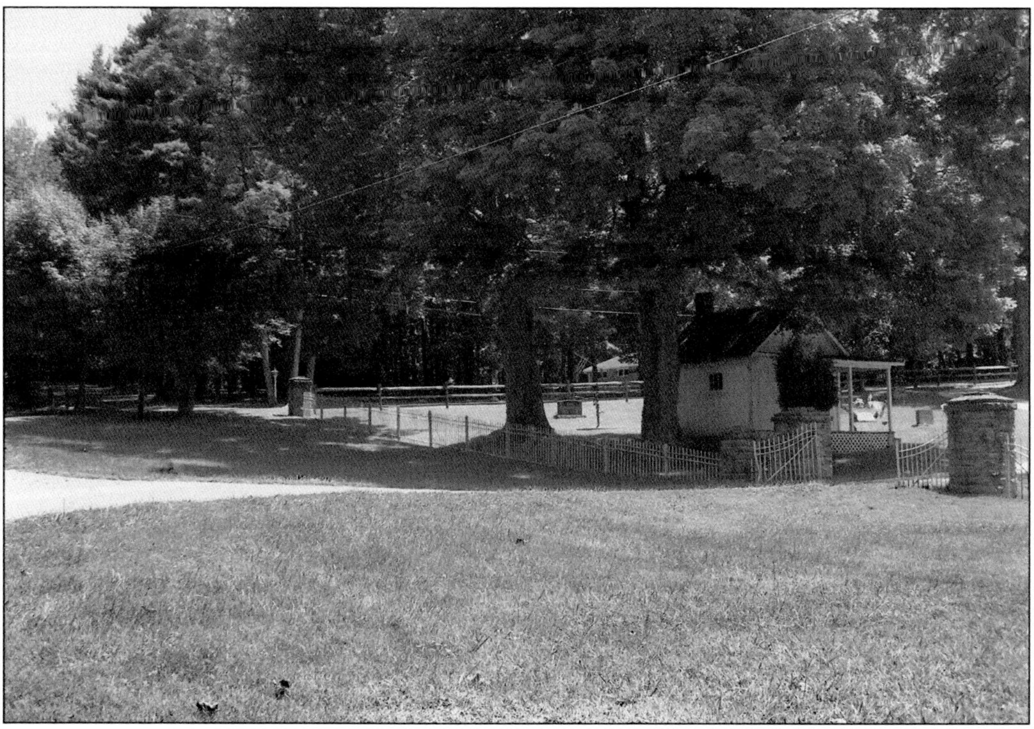

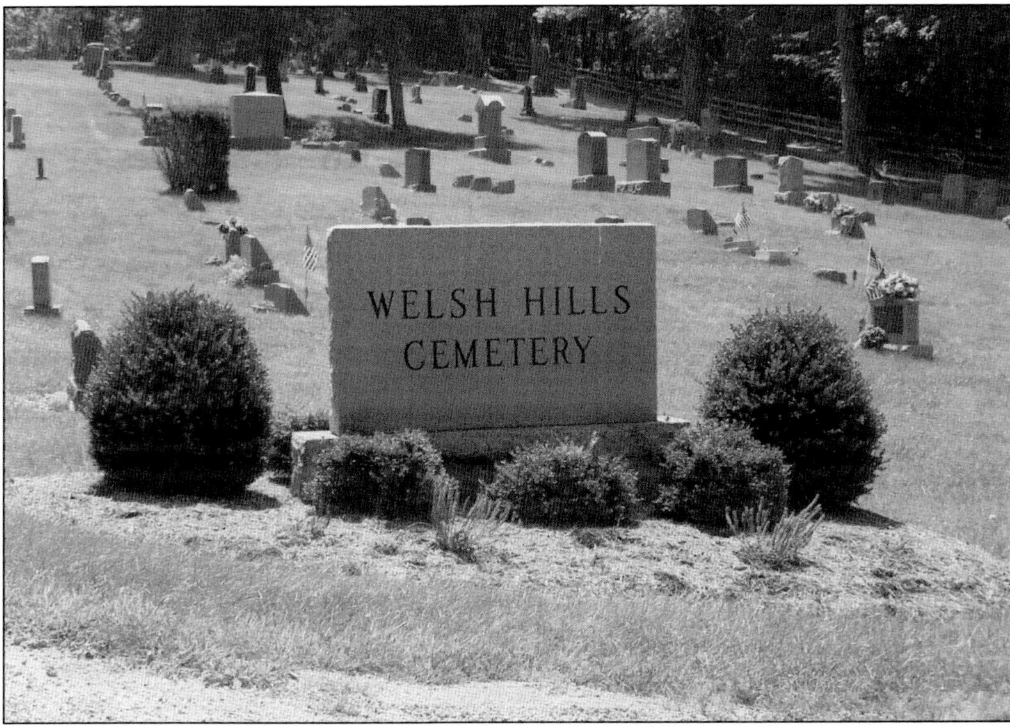


This stone marker is located at the entrance to the Welsh Hills Cemetery. An engraving on the back states: "Established in 1808 by the Original Welsh Settlers of Granville Township." Many of the original settlers are buried here, including Theophilus and Elizabeth Rees. Family names include Rees, Philipps, Griffith, Price, Thomas, Evans, Pittsford, James, Jones, Hughes, Davis, King, Cramer, Williams, Powell, and Roberts. The sculptor Thomas D. Jones selected a simple boulder to mark his gravesite and even carved his own name, leaving the date of his death for another to inscribe. Descendants of the first families continue to use this cemetery as a final resting place. (Both photographs by Janet Philipps Procida.)

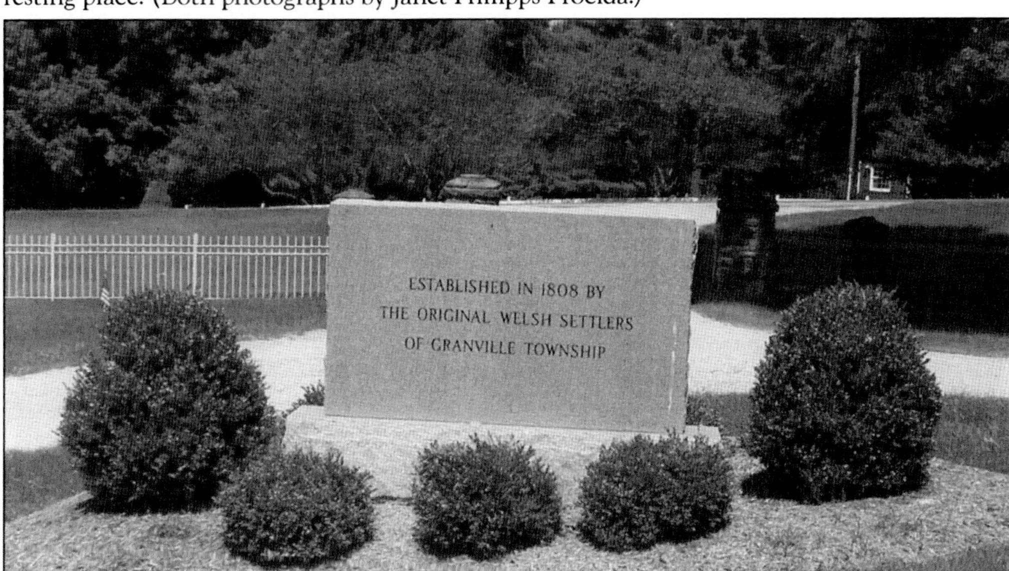

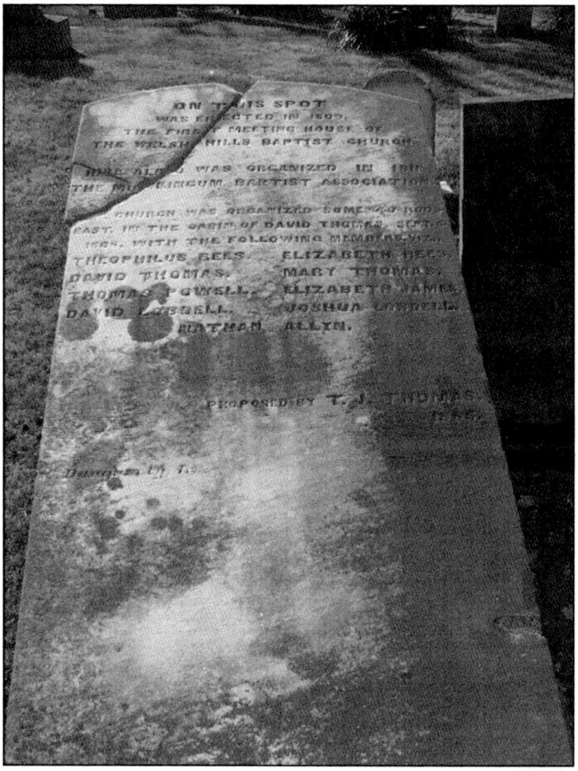

This marker in the Welsh Hills Cemetery commemorates the first Welsh Hills Baptist Church. The text reads, "On this spot was erected in 1809 the first meetinghouse of The Welsh Hills Baptist Church. Here also was organized in 1811 the Muskingum Baptist Association. The church was organized some 40 rods east in the cabin of David Thomas Sept. 4 1808 with the following members viz . . . Theophilus Rees, Elizabeth Rees, David Thomas, Mary Thomas, Thomas Powell, Elizabeth James, David Lobdell, Joshua Lobdell, Nathan Allyn. Proposed by T. J. Thomas 1836."

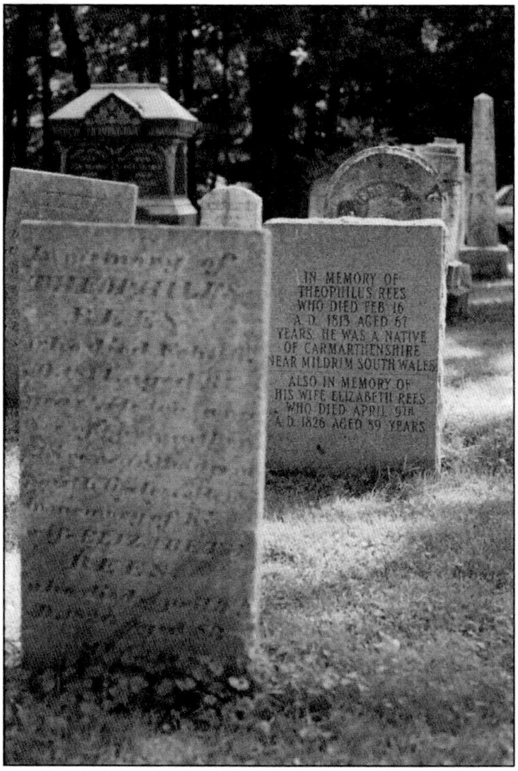


Two tombstones mark the burial place of Theophilus Rees. The original stone marker was placed on his grave when he died in 1814, and descendants purchased the second stone when the original began to disintegrate. The tombstone states that Rees was a native of Carmarthenshire, Wales, near Mildrim (correctly spelled Meidrim). (Courtesy of Carol Philipps.)

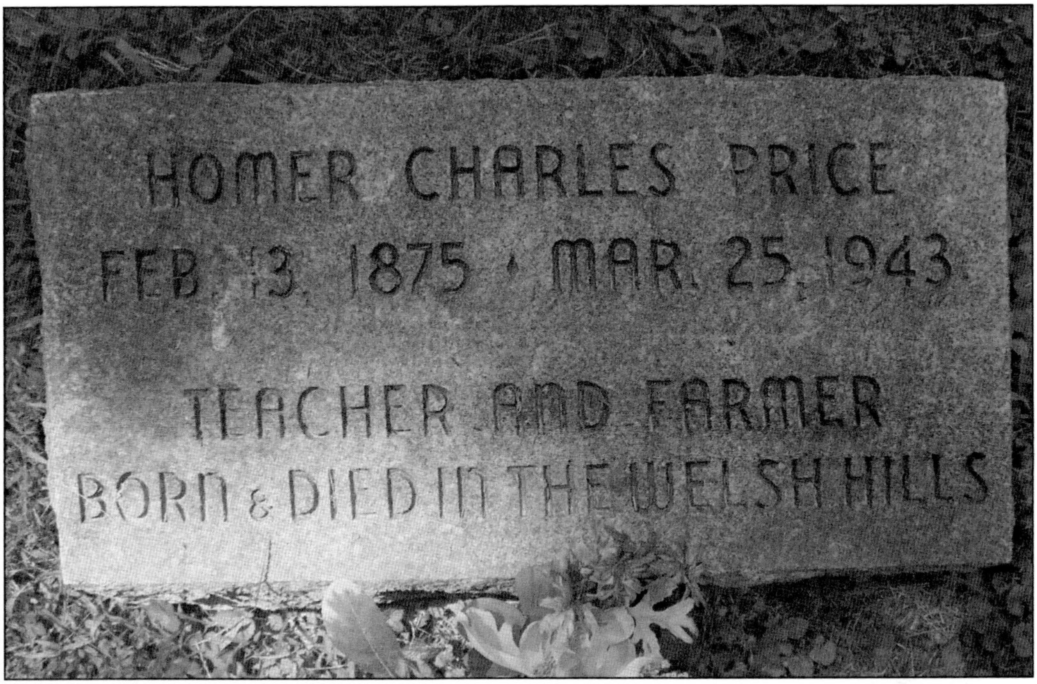


The modest markers for Homer and Gertrude Price downplay their achievements. Homer was a teacher and a farmer, but he was also dean of the College of Agricultural and Domestic Science at Ohio State University. He held degrees from Denison University, Ohio State University, and Cornell University. He served as vice president of the Licking County Farm Association, president of the Ohio State Horticultural Society, and was a deacon for the Welsh Hills Baptist Church for many years. Gertrude was widely known for her work in breeding White Holland turkeys and competed nationally with her prize-winning birds. The couple succeeded in making the Price farm a profitable business venture. (Both photographs by Janet Philipps Procida.)

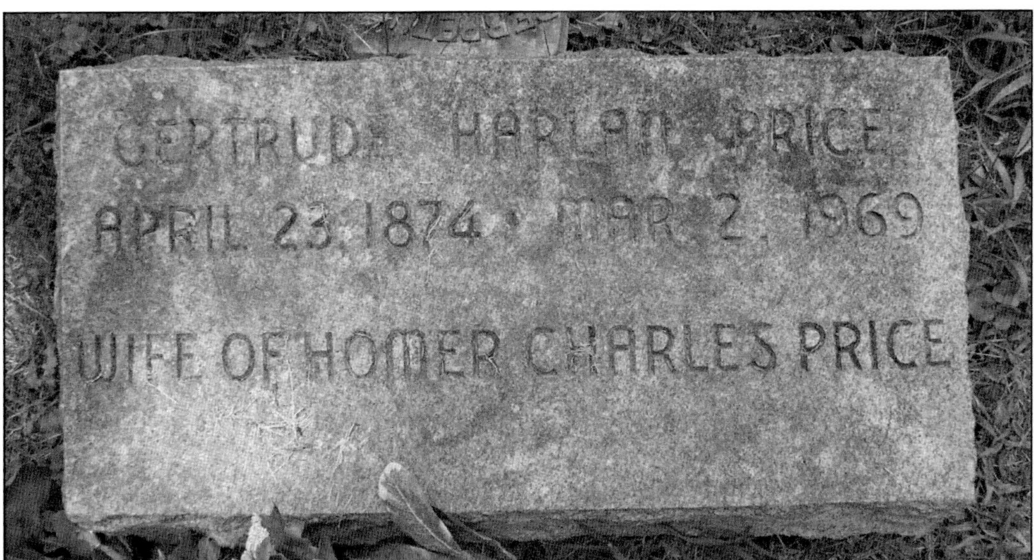

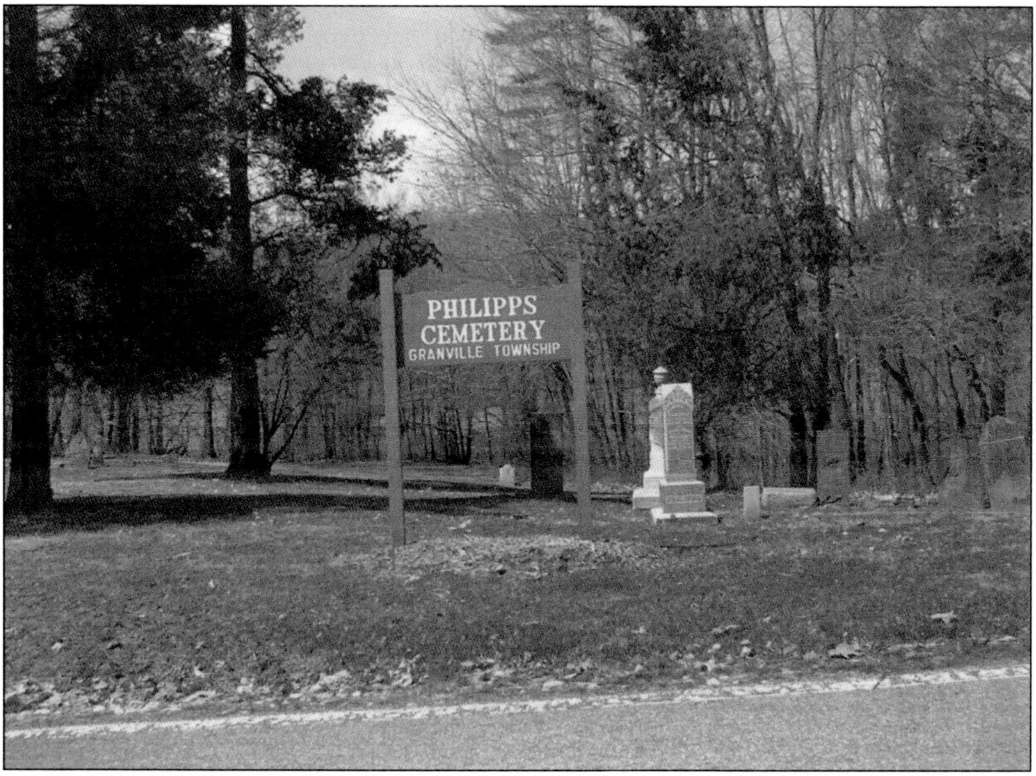


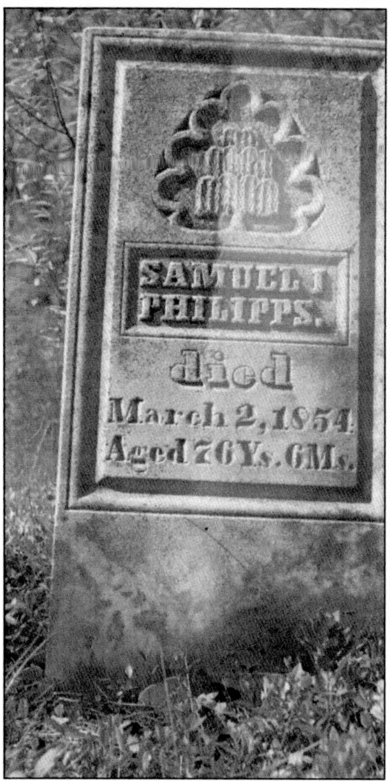


The wooden sign above identifies the Philipps Cemetery located on Philipps Road. Families known to be buried here include Collingham, Cramer, Davis, Davies, Donahue, Evans, Farmer, Hankinson, Hughes, Johnson, Nott, Owens, Phillipps, Platts, Price, Reed, Robinson, Rose, Smith, Turner, Warner, White, Williams, and Wolcott. (Courtesy of Carol Philipps.)

Samuel J. (Joseph) Philipps is buried in the Philipps Cemetery, on property originally owned by Thomas Philipps. Samuel's wife, Lydia, is interred next to him. No new burials have occurred in this cemetery for several decades.

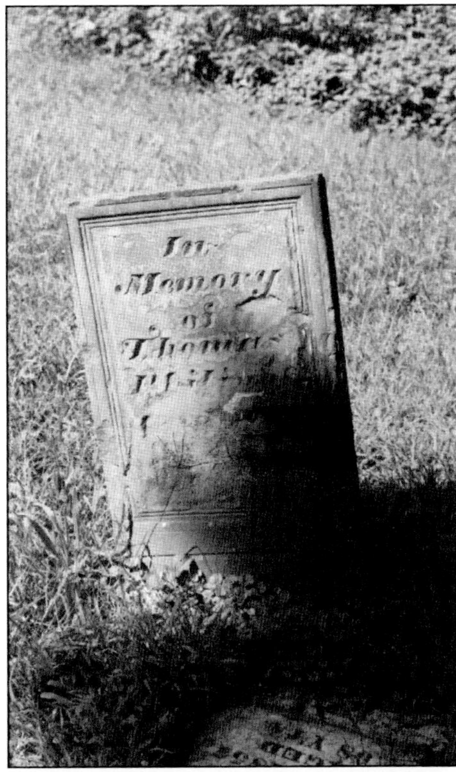


These two gravestones show the burial site of Thomas Philipps. The original sandstone marker is nearly unrecognizable. Philipps's descendants purchased the new gravestone as a replacement. Both tombstones spell the last name as *Phillips*. Stories about Tom Philipps indicate that his name was originally spelled *Phillips* and his wife, Mary, had the maiden name *Philipps*. Thomas is said to have taken the spelling of his wife's name due to her connection with the Philipps family of Picton Castle, Pembrokeshire, Wales. Mary Philipps never resided in the Welsh Hills.

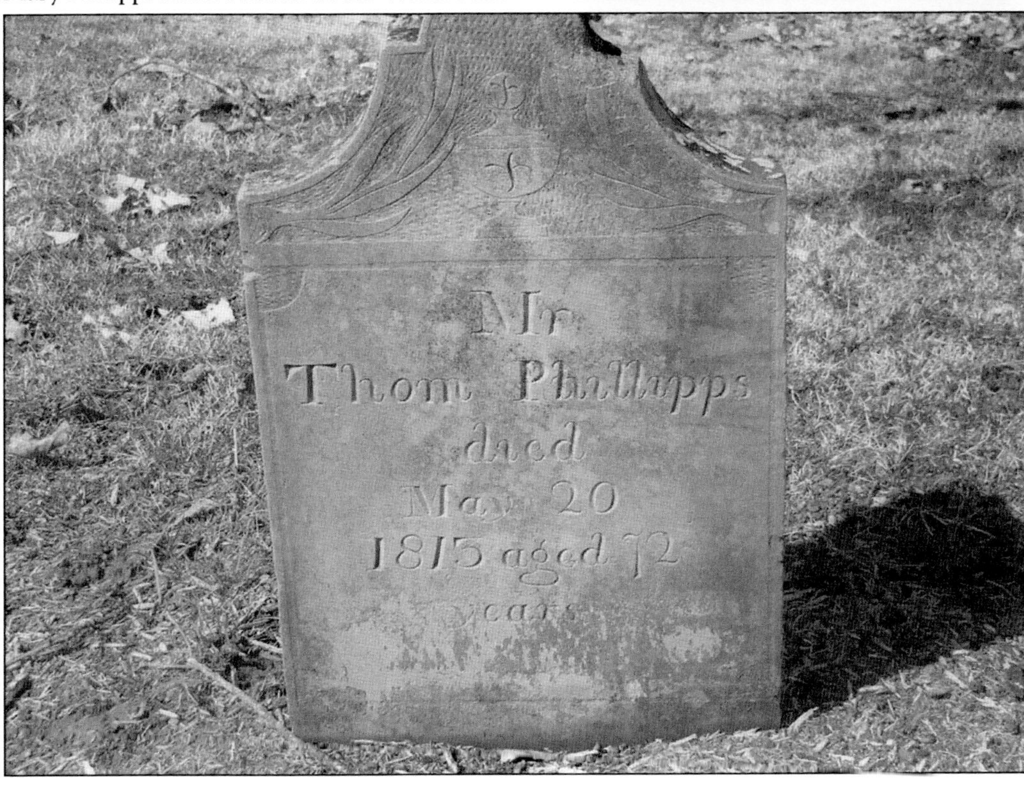

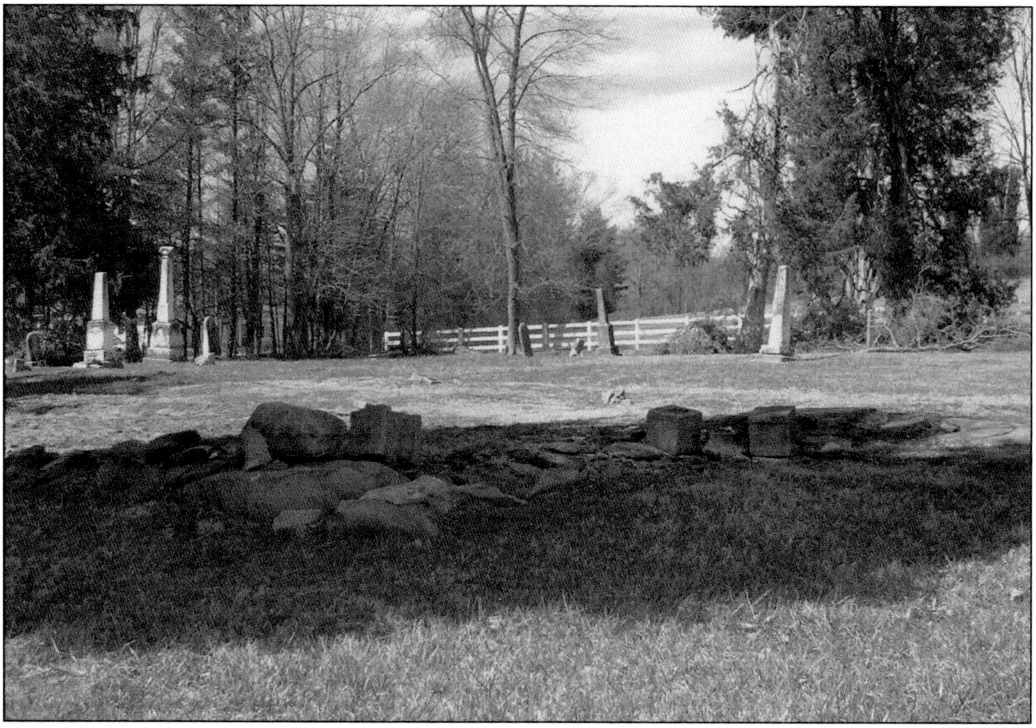

The Welsh Calvinistic Methodist Church cemetery contains the remains of many of the people who attended this church. The structure has been demolished, and all that remains are the stones that served as the foundation, a stone marker that identified the church, and the cemetery. The beautiful hills surrounding the Sharon Valley can be seen in the background. The playing field for the Sharon Valley baseball team was located across the road from the cemetery.

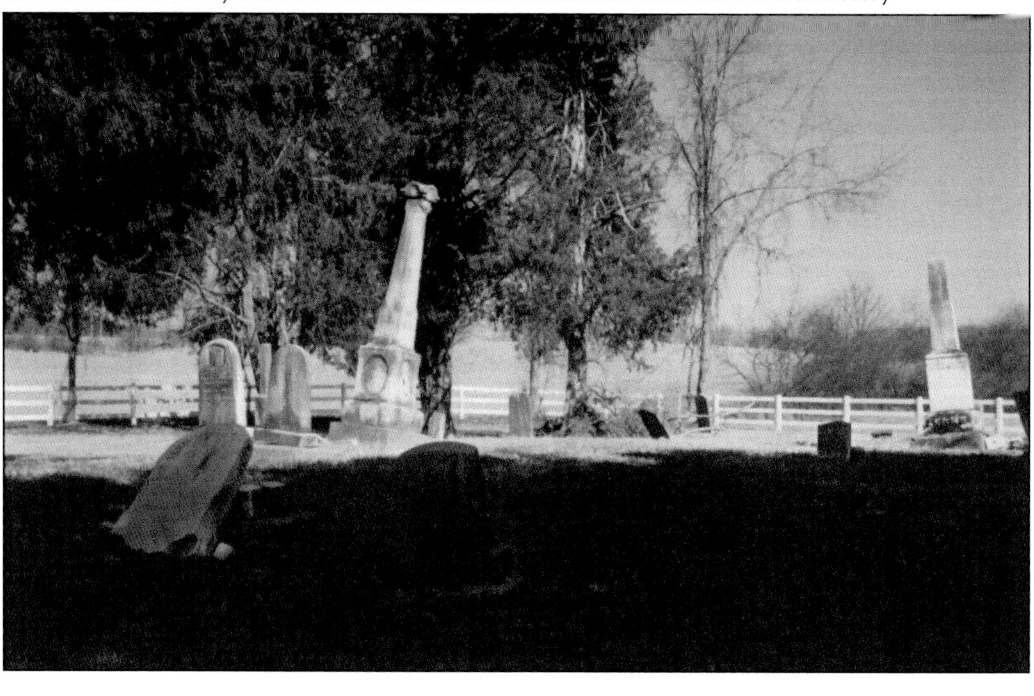

# *Eight*

# INDUSTRY

The Welsh Hills has always been an agrarian community. Early settlers were self-sufficient, and farms were established at the beginning to produce necessary food. The hills abounded with wild animals and birds that provided meat until the pioneers were able to bring cows, sheep, hogs, turkeys, and chickens to their farms. Most initial industries served local families but occasionally provided extra goods to sell in the town of Granville. There was an early grain mill called Cambria Mill located along the Brushy Fork Creek. This mill closed around 1856 when the mill in Granville opened. Flow from the creek was inadequate to operate the mill wheel. Temporary sawmills were set up in open fields for making fence posts and railings. A cider mill located on the Evans farm (also known as the Frederick home) in the 1920s provided a means for local farmers to turn their apples into cider. An earlier noted cider mill was located on North Street and run by "Yankee John Jones." Distilleries were prevalent prior to the war-related tax imposed in the early 1860s. One of the earliest articles of trade was pearl ash, manufactured just east of the Big Spring. Pearl ash was used in the making of soap and glass and was an early ingredient in quick bread (later replaced by baking soda). A woolen mill was located south of the Old Stone Schoolhouse on Welsh Hills Road but failed due to the inadequate source of power. The annual collection of sap from the sugar maple trees was done in the early spring, and maple syrup was made. This tradition was carried on for many generations. Walnut and chestnut trees were plentiful. When land was cleared for farming, a stand of these trees was always saved for collecting the nuts. Many families developed cottage industries that helped supplement their incomes as well as serve the community.

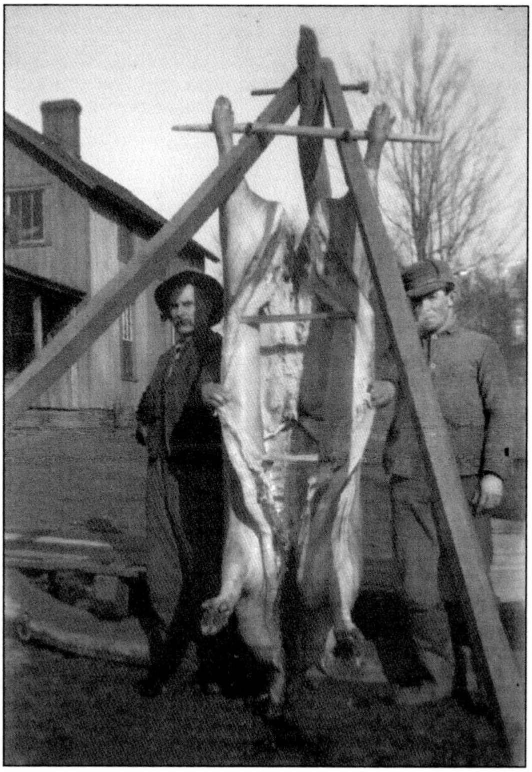

Hog butchering was common in the early days on Welsh Hills farms. In this photograph taken in his front yard, Samuel Jones Philipps stands to the left of the hog. Hogs of this size would feed the immediate and extended families through the winter months. Accounts of the early settlers note that wild boar was hunted in the Hills.

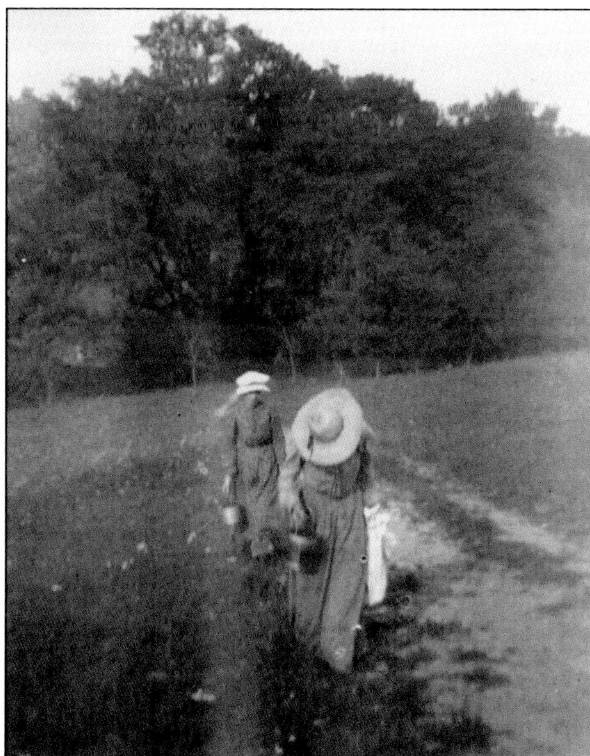

Berry picking was a common summertime activity. The hills were full of wild blackberries and raspberries that ripened in July. Many other native edible plants were found in this area and supplemented the table throughout the year. The Welsh Hills was a good hunting ground for morel mushrooms, also known as sponge mushrooms, as their appearance resembles a sponge.

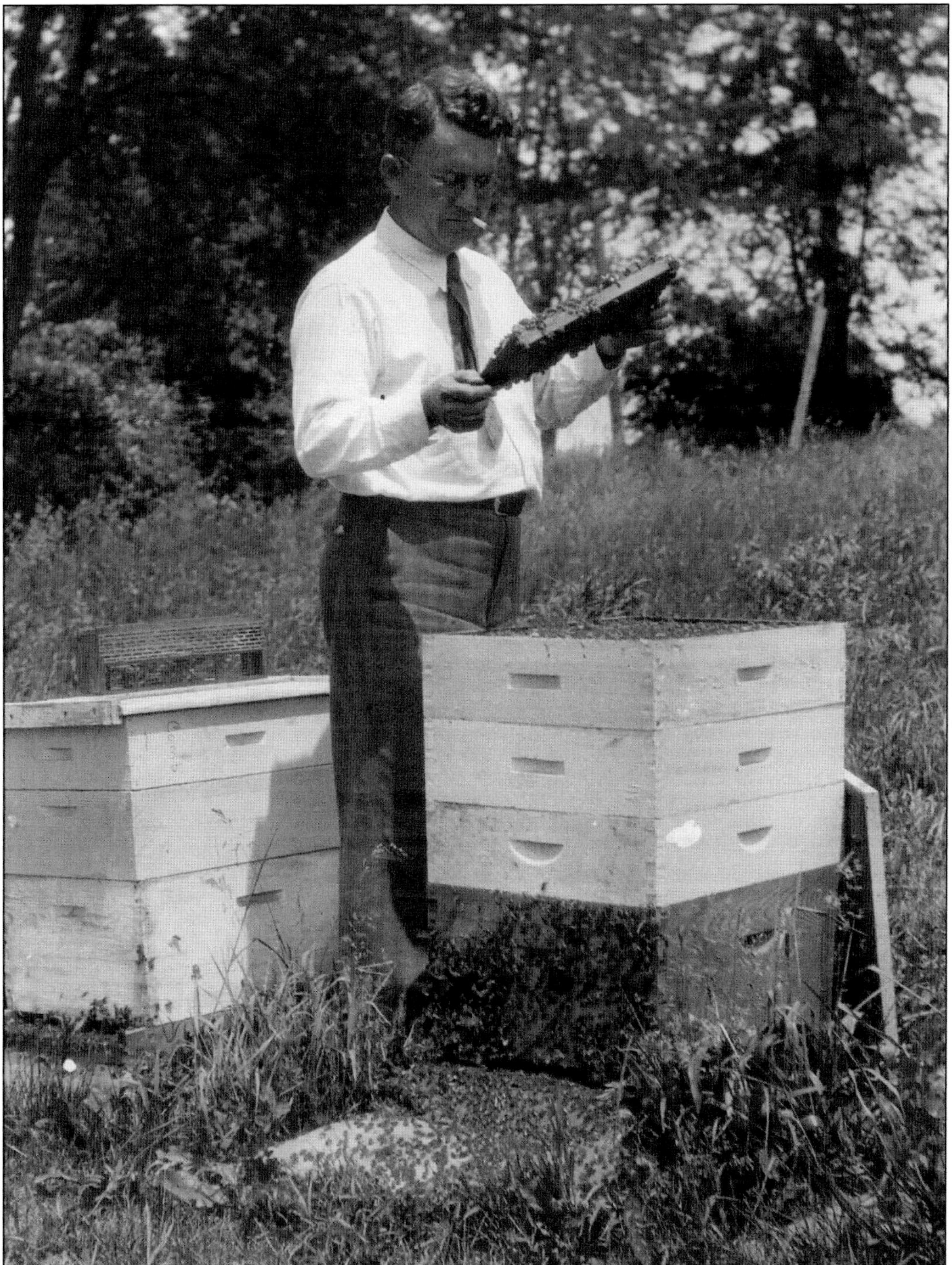

Thomas Warren Philipps was often trying new businesses to make additional income. In the 1920s and 1930s, he and his brother Phil operated the cider mill located on Welsh Hills Road. During the 1920s, Tom tried his hand at beekeeping and supplemented his teacher's salary by raising bees, selling honey, and selling beekeeping equipment. In this photograph, Tom inspects the bee population without the standard protective gear.

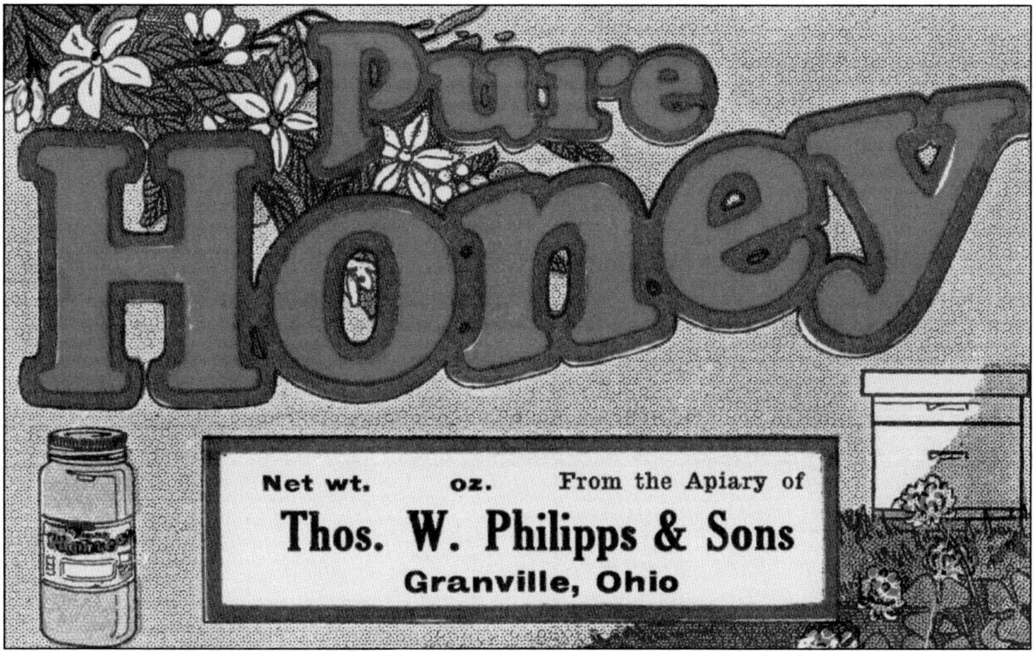


With their bright yellow background and red lettering, these attractive labels were printed for the jars containing honey produced by Thomas Philipps. (Courtesy of Thomas E. Philipps.)

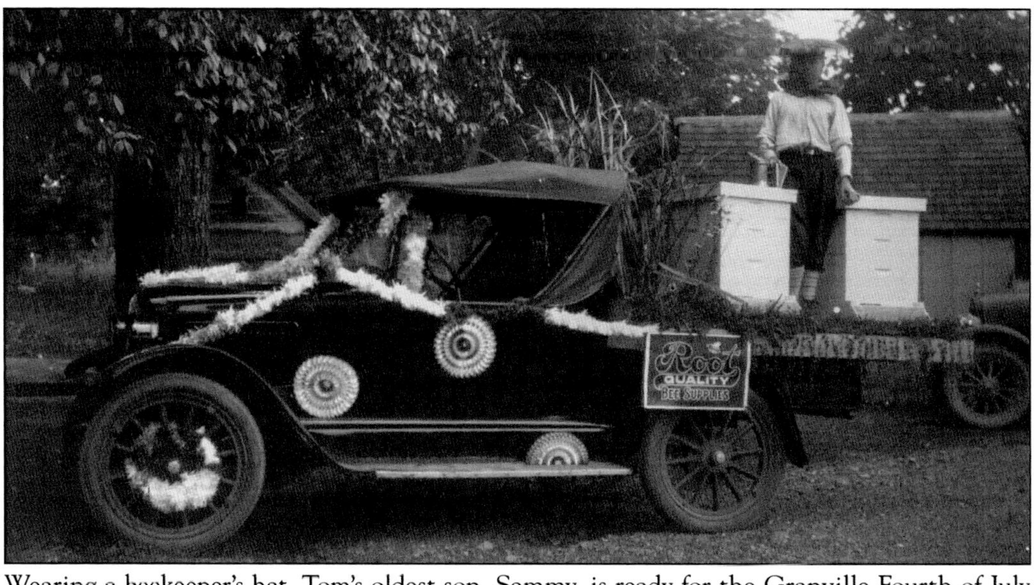


Wearing a beekeeper's hat, Tom's oldest son, Sammy, is ready for the Granville Fourth of July parade. The automobile is a 1925 Ford Model T Runabout with pick-up body. A sign on the truck advertises the beekeeping equipment company. The Granville Fourth of July parade has always been a large celebration for Licking County and continues to be popular today.

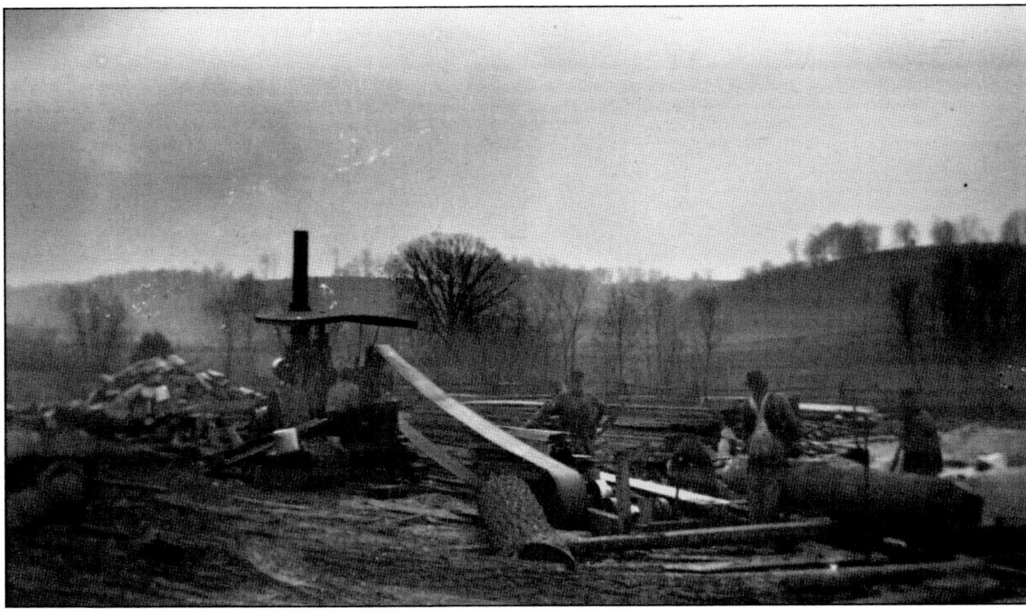

The old sawmill was located at Phil Philipps's farm on Philipps Road. The steam-driven tractor engine that was also used for the threshing machine powered the saw blade. Dr. Sam Wheeler, who lived at his uncle's farm when he was a boy and later wrote about his experience, remembers the sawmill set up in the field. He was given the chore of carrying a bucket of water to put out small fires that would start in the sawdust. Wheeler recalls that the wood slabs cut from the logs were used as fuel and, when the logs sat for a while before going to the mill, the bark would rot and fall off as fox fire. Fox fire is a natural phenomenon caused by luminous fungi on rotting wood that is sometimes visible at night in forests.

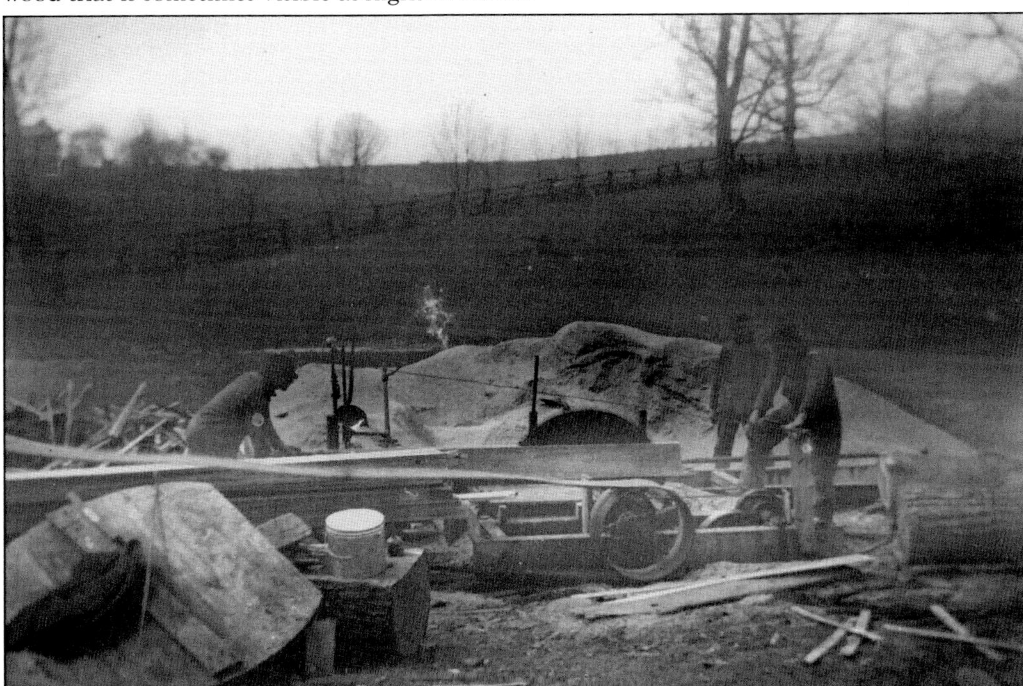

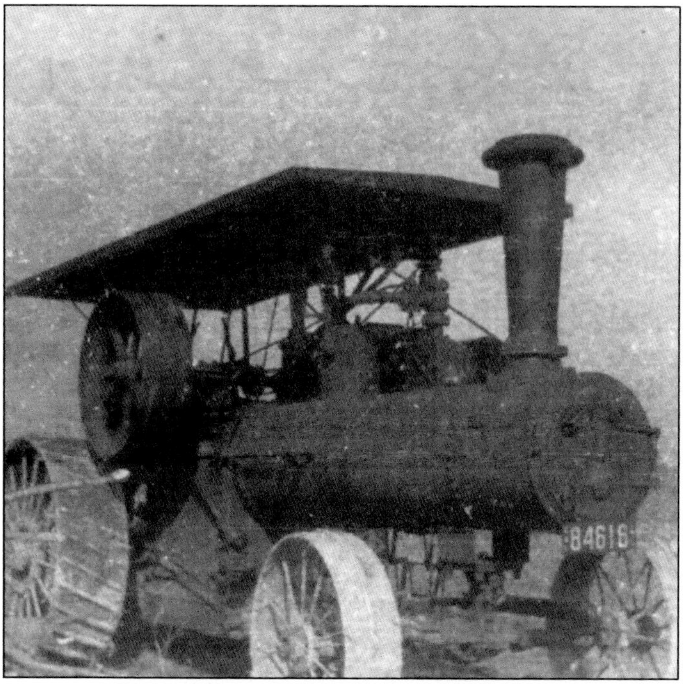


Many farmers in the Welsh Hills used steam-powered tractors during the 1920s and 1930s. Phil Philipps and his brother Tom were partners in the threshing business and owned the tractors seen here. Phil (below, right) and Charlie Hartman (below, left) were two of the men in the Welsh Hills who handled the threshing for local farmers. Phil Philipps's brother-in-law Archie Hankinson would often assist with this work. Phil would always take care of his fields first before moving on to his neighbors'. Phil and Charlie would often compete to see who could complete more fields. (Courtesy of Philip "Bucky" Philipps.)

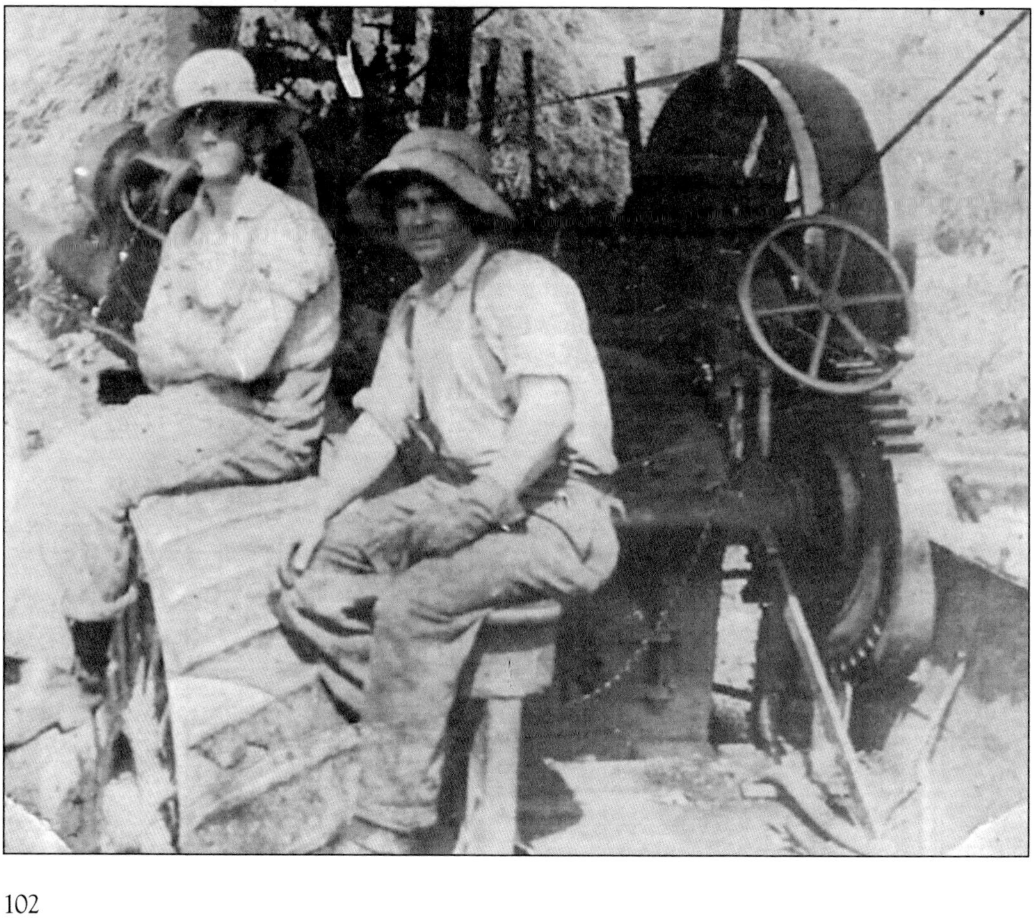

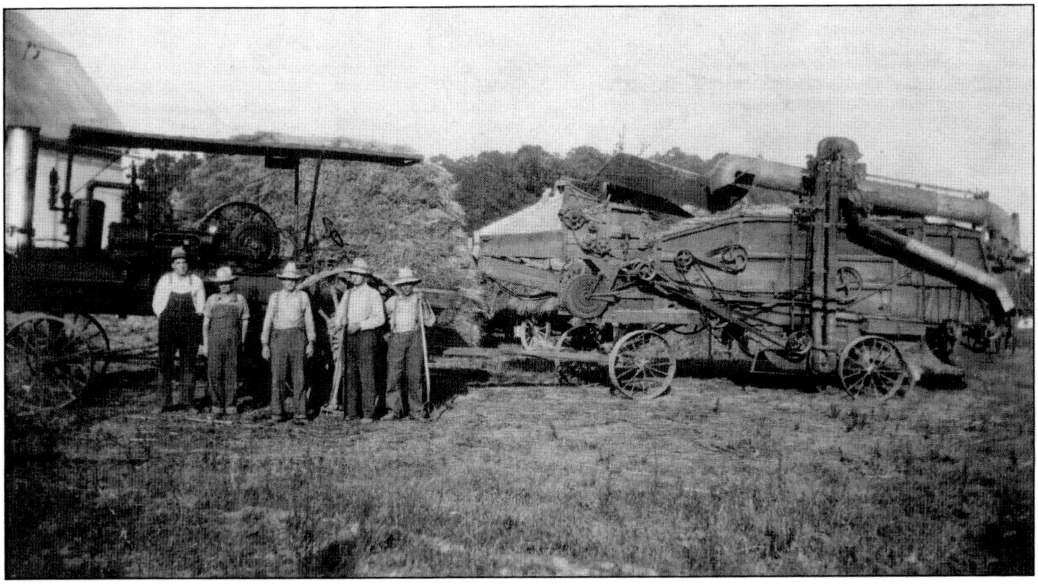

In this photograph taken around 1930, several local farmers who assisted with the annual threshing pose in front of a Peerless steam engine tractor and an Aultman and Taylor Thresher. The tractor and threshing machine were transported from one field to the next until all the farms were completed. Tom Philipps's son Tom remembers carrying water for the steam engine and also recalls the large meals prepared by the women on the farms where they worked. (Courtesy of Philip "Bucky" Philipps.)

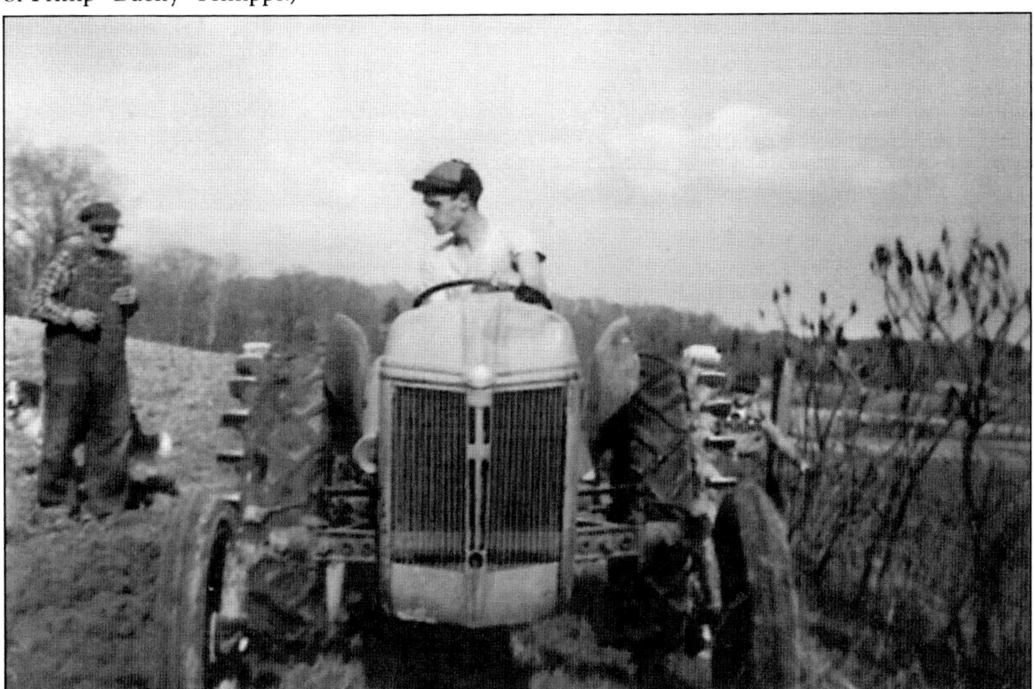

In the 1950s, Kenneth ("Sam") Philipps uses one of the more recent tractors on their farm as his father, Phil, watches in the background. Sam now lives on the family property, which was originally owned by Thomas Philipps from Wales. (Courtesy of Philip "Bucky" Philipps.)

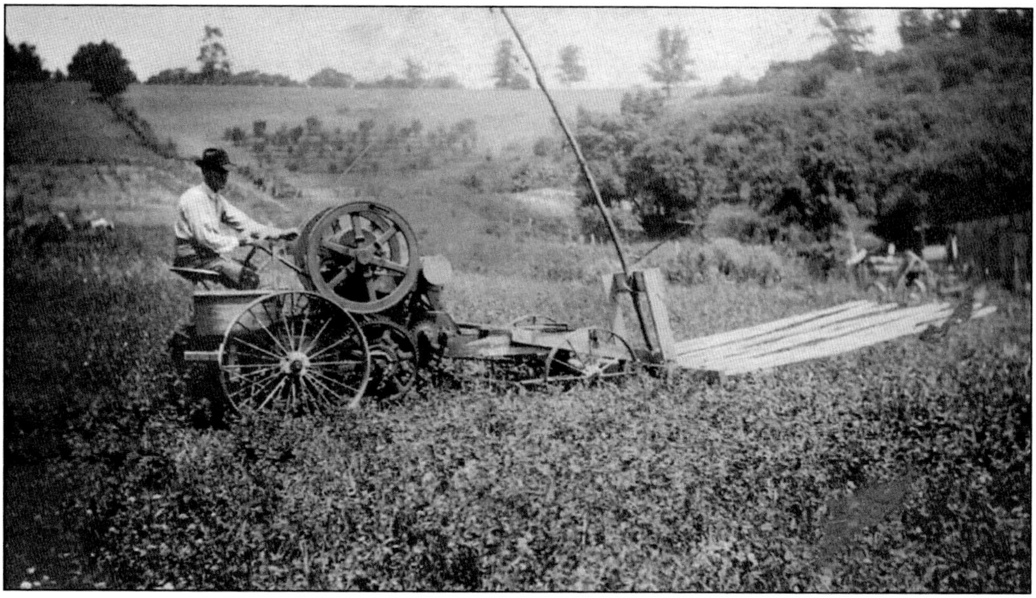

These photographs were labeled "Dick's Tractor" by Thomas Warren Philipps who took the images in the 1920s. The attachment on the front of the tractor is called a buck rake and was used for lifting hay. (Courtesy of Lynda Villars Abbott.)

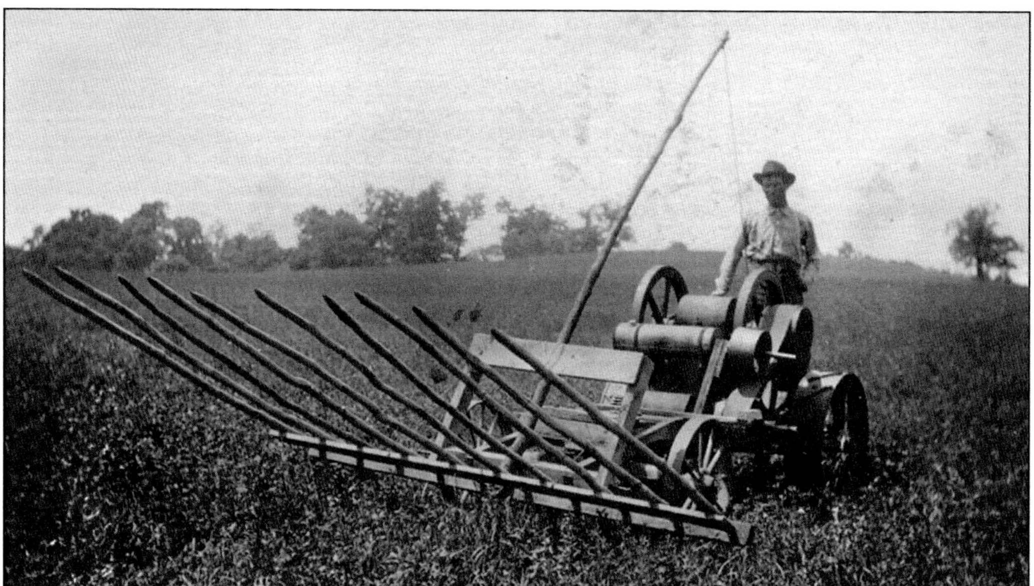

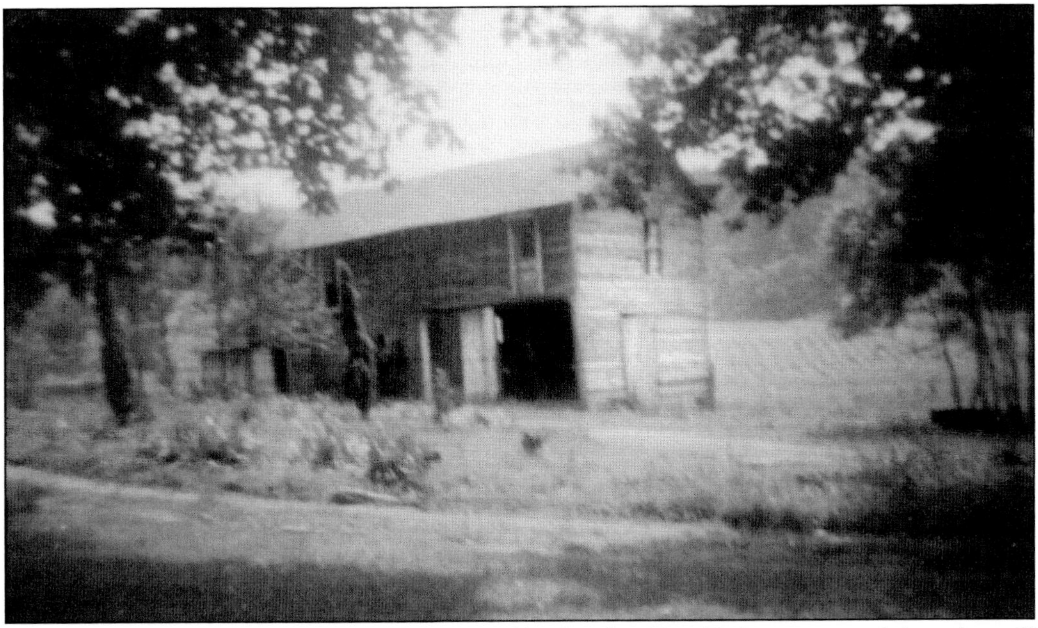

During the 1920s and 1930s, Philip Philipps and his brother Tom Philipps operated the cider mill on the old Frederick property. Farmers from the Welsh Hills brought apples by the wagonload. Tom Philipps still recalls the wagons lined up along Welsh Hills Road waiting to get apples to the press. Each season several barrels of cider were set aside to ferment.

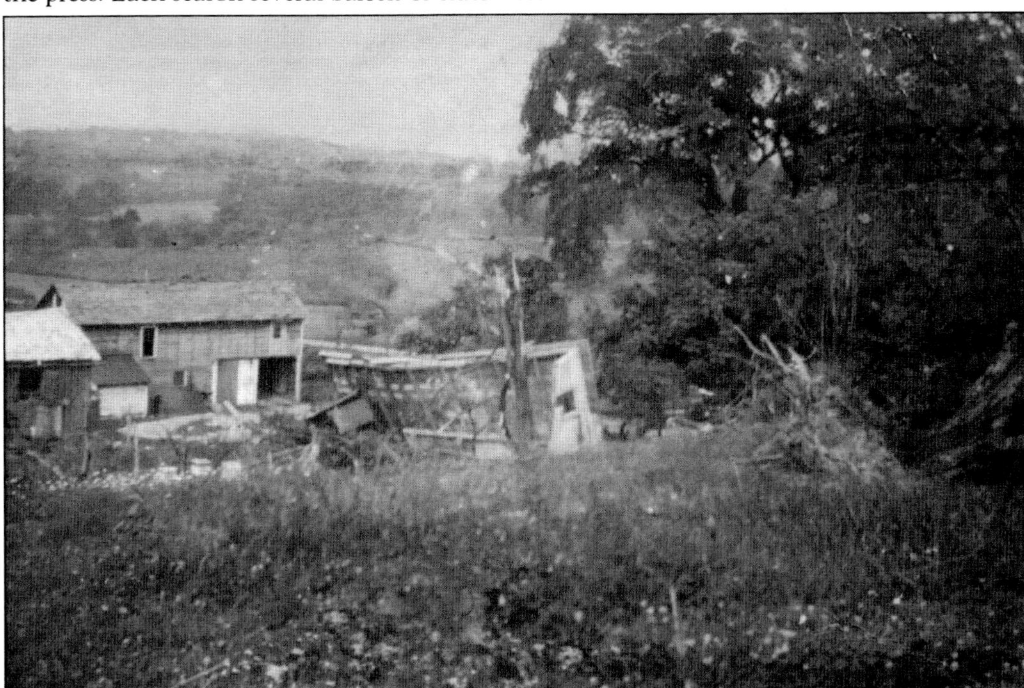

This photograph was taken the morning after a tornado swept through the Welsh Hills. The cider mill is the building at the far left. The structure in the center is a chicken house that was turned upside down.

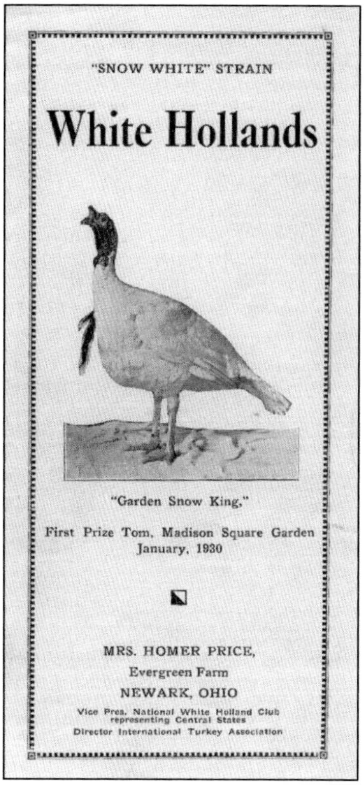

"SNOW WHITE" STRAIN

White Hollands

"Garden Snow King,"

First Prize Tom, Madison Square Garden
January, 1930

MRS. HOMER PRICE,
Evergreen Farm
NEWARK, OHIO

Vice Pres. National White Holland Club
representing Central States
Director International Turkey Association

Gertrude Price used this printed brochure for marketing her White Holland turkeys. Price became an expert on this breed of turkey produced for the quality of its meat. The farm was called Evergreen Farm but was also known as the "Price Fruit Farm." (Courtesy of T. David Price.)

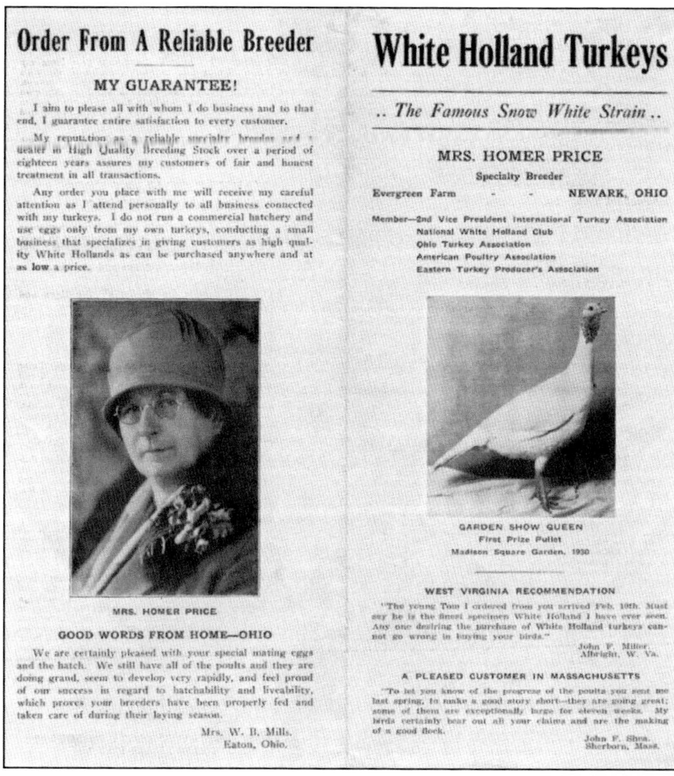

Order From A Reliable Breeder

MY GUARANTEE!

I aim to please all with whom I do business and to that end, I guarantee entire satisfaction to every customer.

My reputation as a reliable specialty breeder and dealer in High Quality Breeding Stock over a period of eighteen years assures my customers of fair and honest treatment in all transactions.

Any order you place with me will receive my careful attention as I attend personally to all business connected with my turkeys. I do not run a commercial hatchery and use eggs only from my own turkeys, conducting a small business that specializes in giving customers as high quality White Hollands as can be purchased anywhere and at as low a price.

MRS. HOMER PRICE

GOOD WORDS FROM HOME—OHIO

We are certainly pleased with your special mating eggs and the hatch. We still have all of the poults and they are doing grand, seem to develop very rapidly, and feel proud of our success in regard to hatchability and liveability, which proves your breeders have been properly fed and taken care of during their laying season.

Mrs. W. B. Mills,
Eaton, Ohio.

White Holland Turkeys

.. The Famous Snow White Strain ..

MRS. HOMER PRICE
Specialty Breeder
Evergreen Farm - - NEWARK, OHIO

Member—2nd Vice President International Turkey Association
National White Holland Club
Ohio Turkey Association
American Poultry Association
Eastern Turkey Producer's Association

GARDEN SHOW QUEEN
First Prize Pullet
Madison Square Garden, 1930

WEST VIRGINIA RECOMMENDATION

"The young Tom I ordered from you arrived Feb. 10th. Must say he is the finest specimen White Holland I have ever seen. Any one desiring the purchase of White Holland turkeys cannot go wrong in buying your birds."

John F. Miller,
Albright, W. Va.

A PLEASED CUSTOMER IN MASSACHUSETTS

"To let you know of the progress of the poults you sent me last spring, to make a good story short—they are going great; some of them are exceptionally large for eleven weeks. My birds certainly bear out all your claims and are the making of a good flock.

John F. Shea,
Sherborn, Mass.

The inside of the brochure includes testimonials from satisfied customers. Gertrude Price bred the turkeys for market and also sold the eggs and poults for breeding to other farmers. Her brochure proudly advocates her prize-winning birds at local and national competitions. One of her hens and one of her toms won first prizes at Madison Square Garden in New York in 1930, and Mayor Fiorello LaGuardia personally congratulated her. (Courtesy of T. David Price.)

# *Nine*

# LIVESTOCK AND PETS

The Welsh Hills has always been a rural community, so the appearance of livestock on farms was a common sight. Early farms known to raise sheep included the Pittsford and Price farms. Families shared the chores of shearing, carding, spinning, and weaving. Edward Price, who brought his skills from Wales, was called "Neddy the Weaver." Dairy cows provided the milk and butter used by farm households. Hogs were butchered and the pork smoked to preserve it. An occasional cow or steer would be butchered as needed. Every farm raised chickens for both eggs and meat, and the Price farm was known for its White Holland turkeys. Before the days of animal control, an abundance of dogs and cats was not uncommon. Dogs were often used when hunting wild animals and birds, and cats took care of the rodent population. Horses and oxen pulled pioneer wagons and buggies, as well as plows and other farm equipment. Some later farmers continued the use of draft horses until tractors and other motorized equipment became standard and affordable.

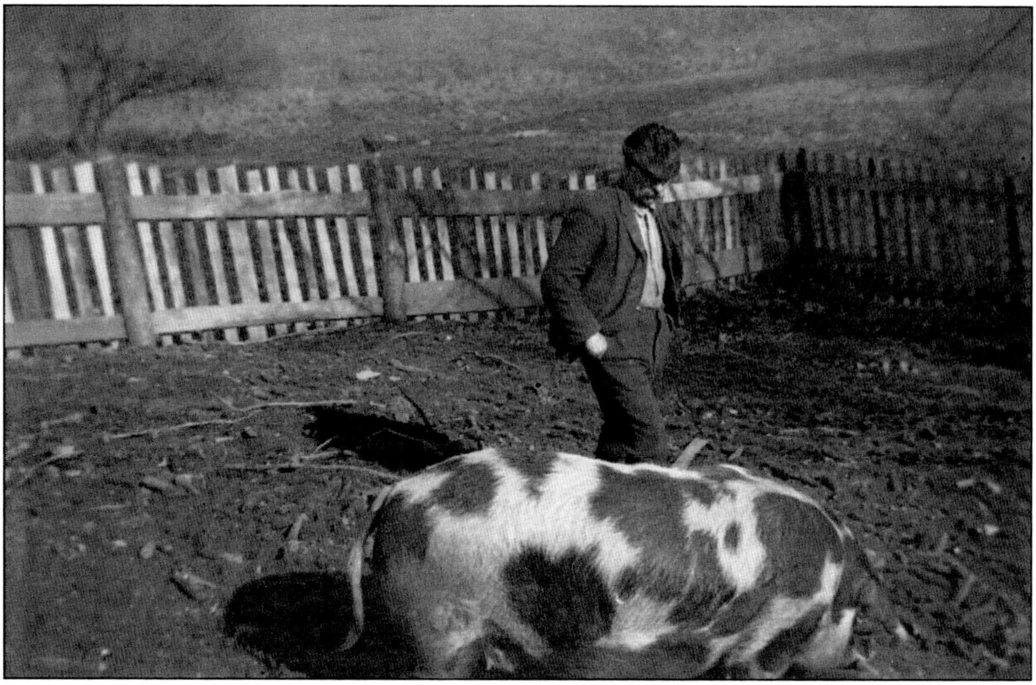

The early farmers in the Welsh Hills were nearly self-sufficient. Samuel Jones Philipps raised cows, hogs, and chickens on his farm and butchered what the family needed for its own consumption. Samuel is shown in this photograph with one of his well-fed hogs.

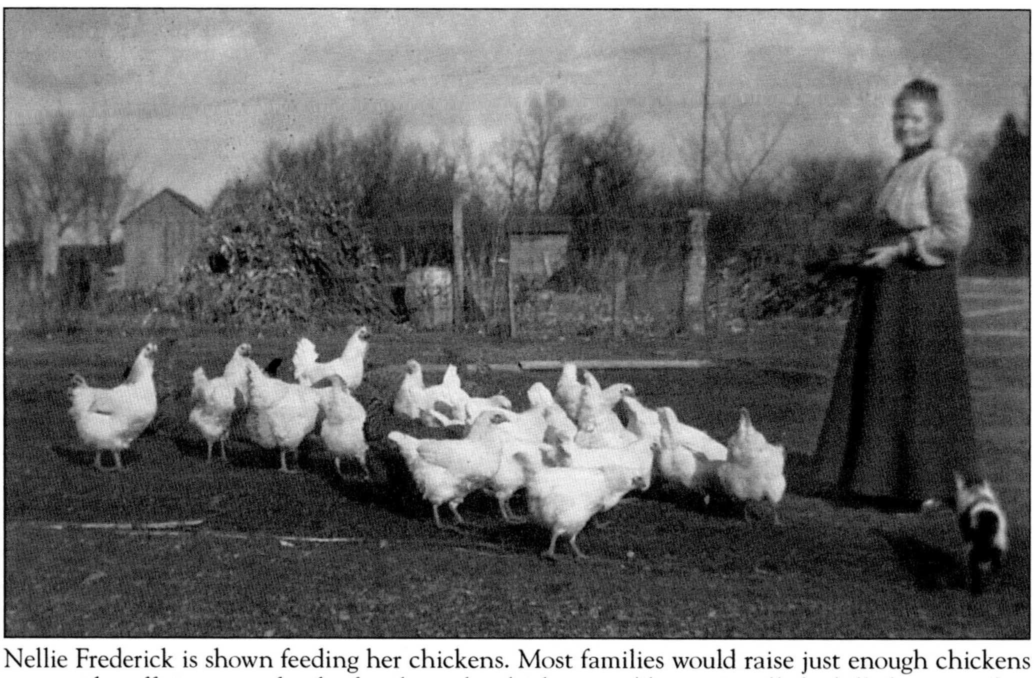

Nellie Frederick is shown feeding her chickens. Most families would raise just enough chickens to provide sufficient eggs for the family, and a chicken would occasionally be killed to provide a meal. In this photograph, a cat watches the chickens, and some of the chickens return its gaze.

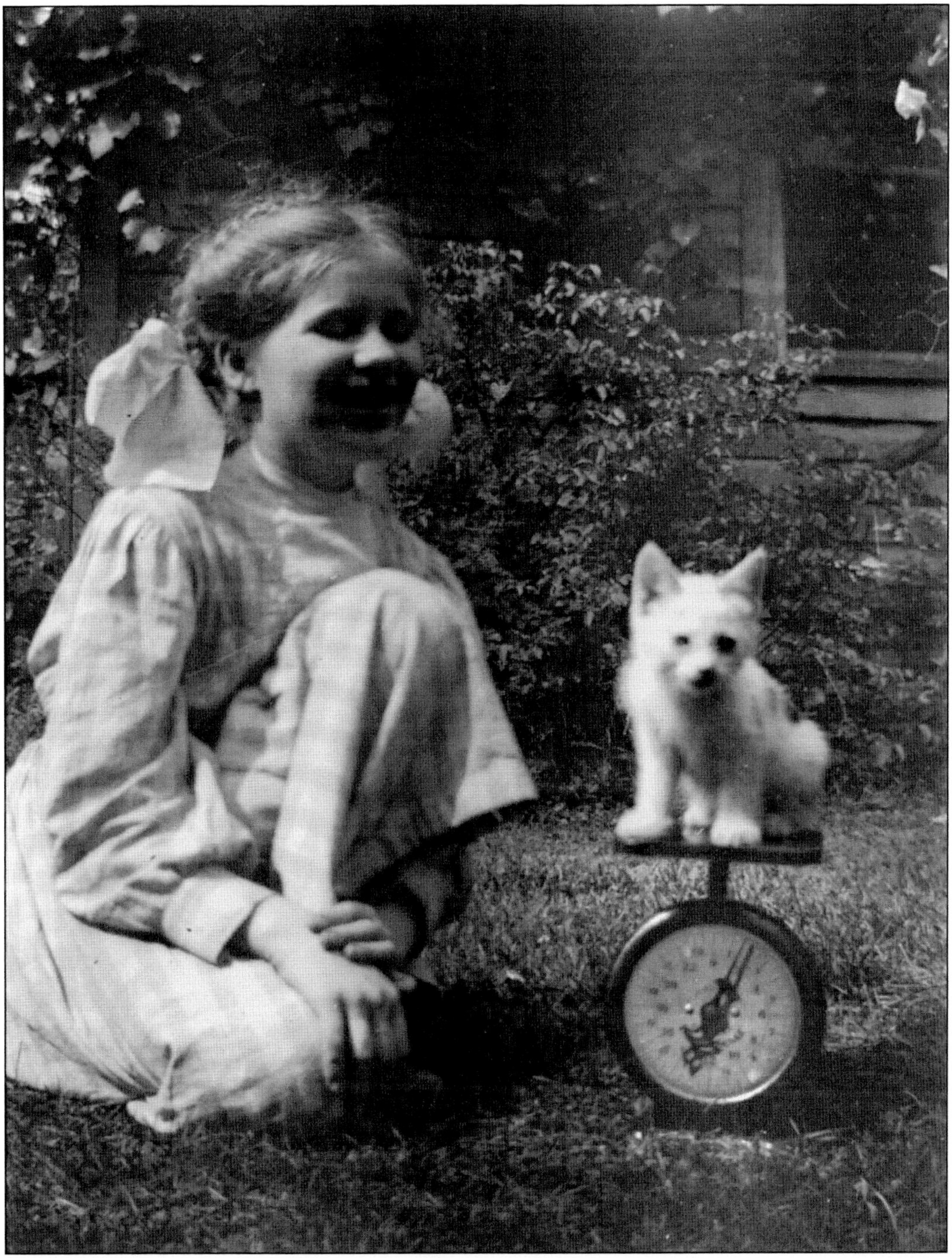

Edris Lucille Rose, granddaughter of Mary Priscilla Philipps and great-great-great-granddaughter of Thomas Philipps, weighs her kitten on the scales. Mary was the sister of Samuel Jones Philipps. As an adult, Edris married George Brown Nichols, and they had four children. She died when she was 32 years old. (Courtesy of Ruth Valentine Sipe.)

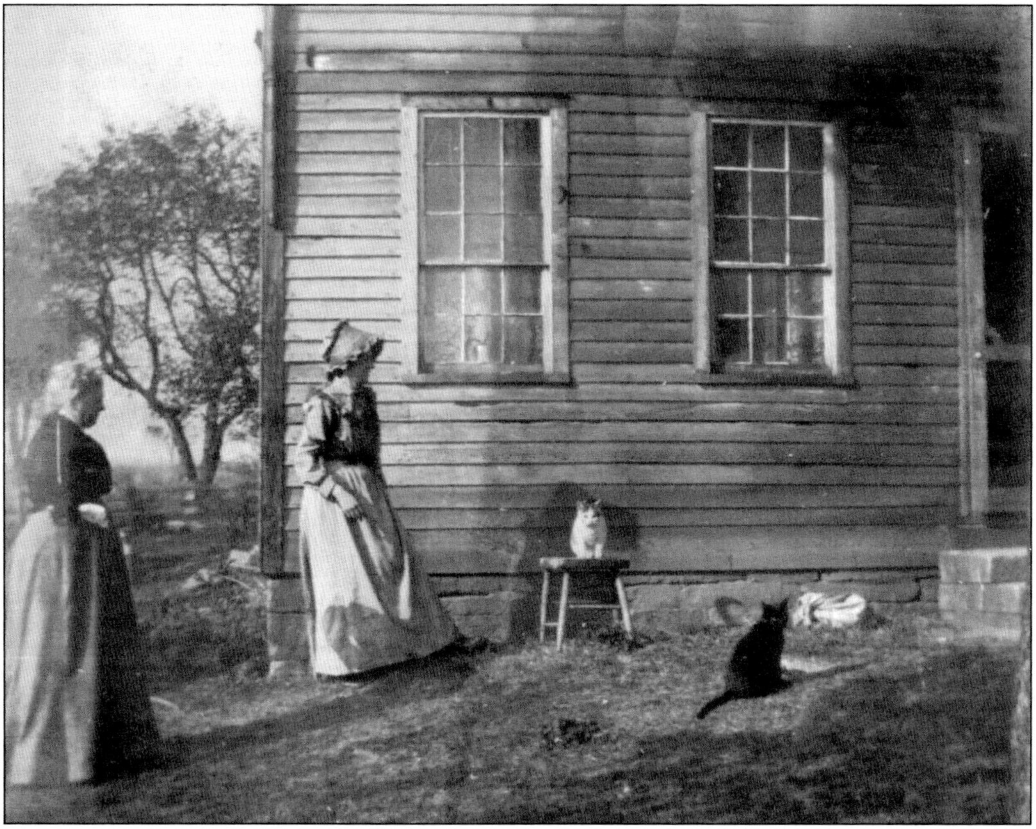

Cats Toosey (cat, left) and Nig (cat, right) and women from the Hankinson family are outside the Hankinson home located on Hankinson Road. This house is now owned by Norm Kennedy. (Courtesy of Mary Ellen Everett.)

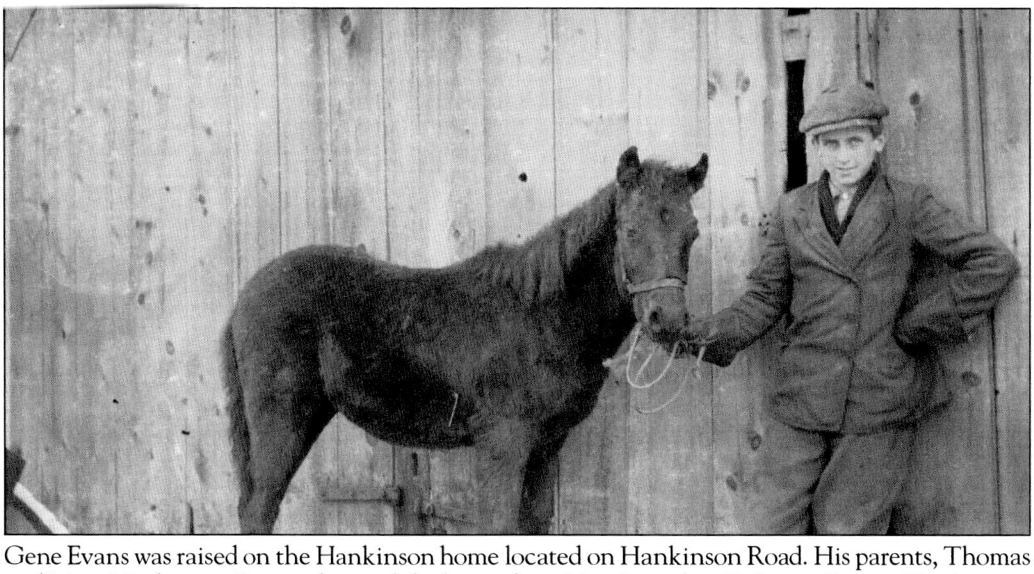

Gene Evans was raised on the Hankinson home located on Hankinson Road. His parents, Thomas and Mary Hankinson Evans, obtained the house from Mary's mother, Rebecca Cramer Hankinson. The farm raised cows, chickens, and horses. Gene was in charge of the care of this foal.

Gertrude Price is shown in this photograph with one of her prize-winning White Holland turkeys. In 1934, Price's turkeys claimed 11 of 12 first prizes in poultry shows in New York City and Harrisburg, Pennsylvania. Her birds received so much acclaim that they were featured in a newsreel. A pair of turkeys was submitted to the world poultry congress in Rome and later sold to an Italian estate. (Courtesy of T. David Price.)

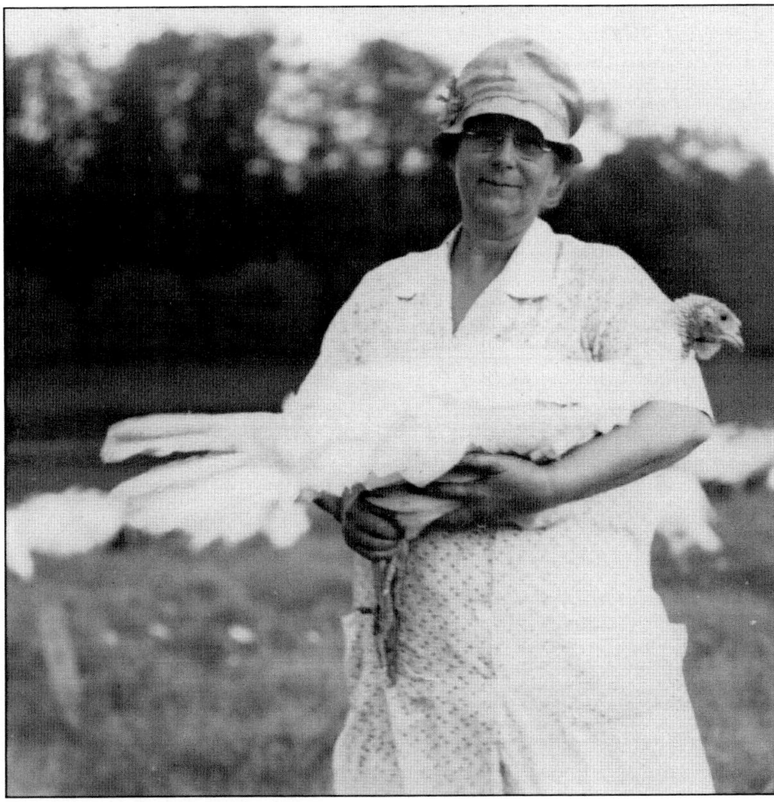

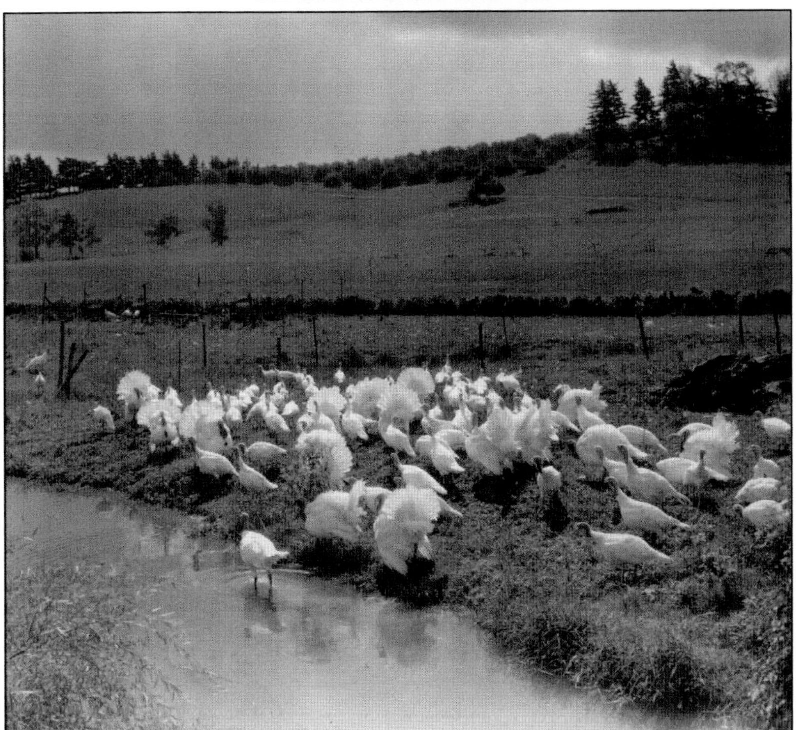

Other residents of the Welsh Hills often saw the flock of White Holland turkeys running around the Price farm. They are flightless birds bred for their excellent meat. Price was an active member of many associations dealing with raising poultry, particularly turkeys, and served as second vice president of the International Turkey Association. (Courtesy of T. David Price.)

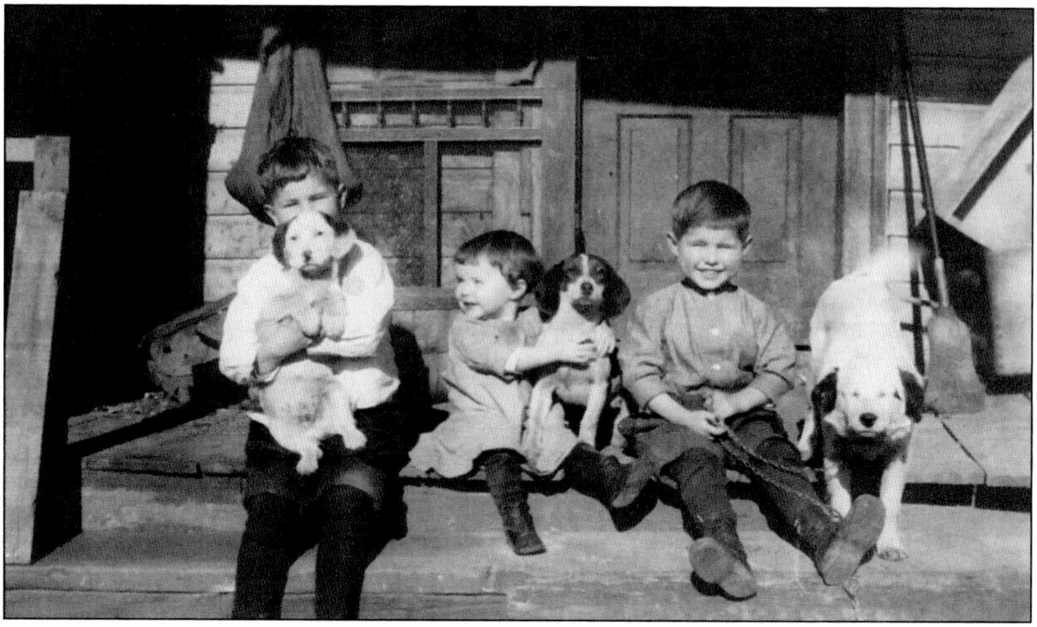

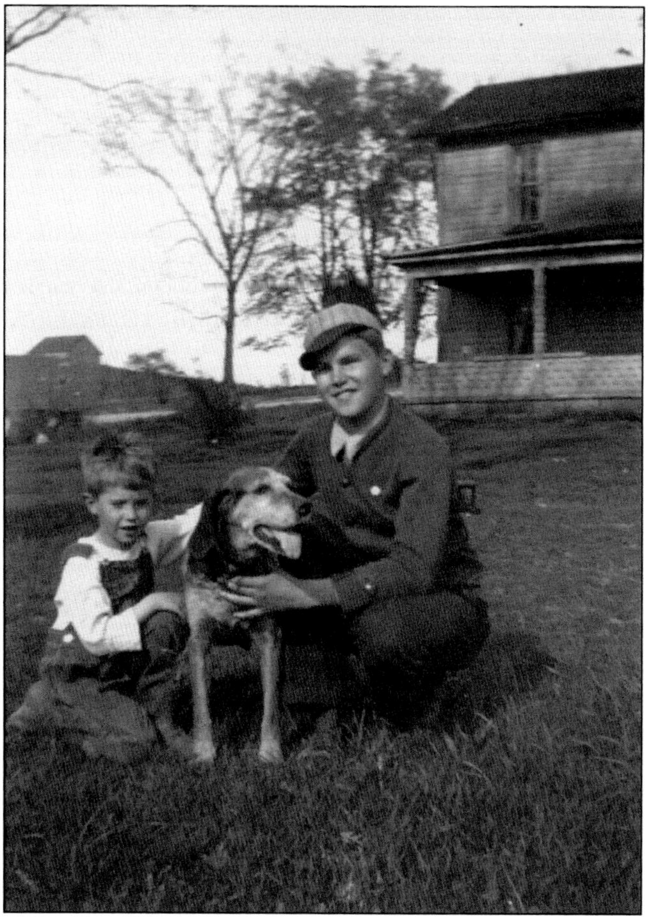

There were never too many dogs on farms in the Welsh Hills. In this photograph above, taken around 1924, three of Thomas Warren Philipps's children pose with their dogs. The children are, from left to right, Sammy, Mary, and Tom. (Courtesy of Thomas E. Philipps.)

Sammy Philipps and his younger brother Lloyd are shown in front of the Frederick home on Welsh Hills Road where they were living at the time. The small building on the hill at the left is on the Hartman property. The hill is devoid of trees in the 1930s. As an adult, Sammy married Helen Hartman and raised their family in this house. (Courtesy of Lloyd Philipps.)

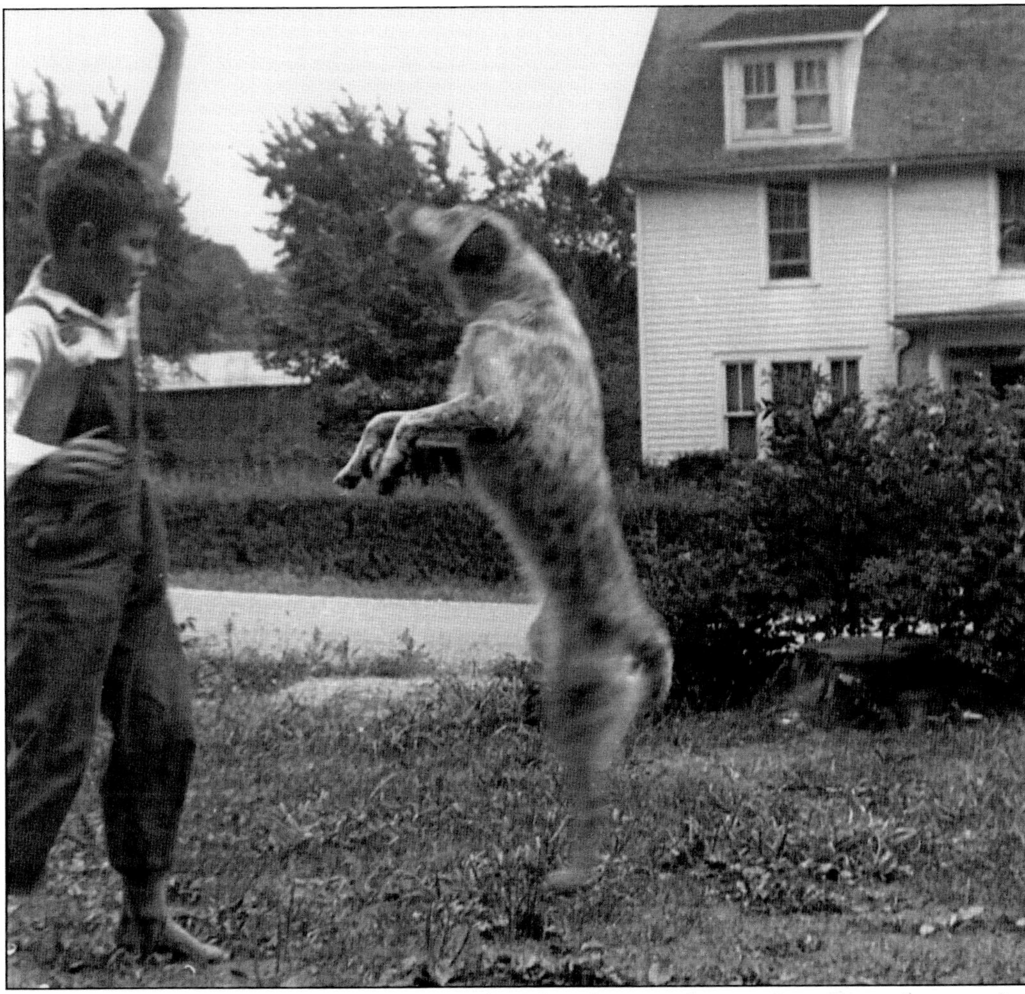

Tommy Philipps is teaching his dog some tricks. This photograph was taken during the time that Thomas and Grace Philipps and their children lived in the old Frederick House on Welsh Hills Road. A Mr. Channel owned the house in the background. The Philipps family owned many farm dogs while living in the Welsh Hills.

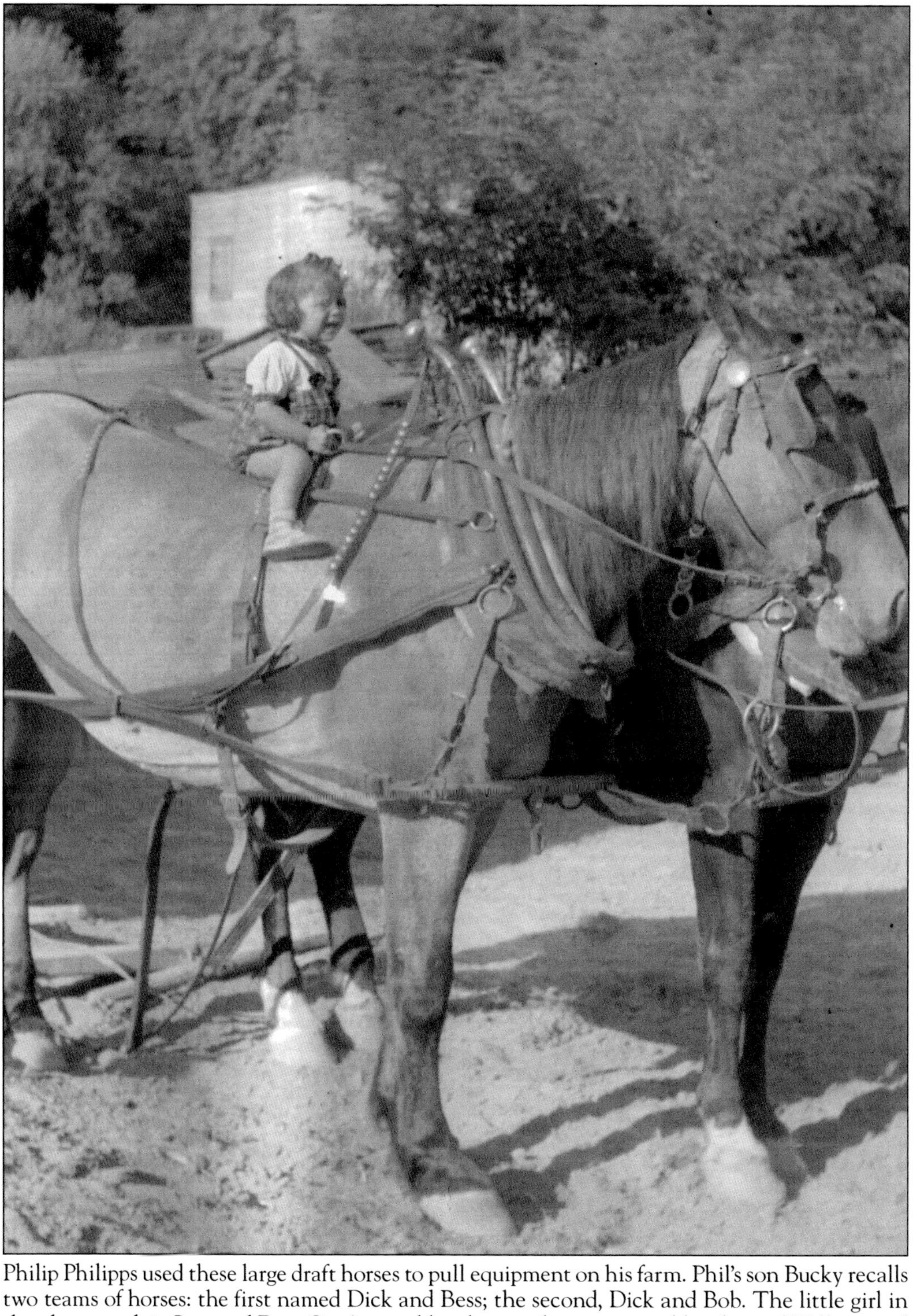

Philip Philipps used these large draft horses to pull equipment on his farm. Phil's son Bucky recalls two teams of horses: the first named Dick and Bess; the second, Dick and Bob. The little girl in the photograph is Sam and Dora Sipe's granddaughter and a great-granddaughter of William and Rebecca Hankinson. She is not very happy sitting on this large animal.

# *Ten*

# Celebrations and Entertainment

When the first settlers arrived, there was little time for entertainment. Celebrations were usually of a religious nature, such as weddings and baptisms. As the community settled, there was more time for recreation. This was often in the form of family gatherings or church picnics. Amusement was regularly centered on necessary chores, like quilting bees, corn husking and wood chopping competitions, and barn raisings. Storytelling was a favorite pastime of many of the older gentlemen. William "Billy" Cramer and Samuel Griffith Philipps were renowned in the Welsh Hills for their storytelling and tall tales.

As more families moved into the Welsh Hills, new activities developed. A literary society was started for the young men and women. Young people also performed plays, and choirs sang at the church and Grange Hall. In the early 1900s, Harvey Williams, a teacher at the Granville School, started the Welsh Hills Band, which consisted of brass instruments and drums. The musicians were local men who were mostly self-taught and performed at special occasions, parades, and picnics. Square dancing became popular in the 1920s and 1930s. Two houses in the Welsh Hills featured rooms large enough to accommodate the dancers. Wade Moreland's house had a large room on the second floor where people came to dance, and he and Charlie Hartman were known as excellent fiddle players.

Young men began taking interest in baseball in the late 1890s. Farm leagues started at this time, and many players developed incredible baseball skills. Woody English, from the nearby town of Fredonia, played against some of these Welsh Hills farm teams as a boy and later went on to the professional leagues.

Stories are plentiful of summer days at the swimming hole, jumping from the hayloft, or running on the hillside, and wintertime was devoted to sledding and ice-skating.

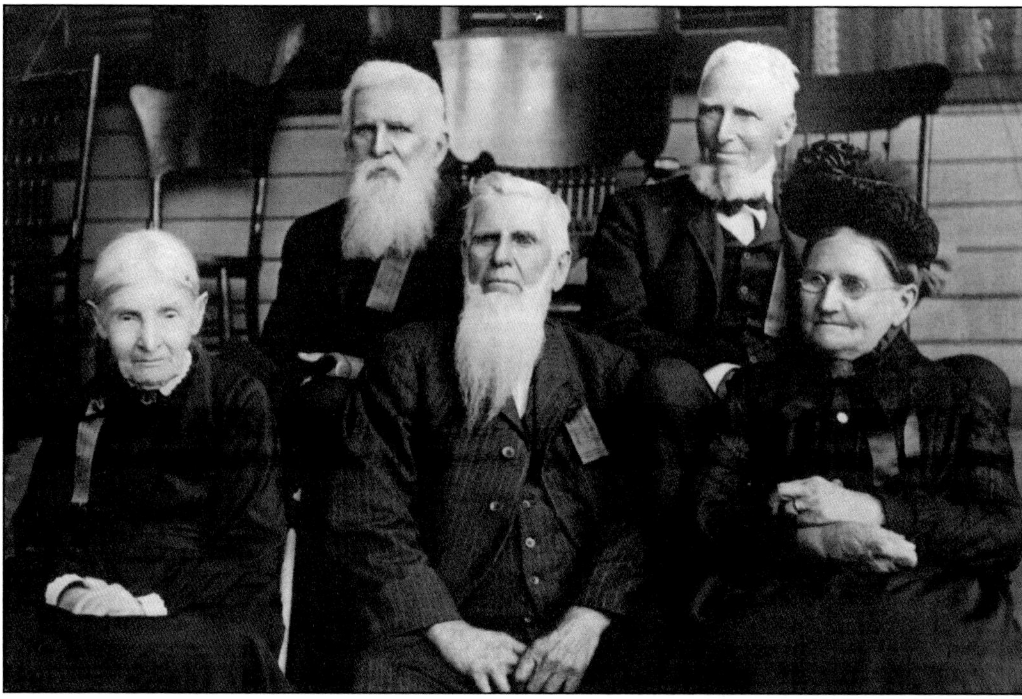

In this 1905 photograph from the centennial celebration of the founding of Granville and the Welsh Hills, these people represent several of the founding families. They are, from left to right, (first row) Esther Williams (wife of John Williams), Richard Jones (brother of David Jones), and Sarah Philipps Jones (wife of David Jones); (second row) David D. Jones and John Williams. They are wearing red ribbons commemorating the event. (Courtesy of Ruth Valentine Sipe.)

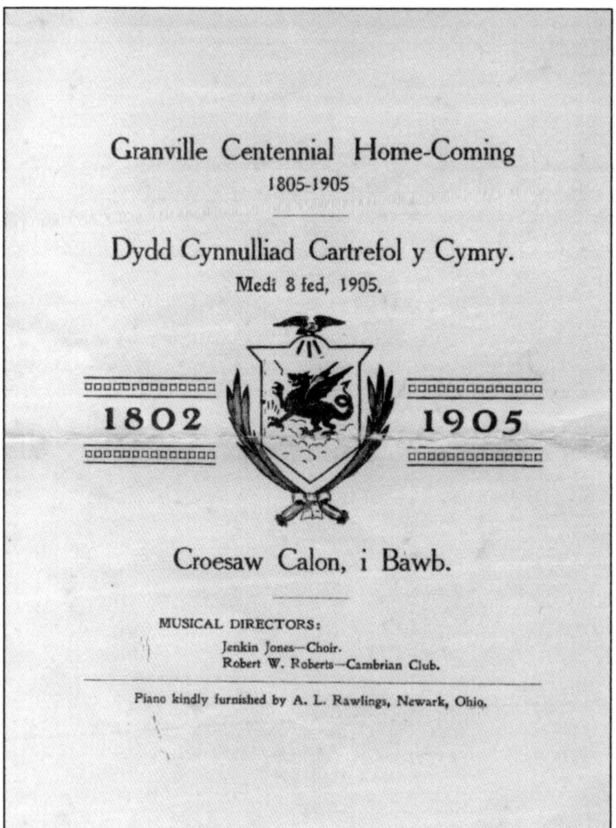

Granville Centennial Home-Coming

1805-1905

Dydd Cynnulliad Cartrefol y Cymry.

Medi 8 fed, 1905.

1802 1905

Croesaw Calon, i Bawb.

MUSICAL DIRECTORS:

Jenkin Jones—Choir.

Robert W. Roberts—Cambrian Club.

Piano kindly furnished by A. L. Rawlings, Newark, Ohio.

The cover of the centennial program commemorates the 1802 founding of the Welsh Hills and the 1805 founding of the town of Granville. The symbol in the center shows an American eagle and a Welsh dragon. The Welsh words loosely translate "Welshmen Homecoming Day, September 8, 1905," and "Heartfelt Welcome to All." (Courtesy of Thomas E. Philipps.)

**Programme**

9:30 to 11:00 A. M. Reception at the Welsh Church.
11:30 A. M. Dinner corner of Granger and Broadway.

**Afternoon Session.**

Invocation . . . B. Gwernidd Newton, Pittsburg, Pa.
Welcome Address by the President
Addresses, the order at the discretion of the President
Our Welsh Forefathers . William Harvey Jones, Columbus, O.
Organization and History of the Welsh Churches.
The Congregational Church, . Thomas James, Granville
The Calvinistic Methodist Church.
The Welsh Hills Baptist Church.
Poem, in Welsh, by Theophilus Rees, read by Griffith D. Jones.
Some Welsh Characteristics, . Prof. C. L. Williams, Granville
The True Welsh American, . J. R. Davies, Esq., Newark
The Welsh People, . Rev. John Hammond, Columbus
Some Trace of Welsh Character, . Hon. J. B. Jones, Newark
The Old Welsh Ministers, . Rev. J. M. Thomas, Columbus
Welsh in the Civil War . . . C. B. Evans, Granville
Welsh Americans, . . J. M. Lewis, Esq., Columbus
The Family of "King" Jones, . . O. C. Jones, Newark
Solo, (Selected) . . . . J. Howard Jones, Newark
Selections for the program for the Evening on next page.

The activities from this program are for the Welsh portion of the centennial celebration. All of the speakers were descendants of Welsh settlers, and William Harvey Jones was a local historian. The evening schedule included songs sung in the Welsh language by the choir and the Cambrian Club. Parts of the festivities took place at Welsh Hills Baptist Church. (Courtesy of Thomas E. Philipps.)

**Evening Concert.**

Moderator, . . . . . . Rev. B. Gwernidd Newton
Order of pieces to be arranged by the Moderator.
Address, by the Moderator.
By The Cambrian Club:
"Harlech War Song," . . . . . . Gwilym Gwent
"Y Delyn Aur," (The Golden Harp), Arranged by D. Pugh Evans
"Ar hyd y nos," (Allthrough the Night), . Dr. Rhys Herbert
Welsh Airs:
"Dafydd y Gareg Wen," (David of the White Rock),
"Cader Idris," (Jennie Jones),
"Morfa Rhuddlan," (Plains of Rhuddlan),
Arranged by Dr. Roland Rogers
"Myfanwy," (Arabella), . . . . . . Dr. Parry
"Seranade," (Lovely Maid), . . . . . Dr. Parry
"Old Folks at Home," Arranged by Perkins.
"Life of Youth," (Valse de Concert), . . Adam Geibel
"Come Bounteous May," (Old English Glee), . . Shoffarth
"By Celia's Arbor," (Old English Glee), . . . Horsely
Duett, "Anhawdd rhoddi hen Delynau," (Harps Lament),
. . . . . . Owain Alaw
Choruses by the Choir and the Cambrian Club:
"Aberystwyth," "Crug y bar," "Babel," "Hen wlad fyn hadau," (The Land of My Fathers), "America," "Llanfair," "Moriah," and others.

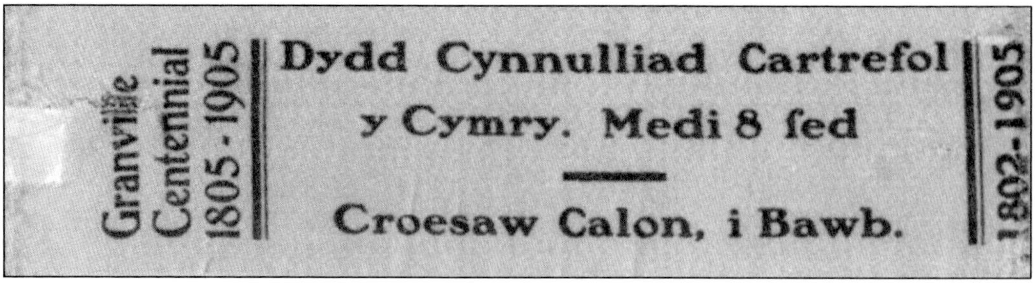


The Welsh participants in the centennial celebration wore red ribbons with Welsh inscriptions. The ribbon above was worn during the 1905 centennial and is loosely interpreted as "Welshmen Home-Coming Day, September 8, 1905," and "Heartfelt Welcome to All." The ribbon seen below was prepared for the bicentennial celebration in 2005 and translates as "Welsh Heritage Weekend May 20–22, Pioneer Spirit Lives On." (Courtesy of Ruth Valentine Sipe and Carol Philipps.)

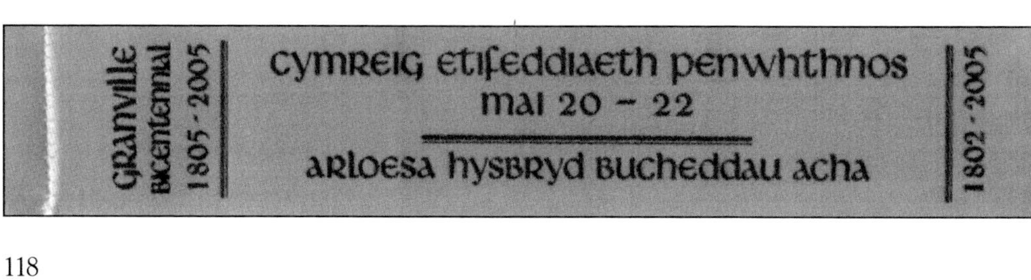

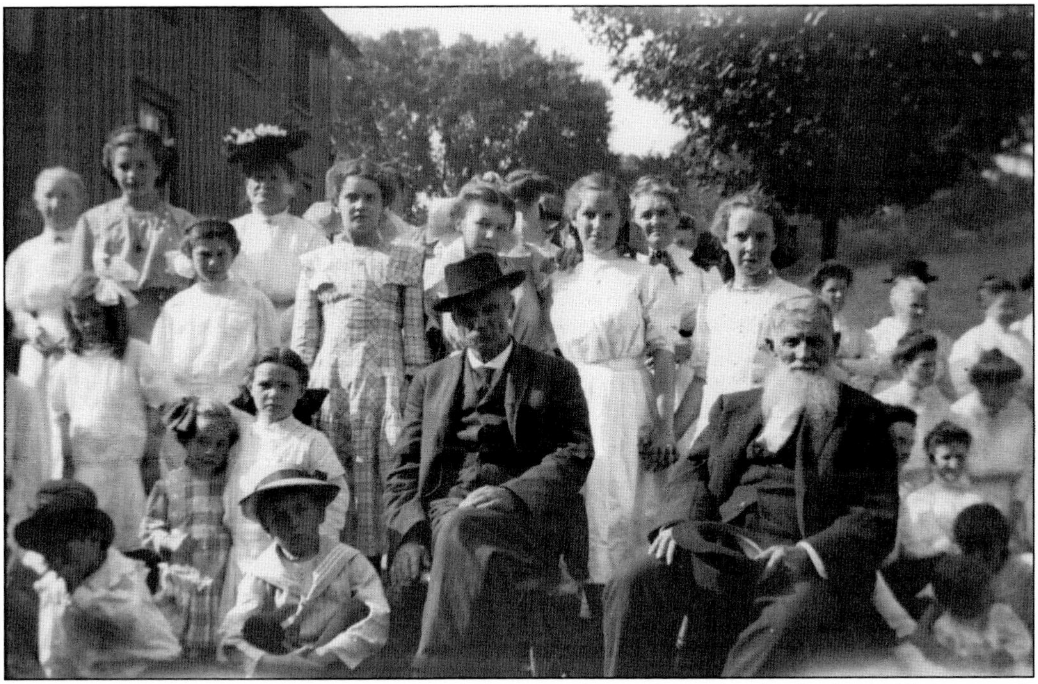

Family reunions were cause for celebration in the 1800s and continue to this day. In this 1905 photograph taken at his home, his children and relatives surround Philipps family patriarch Samuel Jones Philipps (front center wearing hat). His youngest daughter, Edith, stands over his left shoulder.

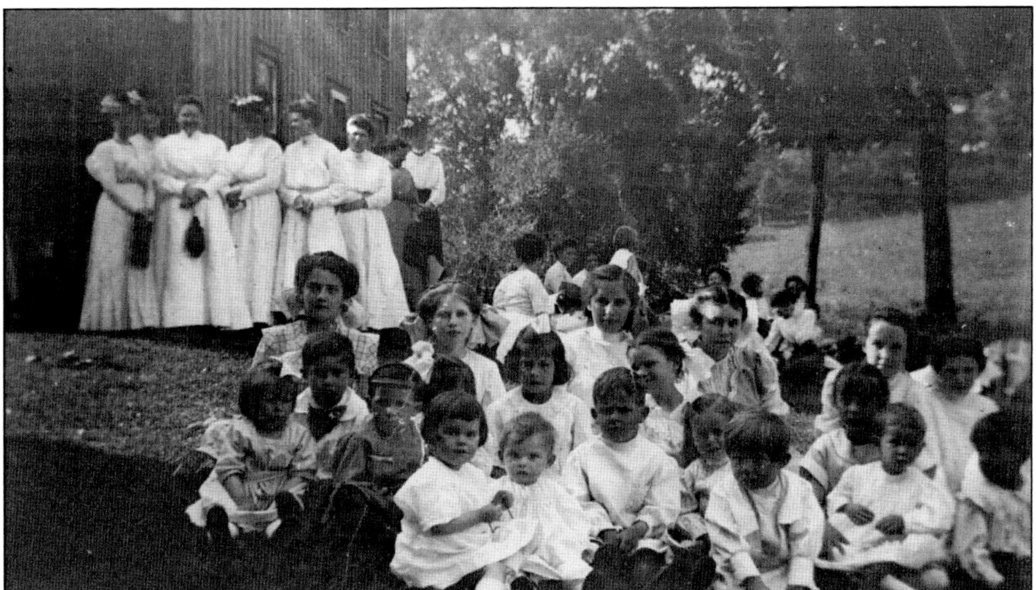

The children sit patiently to have their picture taken at the Philipps reunion, while their mothers keep an eye on them. Joyce Weiser (far left, wearing a hair ribbon) is the granddaughter of Jake and Nellie Frederick. Edris Lucile Rose (back row, second from left) is the granddaughter of Mary Philipps, Samuel Jones Philipps's sister. Edith Philipps (back row, third from left) is Samuel's youngest daughter.

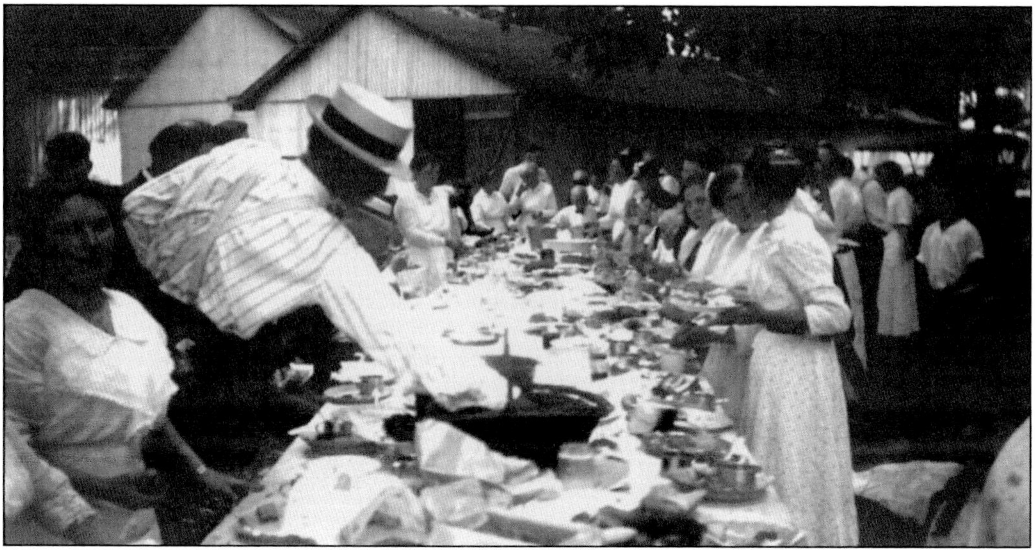

The Williams family gathered every year for a reunion, such as the August 2, 1916, picnic in the image above. The background of the 1928 photograph (below) clearly shows the Williams house on Welsh Hills Road, which hosted the family events. Many families from the Welsh Hills were interrelated, and it was not uncommon to see the same people attend all the different family reunions. Thomas Philipps (seated on the ground at the far right in the 1928 image) was known to attend the Philipps, Rees, Hankinson, Williams, Griffith, and Knight family gatherings. (Courtesy of Mary Villars and Carol Philipps.)

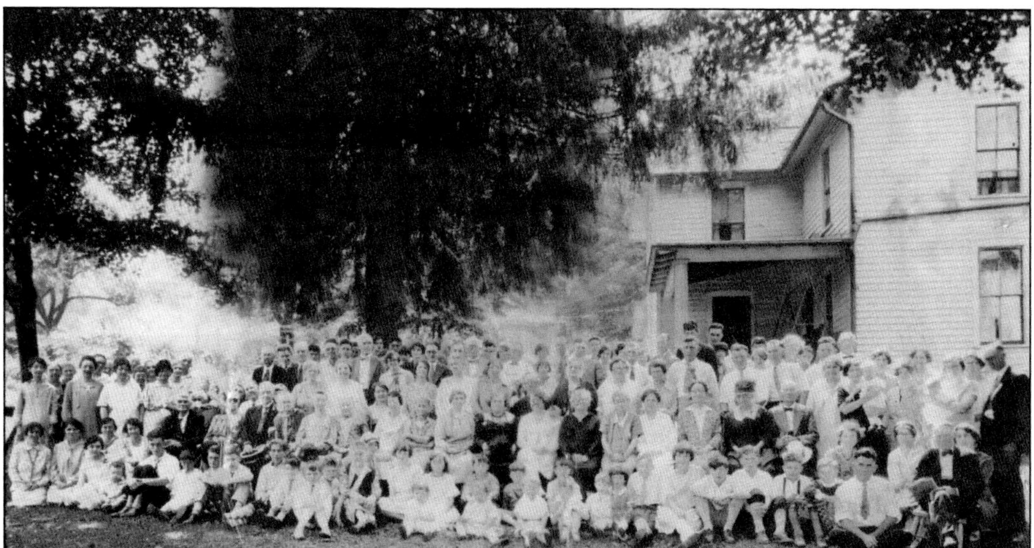

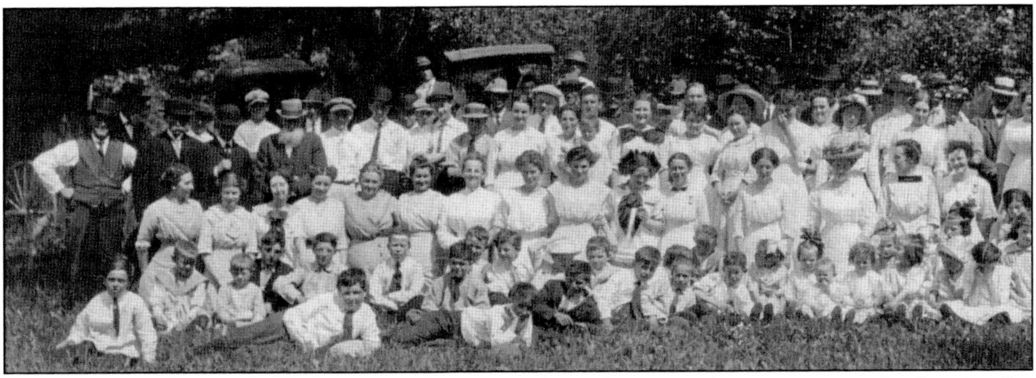

This photograph shows a very large gathering of Hankinson relatives, many who live in the Welsh Hills. Members of the extended family, who lived in Perry County on a farm known as Hankinson Hollow, also appear in this image. Some of the Hankinson cousins lived in New Jersey and would come to visit the Ohio cousins. Will Henry (third row, second from left) is a New Jersey relative.

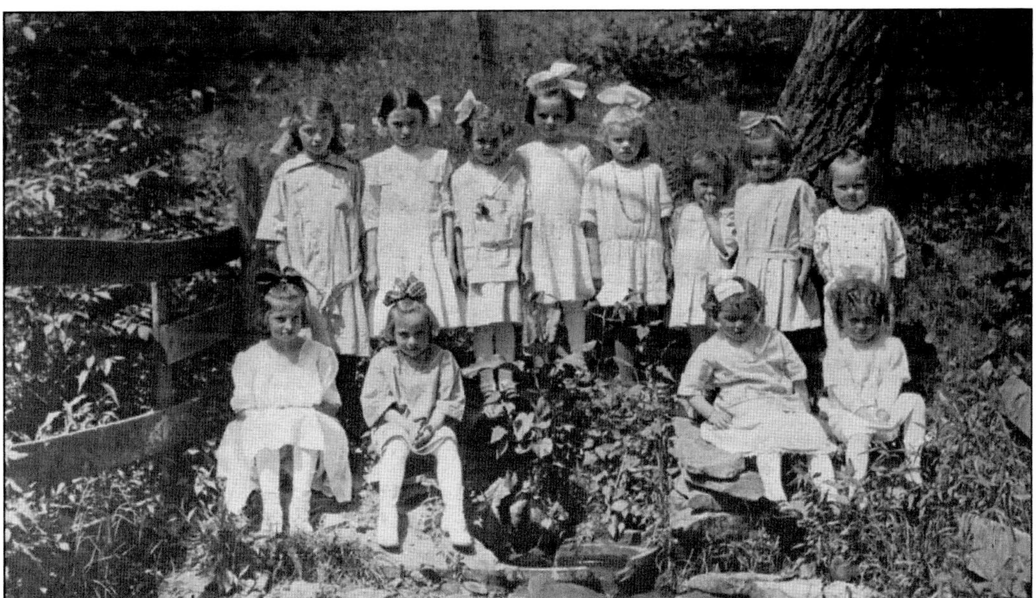

A separate photograph was taken of the young girls. Lucy Hankinson (second row, fourth from right) is the daughter of Hayes and Mami Hankinson. The Hankinson clan was quite large, and many of the family members remained in or near the Welsh Hills. Family gatherings were well attended. A Hankinson reunion is still held every year at Big Spring Farm.

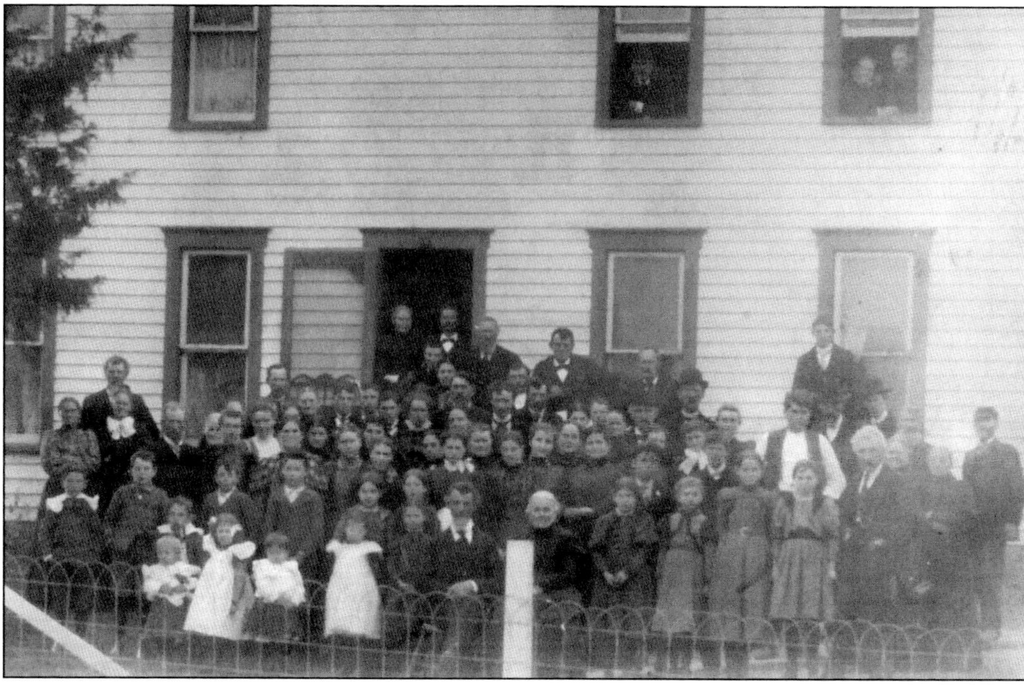

This photograph was taken in 1908 at the celebration of 40 years of marriage between William and Rebecca Hankinson, seated at the front center of this group. Their children, grandchildren, brothers, sisters, and cousins are all gathered for this occasion. Thomas W. Philipps took the photograph at the Hankinson home on Hankinson Road.

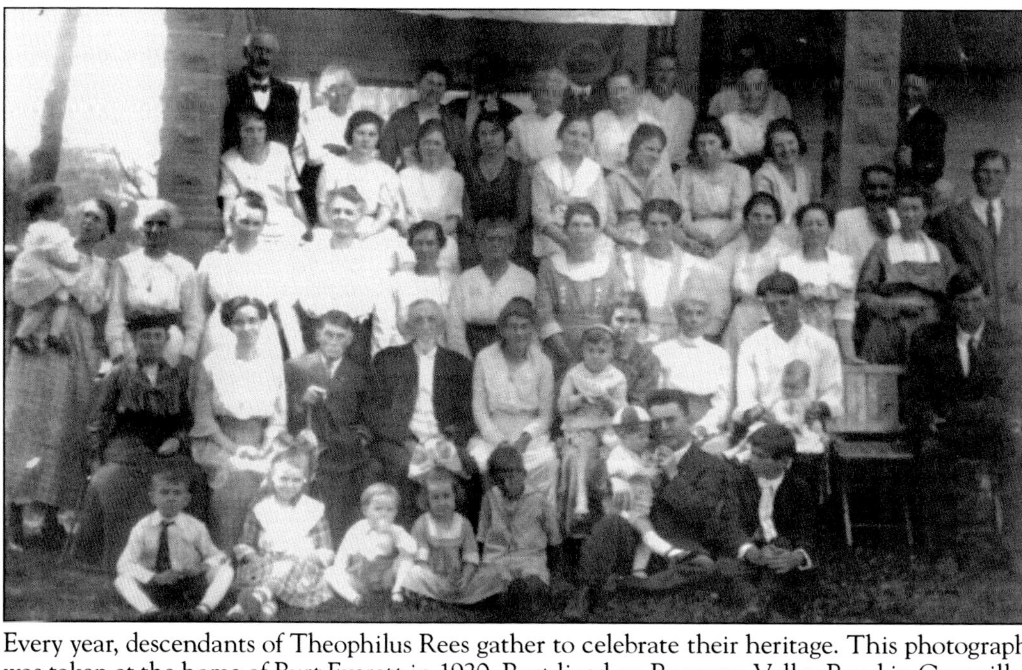

Every year, descendants of Theophilus Rees gather to celebrate their heritage. This photograph was taken at the home of Burt Everett in 1920. Burt lived on Raccoon Valley Road in Granville. Descendants with surnames Philipps, Hankinson, Evans, Thomas, and Rees are represented in this image. The annual combined Rees and Philipps reunions continue today.

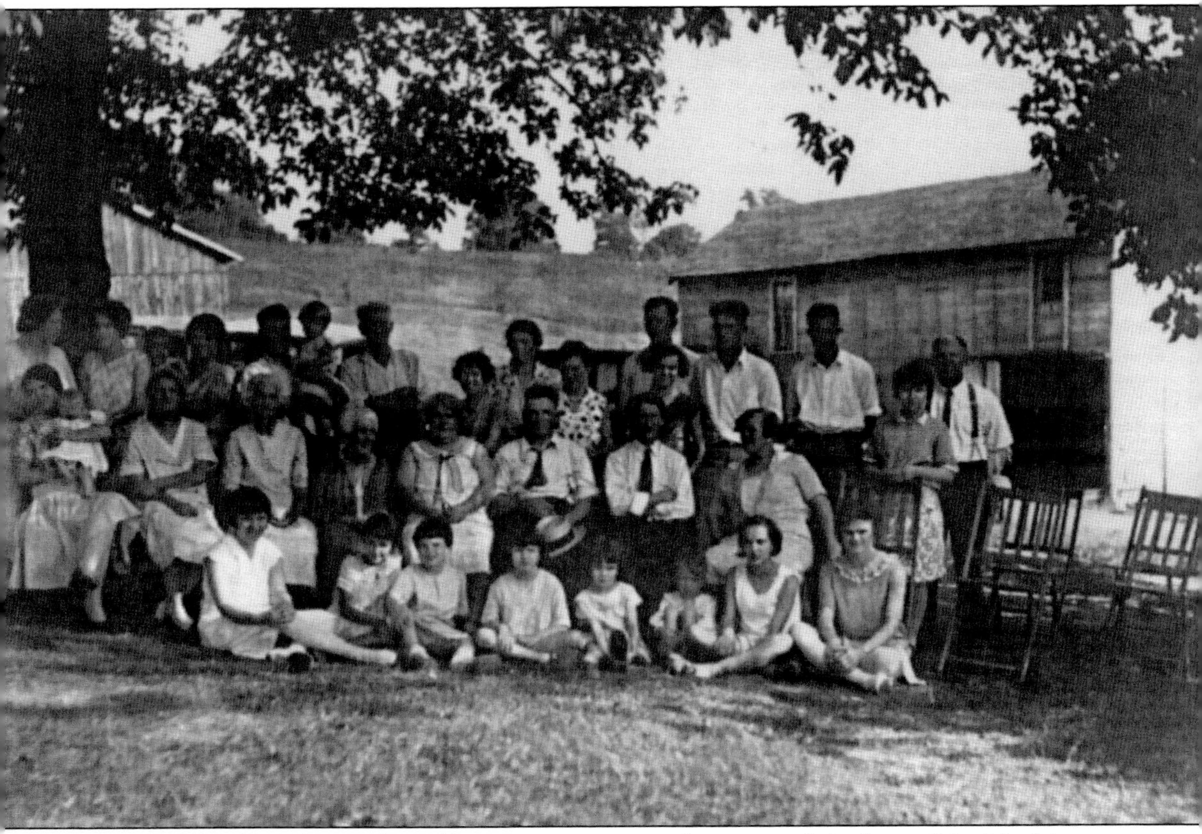

Extended families often gathered for picnics or a special occasion. Members of the Hankinson, Philipps, Evans, and Sipe families pose for this c. 1928 photograph at the old Jake Frederick property, where Tom and Grace Philipps were living at the time. They are, from left to right, as follows: (first row) Alberta Sipe, Alyce Sipe, Mary Philipps, Helen Sipe, unknown, Lloyd Philipps, Phyllis Sipe, and Lucy Hankinson; (second row) Adaline Sipe holding Wilma Philipps, Dora Sipe, Mary Evans, Rebecca Hankinson, Susie Barber, Pete Barber, Vernon Taylor, Pearl Taylor, and Ruth Valentine Sipe; (third row) Thelma Sipe, Anna Mae Sipe, Bertha Philipps holding her son Philip, Phil Philipps holding his daughter Phyllis, Tom Evans, Elsie Barber, Grace Philipps, Ruth Barber, Burdelle Evans, unknown behind Burdelle, Gene Evans, Archie Hankinson, and Sam Sipe. The old cider mill is in the background.

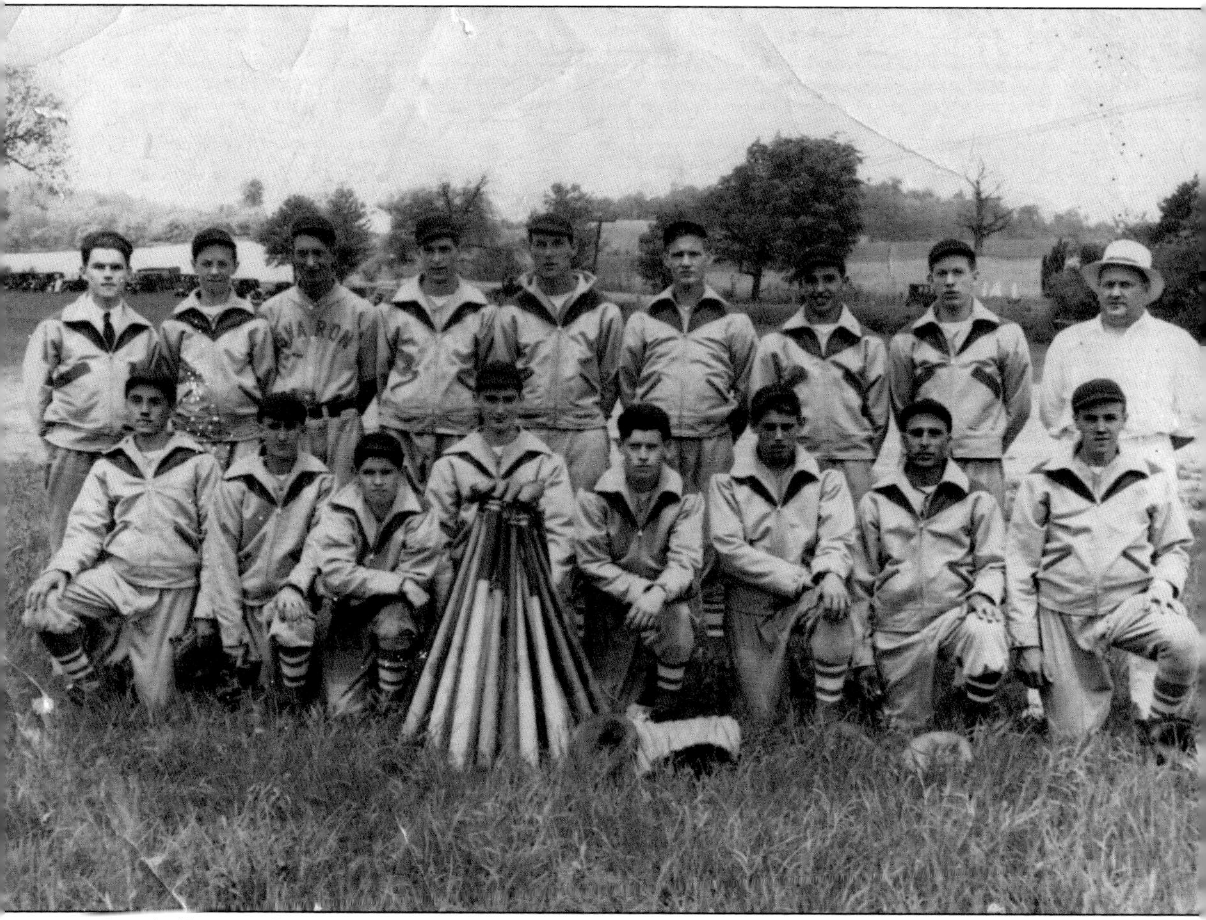

Baseball was a favorite pastime for many young men in the Welsh Hills. Several teams were established to play each other as well as teams from outside the area. The 1936 Sharon Valley team played in a field located across from the Welsh Calvinistic Methodist Church on Sharon Valley Road. Players are, from left to right, (first row) Bill Hartman, John Milner, Tom Philipps, George Daniels, Marshall Hankinson, Fred Hartman, Ralph Smith, and Carl Jones; (second row) Sam Philipps, Ray Jones, Bill Tavener, Charles Hartman, Lester Foster, John Tavener, Al Marzano, Jess Kinser, and coach Curtis Berry. Curtis Berry was the Newark police chief at the time and was able to solicit sponsors to pay for uniforms and equipment. Farm teams had been playing in the Welsh Hills for several generations. (Courtesy of Thomas E. Philipps.)

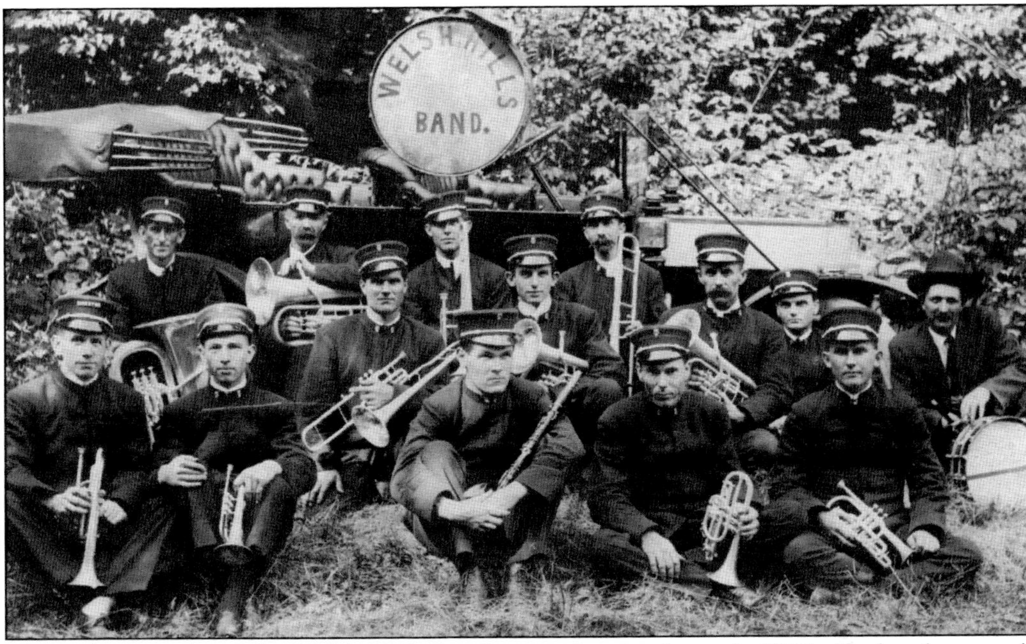


These photographs of the Welsh Hills Band were taken in the early 1900s. In the photograph above are, from left to right, (first row) Harvey Williams (founder and organizer of the band), Willis Parry, Charlie Thompson, Herb Griffith, and Thomas Philipps; (second row) Phil Philipps, Archie Hankinson, and Guy Griffith; (third row) Charlie Hartman, Ed Wright, Albert Hankinson, Sam Parry, Simon Jones, and Wib Raffey. In the photograph below are, from left to right, (first row) Frank Hartman, Sam Parry, B. Williams, Simon Jones, Albert Hankinson, Phil Philipps, and Charlie Thompson; (second row) Ed Wright, Archie Hankinson, Guy Griffith, Charlie Hartman, J. Hankinson, Herb Griffith, Willis Parry, and Harvey Williams. The band performed for special functions and public events and marched in the Fourth of July parades. Most of the members received no formal training, but people recall that they were good performers. (Courtesy of Philip "Bucky" Philipps and Thomas E. Philipps.)

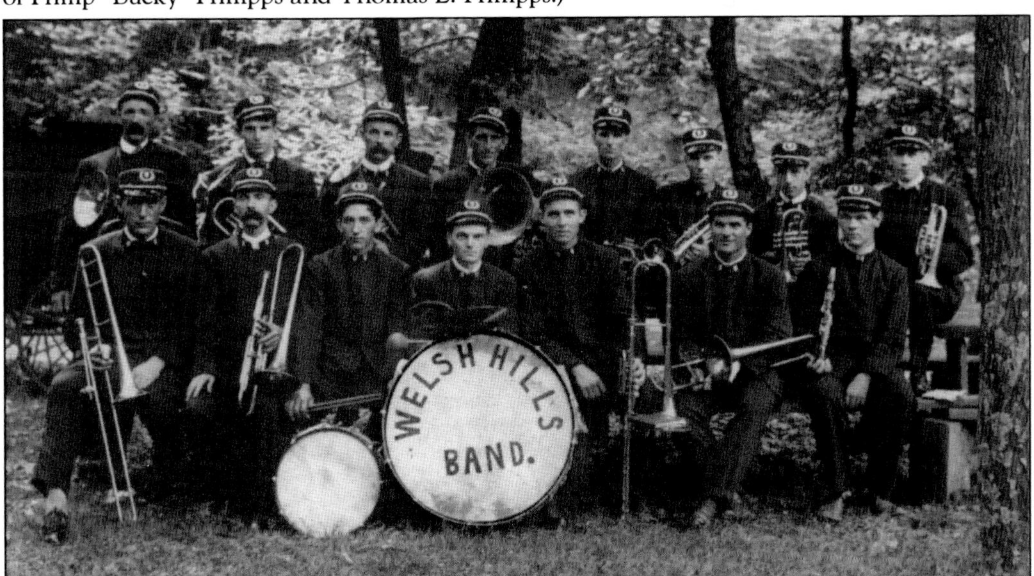

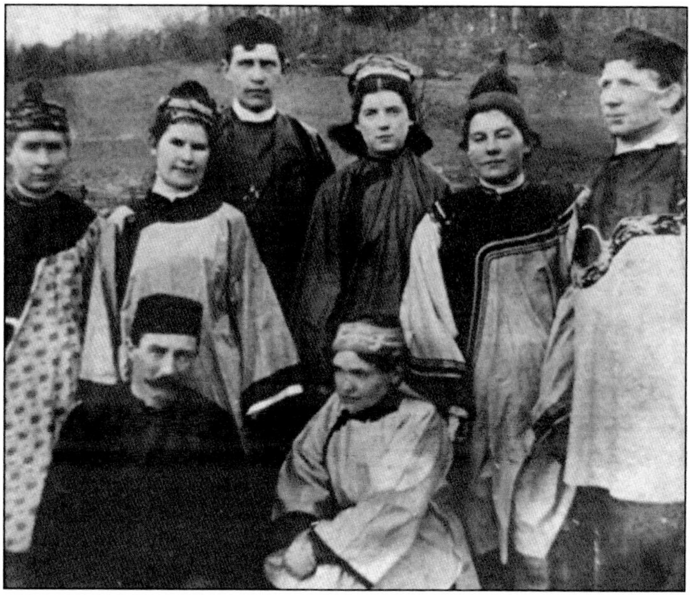

Another form of entertainment was acting. In this photograph from the early 1900s, the group is wearing special costumes for its performance. The woman standing second from the left is Mamie Philipps, daughter of Samuel Jones and Wilhelmina Philipps, and the woman standing fourth from the left is Dora Hankinson, daughter of William and Rebecca Hankinson. Mamie and Dora were cousins. The performance was most likely held at the Welsh Hills Grange Hall that contained a large room with a stage.

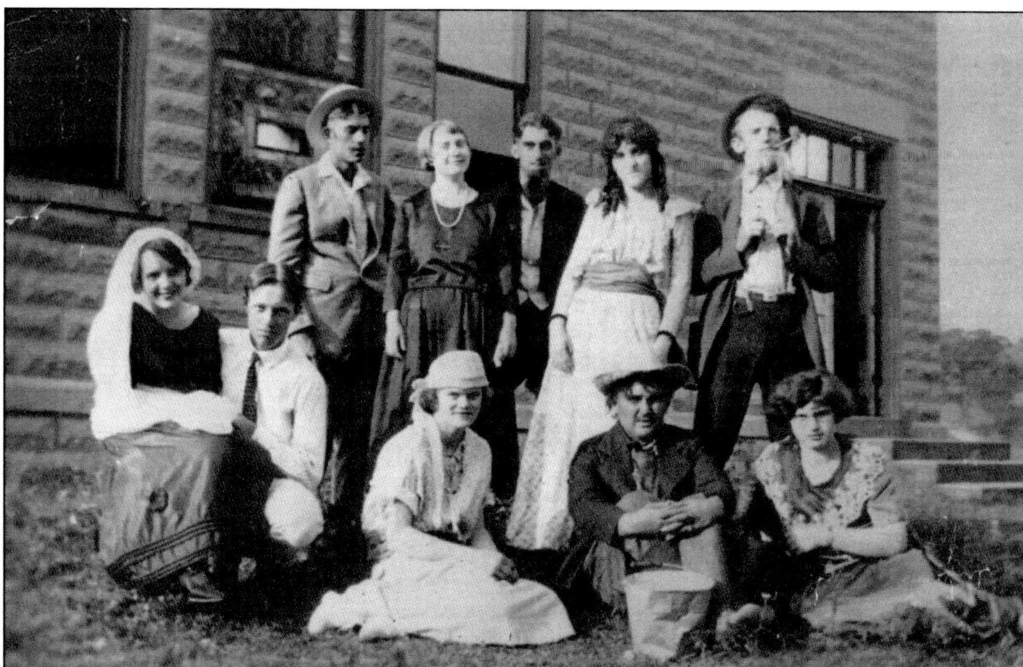

This group seated in front of the Welsh Hills Baptist Church is dressed in costume for the play *Deacon Jones*. The church and the Welsh Hills Grange Hall were used for entertainment, and plays were often performed. Cast members are, from left to right, (first row) Adaline and Clifford Foster, Lucy Hankinson, Thomas Philipps ("the villain"), and unidentified; (second row) two unidentified, Gene Evans, unidentified, and Archie Hankinson.

# BIBLIOGRAPHY

Brister, E. M. P. *Centennial History of the City of Newark and Licking County, Ohio, Volume I and II*. Chicago and Columbus, OH: S. J. Clarke Publishing Company, 1909.

Bushnell, Rev. Henry. *The History of Granville, Etna and Kirkersville, Ohio*. Columbus, OH: Press of Hann and Adair, 1889.

Gallant, Thomas F. *Early Public Schools of Granville and Granville Township*. Granville, Ohio: Granville Historical Society, 1981.

Hill, N. N. Jr. *History of Licking County Ohio, 1881*. Newark, Ohio: A. A. Graham and Company, 1881.

Jones, William Harvey. "The Welsh Hills: The Story of a Pioneer Community." Paper prepared for the 1905 Granville Centennial.

Smucker, Isaac. "History of the Welsh Settlements in Licking County, Ohio, The Characteristics of our Welsh Pioneers—Their Church History, with Biographical Sketches of Our Leading Welshmen." Newark, Ohio: Wilson and Clark Printers, American Office, April 5, 1869.

www.arcadiapublishing.com

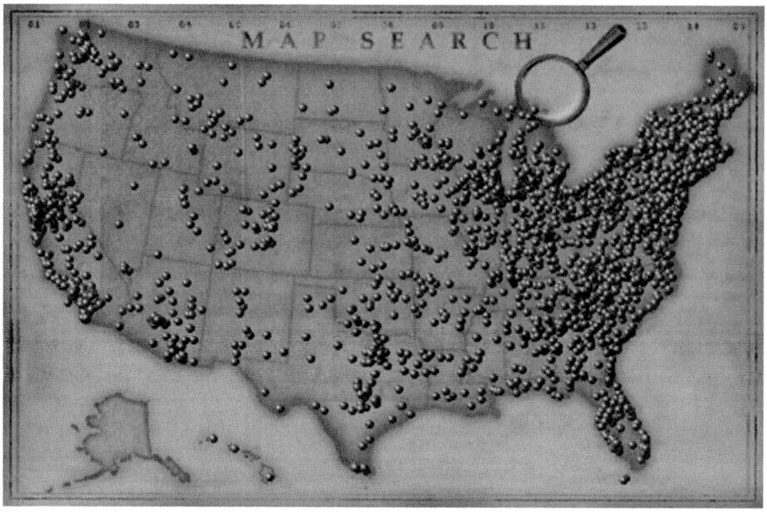


Discover books about the town where you grew up, the cities where your friends and families live, the town where your parents met, or even that retirement spot you've been dreaming about. Our Web site provides history lovers with exclusive deals, advanced notification about new titles, e-mail alerts of author events, and much more.

MADE IN THE USA

Arcadia Publishing, the leading local history publisher in the United States, is committed to making history accessible and meaningful through publishing books that celebrate and preserve the heritage of America's people and places. Consistent with our mission to preserve history on a local level, this book was printed in South Carolina on American-made paper and manufactured entirely in the United States.

This book carries the accredited Forest Stewardship Council (FSC) label and is printed on 100 percent FSC-certified paper. Products carrying the FSC label are independently certified to assure consumers that they come from forests that are managed to meet the social, economic, and ecological needs of present and future generations.

FSC
Mixed Sources
Product group from well-managed forests and other controlled sources

Cert no. SW-COC-001530
www.fsc.org
© 1996 Forest Stewardship Council

Find Your Place in History.